NEW QUESTIONS, NEW INSIGHTS, NEW APPROACHES

CONTRIBUTIONS TO THE RESEARCH FORUM AT THE WORLD SUMMIT ON MEDIA FOR CHILDREN AND YOUTH 2010

YEARBOOK 2011

NEW QUESTIONS, NEW INSIGHTS, NEW APPROACHES

CONTRIBUTIONS TO THE RESEARCH FORUM AT THE WORLD SUMMIT ON MEDIA FOR CHILDREN AND YOUTH 2010

EDITORS: CECILIA VON FEILITZEN, ULLA CARLSSON & CATHARINA BUCHT

The International Clearinghouse on Children, Youth and Media

NORDICOM
University of Gothenburg

Yearbook 2011

New Questions, New Insights, New Approaches

Contributions to the Research Forum at the World Summit on Media For Children and Youth 2010

Editors:
Cecilia von Feilitzen, Ulla Carlsson, Catharina Bucht

ISSN 1651-6028
ISBN 978-91-86523-21-3

Published by:
The International Clearinghouse on Children, Youth and Media
Series editor: Ulla Carlsson

Nordicom
University of Gothenburg
Box 713
SE 405 30 GÖTEBORG
Sweden

Cover by:
Karin Persson

Printed by:
Litorapid Media AB, Göteborg, Sweden, 2011
Environmental certification according to ISO 14001

Contents

Foreword

Rapid and dramatically changing digital and converging media and communication processes have given rise to new questions about the relations between children, youth and media. These processes have prompted many in research and in the debate to reformulate and re-approach basic questions at new levels and from new perspectives. By elucidating, broadening and contextualizing knowledge about young people and media from a global point of view, we also discover the very different media situations in various parts of the world.

In cooperation with the hosts of the World Summit on Media for Children and Youth in 2010, Karlstad, Sweden, The International Clearinghouse on Children, Youth and Media at Nordicom organized a Research Forum with different sessions in the summit programme. The aim of each session was to provide a space for an exchange of knowledge and a dialogue between the different groups of delegates at the summit and for researchers to reach out to interested parties in and outside the research community – teachers, media professionals, decision makers, regulators, etc. A constructive dialogue between representatives of different professions and positions is vital for further progress in realizing children's rights. The current Yearbook is based on the presentations made at the sessions of the Forum.

Under the overriding theme of the introductory Plenary Session "New Questions, New Insights, New Approaches", The Clearinghouse Research Forum had four more sessions with panels on different themes:

- Media Literacy and Education
- Children, Media, Consumption and Health
- Media Ethics and Social Responsibility
- Communication for Social Change

In these five panels, there were 25 presentations of topical research by a range of the most outstanding scholars from Africa, Asia, Europe, Latin America and North America. For this book, they reworked their contributions to provide slightly extended articles.

In this rich, broad and varied material dealing with practical and theoretical research cases, a multitude of insights can be found.

For children and youth, the many media platforms of today are often combined into the trinity of internet, television and mobile phone. They intersperse a myriad of optional applications providing increasing possibilities to engage individual users' interests and mark their activities. This circumstance, which also implies that the space of the public sphere is becoming ever more media centred, gives new opportunities for people to communicate, create, and participate. Yet social networking, blogging, producing alternative media contents on the internet, etc., are possible only for those who have access to these media. For example, even if there were more than five billion mobile phone subscriptions in the world in 2010,[1] internet users were only 29 per cent of the world's population.[2] Clearly emerging from the book's articles are the deep structural media divides within and between countries – divides that in their turn depend on economic, social, political and cultural inequalities in society that are much more sluggish.

One recurrent theme related to children, youth and media, which has strongly intensified during the past three decades and is also found in this book, is the need for media literacy education. In these contexts media literacy means, besides having access to digital and other media, the ability to scrutinize the media and media contents in a critical way, to express one's own views through the media and to creatively take part in production of media contents. Although media production is becoming easier with the advent of new and cheaper technologies, it is vitally important that these opportunities reach all young people. That is, also reaching children and youth in poor, discriminated and peripheral parts of the world, and in more or less disregarded situations constructed by power relations based on gender, ethnicity, class, low literacy, lack of education, etc. Living in such areas and situations is a reality for the majority of young people in the world.

There is hope that media literacy will also include young people's participation in the public sphere as citizens. This could be a way to balance the risks and potentially harmful influences of media output, which, seen globally, is becoming more and more commercialized. New kinds of individualized, interactive and "dynamic" advertising and marketing are increasingly targeting and seeking to involve children and young people as consumers – at the same time as local programmes, software, etc., of high quality aimed at children often are scarce.

There are certainly many examples of how youth across the world act in their local communities as citizens, creating alternative media, offering resistance to existing circumstances, and communicating for social change. This book offers several such examples.

But it is unrealistic to believe that problematic media influences can be counteracted by the children themselves, acting as independent agents and "self-regulators". This cannot be achieved even if it is supported by a subject-to-subject interplay with civil society – parents, teachers, peers, voluntary organizations, etc. Children's everyday lives are permeated by media use and their life situations are highly diverse and unequal – not all children have such collective support.

And although there are examples, some included in this book, of the media helping to reduce serious health problems in collaboration with other societal forces, there are other examples of the media contributing to worsening health. When the media fail to inform about facts and instead heavily emphasize entertainment, underpin and encourage stereotypes about, e.g., gender and sexuality, and/or give the impression that more consumption will make you happy, no progress in this area is made.

It is therefore imperative that the media strive to act more ethically and responsibly. If they cannot do so on their own, due to their dependence on trade and industry marketing, they must be supported and followed up by responsible societal policy.

Several articles in the book show that the media will certainly be more attractive to children and young people if they try to see needs and problems from the perspective of the third of the world's population under 18 years of age (or the almost half of the world's population under 25 years). Children's needs and problems as they express them, concern, among other things, justice, equality and solidarity, engagement in societal issues, and a culture one is familiar with. The media's work towards addressing these issues is indispensable.

It is our hope that these insights, spread to a wider audience, will be further integrated into local and multilateral communicative actions aimed at implementing the rights of children.

Let us conclude by thanking all contributors to the Research Forum and this Yearbook. We also wish to thank the team of the World Summit on Media for Children and Youth in Karlstad for their excellent organization and cooperation. Finally, we would like to express our deep gratitude to the Nordic Council of Ministers, whose support made the Research Forum and Yearbook possible. The Nordic Ministers of Culture have made globalization one of their top priorities, unified in the strategy: "Creativity – the Nordic response to globalization", of which the Research Forum and this Yearbook are a part.

Göteborg in May 2011

Cecilia von Feilitzen *Ulla Carlsson* *Catharina Bucht*

Notes

1. http://www.itu.int/ITU-D/ict/statistics
2. http://www.internetworldstats.com

Plenary Session on
New Questions, New Insights, New Approaches

Introduction to the Research Forum Plenary Session

Young People in the Digital Media Culture

Ulla Carlsson

New media landscapes have transformed the social functions of media and communication. In the midst of this development are our young. Young people of today share ideas, thoughts and values through mass media, music and a variety of internet platforms. All over the world they are organizing themselves and networking in many different ways.

But opportunity is not equal for all.

Children and youth represent more than one-third of the world population. In the least developed countries young people account for nearly 70 percent, whereas in the industrialized regions of the world the figure is less than 25 per cent (UN Population Division, 2009). More than half of the young people live in poverty. Many of them lack access to media, information and knowledge. It is a world of poverty with social and economic exclusion, poor schools, gender discrimination, unemployment and inadequate health systems. A world seems far away where young people, not least girls, have good opportunities to express their own views and have their opinions respected.

The Nordic countries, the region you are visiting this week, are reckoned among the other, "well situated" parts of the world, where education and health care are universal and the prospects of gainful employment are good. Nearly everyone has access to mobile telephones and 90 per cent have internet access at home; newspaper and book reading continues to be widespread and frequent.

The mission of The International Clearinghouse on Children Youth and Media is to cast light on what is currently known about children, youth and media from a global point of view. One might say that we also help to bring order to a complex subject area, where many diverse views and interests converge, and consensus in the research community sometimes is lacking. It is our hope that bringing together a disparate body of research findings and ideas about young people and the media will contribute and stimulate to further research in the field.

Our Clearinghouse has published twelve yearbooks to date – you have received the one for 2010 here at the World Summit. In the yearbooks, researchers and experts from all the corners of the world have treated a wide variety of issues from many different perspectives. The global dimension is a core principle in the work of the Clearinghouse with respect to both the content we publish and distribute, and the contributors who produce it. This Yearbook represents a departure from that hallowed principle of global representation. The focus rests on children, youth and media in a digitized media culture based on work being done in the research communities of Denmark, Finland, Iceland, Norway and Sweden. But, we hope that the issues treated here will interest a broad range of readers all over the world.

So, we are convinced of the importance of research – knowledge lies at the core of how the most important issues regarding children, youth and media will be treated. Meaningful strategy documents and goal-oriented programs need to be based on knowledge from both research and experience.

Issues of democracy and development are central – not least the questions, how to bridge the knowledge divides in the world, and how to use media and communication both as tools and as a way of articulating processes of development and social change. We should do well to recall that throughout history, young people have often been active participants in the manifestation of social change, and most times their creative uses of media and innovative practices of communication have been crucial in the process. Consider, for example, the key roles young people play in citizen media, or in campaigning for political freedom, freedom of expression, fair trade and HIV/AIDS prevention (Tufte & Enghel, 2009).

The communication society of today has enormous potential regarding our planet, not least for those who are young today – we gain access to cultures and knowledge that used to be beyond our horizons. But in many parts of the world, there are fears that globalization poses a mortal threat to uniqueness, that media are in control of the globalized cultural sphere. At the same time the world seems to retreat further from us. People defend their identities, and when common culture can no longer be maintained as it once could be, stockades are raised around local cultures, religious beliefs and communities. Transcendance of boundaries and defense of boundaries are twin aspects of the globalization process.

Globalization processes force us not only to focus more on transnational phenomena in general, but also to highlight difference. We have to argue for a stronger focus on regional and national inequalities and social transformation. About 60-70 per cent of the inequality that exists today is inequality between nations; two hundred years ago 90 per cent of the inequality was within countries (Bourguignon & Morrison, 2002). Thus, the gap between wealthy and poor countries has increased dramatically over the past two hundred years.

So, more than ever we need mutual understanding of both local and global media cultures. Often, however, we lack the knowledge, indicators and measuring tools that would help us to explore the insights we need to reach these goals. The development of such resources allows us to follow developments in the rapidly changing media field, nationally, regionally and internationally, and to bring the emergence of new phenomena and relationships to light.

Research communities have to create platforms to achieve long-term goals through national, regional and international collaboration. We have to build on past work, but break new ground. We need fresh, unexpected insights and new comparative research questions. We need to develop analytical frameworks that will guide comparative analysis of media cultures – much more open to holistic perspectives. Without that we run an obvious risk that certain factors will grow out of proportion.

And, there is an urgent need for the agenda to become sensitized to different cultural contexts and intercultural approaches to a much higher degree than has been the case to date. We need to learn more from one another, to share knowledge, ideas and context.

That will be crucial to our ability to deal adequately with the difficult issues regarding young people and media on the global, regional and local arenas in the future. These issues touch on vital democratic values – what kind of society do we want, and who is this 'we'? (Mansell, 2009). The protection of human rights and freedom of expression, ensuring universal access to the internet as a public service, and promoting media literacy are key priorities.

And now, we have, I must say, two highly qualified contributors to this plenary session, brimming with knowledge from long scientific, and professional, experiences.

I am afraid that my few words of introduction can hardly do them justice.

Dr. Dafna Lemish is Professor of Communication from Tel Aviv University in Israel, and the Center on Media and Child Health at Harvard University, USA.[1] She is the editor of the *Journal of Children and Media* and has published extensively in the area of children and media. Her presentation today is based on her new book: *Screening Gender on Children's Television: The Views of Producers around the World* (2010).

Dr. Ibrahim Saleh is Convenor of Political communication at the Centre for Film and Media Studies in the University of Cape Town. Saleh is a Fulbright scholar and a senior media expert in the Media Sustainability Index (MSI) of Middle East & North Africa (MENA). Saleh also chairs the Journalism Research and Education Section in the International Association for Media and Communication Research (IAMCR), and a Global Partner Organization of the UN Alliance of Civilizations (AoC) Media Literacy Education Clearinghouse.

Note

1. She became in the Autumn of 2010 Professor and Chair of the Department of Radio-TV, College of Mass Communication & Media Arts, Southern Illinois University, USA.

References

Bourguignon, F & Morrisson, C: Inequality among World Citizens: 1820-1992. *The American Economic Review*, 92(2002)4

Carlsson, U (ed.): *Children and Youth in the Digital Media Culture. From a Nordic Horizon*. The International Clearinghouse on Children, Youth and Media, Nordicom, University of Gothenburg, 2010 (Yearbook 2010)

Mansell, R: *Power, Media Culture and New Media*. London School of Economics and Political Science, 2009, LSE Research Online (http://eprints.lse.ac.uk)

Population Ageing and Development. UN Population Division, 2009 (www.un.org/esa/population/publications/ageing/ageing2009.htm)

Tufte, T & Enghel, F (eds.): *Youth Engaging with the World. Media, Communication and Social Change*. The International Clearinghouse on Children, Youth and Media, Nordicom, University of Gothenburg, 2009 (Yearbook 2009)

Eight Working Principles for Change in Children's Television

The Views of Producers around The World[1]

Dafna Lemish

As part of an exploration of ways to create better television for children around the world, I decided to seek the advice and to draw upon the accumulated knowledge and expertise of producers of quality television for children around the world. Over the course of four years, I talked to 135 media professionals from 65 countries in all continents, whom I personally met in various international events for children's media, including, among others: *Prix Jeunesse International festivals* in Munich in 2004, 2006 and 2008; the *Japan Prize* in Tokyo in 2006; *Basel-Karlsruhe Forum* in Basel in 2007; and *The 5th World Summit on Media for Children* in Johannesburg in 2007.

Interviews included questions about the producers' own personal career development; their current work; their perceptions of social issues in their culture and in television for children in their country; their impressions of social representations in their own and others' work that they have viewed in the festivals; their suggestions and aspirations for change, and the like. Almost all interviews were tape-recorded and transcribed verbatim, and, since most interviewees were not native English speakers, were also lightly edited for English, trying to preserve the style and flavor of the original conversation. The transcripts were later submitted to a grounded thematic analysis of the main issues that surfaced in the interviews. I took their dreams, advice, frustrations, and questions with me to the libraries in an attempt to integrate grounded professional knowledge with academic analytical and theoretical frames. Thus, the social action research project that evolved now also illuminates potential benefits of integrating professional and academic ways of knowing about the media and social world.

The aim of this article is to provide an abbreviated version of the conceptual framework for producing better content on television for children around the world that emerged in this study. To do so, eight grounded main principles are presented that are at the heart of what the media professionals interviewed shared with me:

Equality

- Equality is advanced when boys and girls are treated equally as well as offered equal roles and opportunities on television, all the while recognizing and respecting their differences.

The central, underlying assumption driving interviewees' observations was the need for gender equality in programming for children. Interviewees believed that boys and girls should have equal rights, equal opportunities, and equal responsibilities; and that both genders should be given the same care and nourishment to promote their well-being and materialize their potentialities, to live a dignified life of self worth and fulfillment, and to become productive participants in their families and communities. According to the most salient view, males and females need to be on the screen in equal numbers, in all genres, because their presence symbolizes their actual or the need for real presence on equal terms. For many interviewees, gender equality meant allowing both boys and girls to own the same personality characteristics, to occupy the same roles and professions, to have the same position in the story. More specifically, interviewees talked about "role-reversal" where roles traditionally associated with one gender are portrayed by the other one: boys aspiring to be ballet dancers, hospital nurses, or teachers and girls aspiring to be bus drivers, boxers, or scientists; boys engaged in sewing, cooking, and taking care of young siblings while girls play sports, lead a group, and operate technology.

One comment repeated by many was the desire to be able to show girls in leadership roles and boys in nurturing ones. Leona (Philippines), for example, said:

> [...] depicting boys and girls free to be who they are, [...] being careful to cast characters and create stories that show the diversity of roles of men and women and girls and boys, that emphasize relationships of equals. We have story lines that would challenge stereotypes, for example, of what girls can and cannot do, or of boys being suppressed in expressing their emotions.

This vision includes the ability to present the entire range of emotions in both boys and girls without being restricted by social expectations that boys conceal their vulnerability and girls control their inner energies. Equality for boys meant, for interviewees, allowing them to express themselves and to display nurturing and caring qualities. On the other hand, equality for girls meant developing characters that are smart, independent, and assertive, who are allowed to be humorous and strong. Above all, producers want to see boys who have given up on aggression being the focal of their driving force; and girls who have given up on sexual flirtations, as their perceived strength. They wanted to see boys and girls who empower themselves in other, more constructive and diverse ways.

Diversity

- Diversity is achieved when children are represented through a wide range and variety of characters, both within each social category of gender, race, ethnicity, etc., as well as across all possible groups.

The principle of diversity calls for attention to be directed to the intersections between all other central human circumstances and characteristics that interact to construct identities: gender, race, ethnicity, class, religion, language, geography, history, abilities, age, sexuality, and family. The position was clear: When there is only one character in the program representing a human group, she or he is expected to stand for all. In this situation one human characteristic is the most striking feature, a fact that lends itself to stereotyping. In contrast, when there are many girls (and boys), characters can exhibit a variety of characteristics and qualities, can appear in different forms and shapes and as a combination of many possibilities.

Diversity was a major concern expressed by many producers. Abby (U.S.) for example said:

> I think diversity is a huge issue in this country [...] African Americans, Hispanics, Asians [...] there is very little diversity in children's television [...]. Race, religion, culture – trying to become a united country, we need to also recognize that we are a diversified country, we are different, we respect people who are different. We need to say to children that we are human beings [...].

Svein (Norway), described diversity issues related to recent immigration waves from around the world, a concern expressed by many North European interviewees:

> We try to raise the status of children coming from other countries [...] as there are a lot of immigrant children [...].. We have to reflect that in all of our programs [...]. We have to show children from Turkey and Pakistan, and also from Asia – Korea, Vietnam. A lot of the children have been born here and they are mixed in the Norwegian society more than their parents, and that's where some of the conflicts are. And we have to deal with it on television.

Elaine (Brazil) framed the discussion of diversity in terms of presenting to children a society of inclusion:

> An issue for us is much more the issue of inclusion, [...]. When we talk about inclusion we are talking about the blacks, and the poor, the disabled, the Indians.

Overall, participants' framing of diversity assumed a position of multi-culturalism and tolerance for difference expressed by means of representations consistent with changing configurations of societies and the challenges involved in shifting away from the hegemonic whiteness on television. Diversity is required everywhere, in all forms and types of characters in fiction and non-fiction formats, both front-stage and backstage. Different body and facial shapes and skin colors, costuming and apparel of all cultural styles and fashions, languages and accents, home interiors and foods, customs and religious traditions. It should reflect the urban and the rural ways of life, as well as the various classes that constitute and are representative of children's worlds. Good characters and exciting stories can appear in all colors, shapes, and forms.

Complexity

- The principle of complexity embraces, in some degree, the "different but equal" position and, in practice, seeks to broaden the possibilities and traits for both boys and girls by producing more complex, rounded, and non-stereotypical characters.

The need for character-complexity was one of the central arguments raised by interviewees, given their widespread critique of the general presence of under-developed characters and stereotyping. Their arguments claimed that uni-dimensional characters, built upon one specific trait (e.g., being the "bitch-blond" or "goody-book reader" girl; the "bully" or "geek" boy), lend themselves to simplicity, stereotyping, and under-developed plots.

While the principle of diversity discussed above focuses on the inclusion of a variety of character types, the principle of complexity requires that each character will be a "well-rounded", non-stereotypical, complete human being. So while diversity focuses on the "between character" principle, complexity centers on the "within" character principle. Stated in a different manner, a program may have many diverse characters, yet some or all may be very stereotypical and lack complexity.

Julie (U.K.) provided a detailed explanation advocating for complexity:

> [...] I think the more complex we can make our characters, the more sides of them that we can show, [...] the richer the characters are, and the more we address that issue. I think it's important not to oversimplify any characters [...] What's really important is: Do we believe these characters? Do we understand them in that context? Do we think they feel what they feel and behave how they behave?

The principle of complexity embraces, to some degree, the understanding of "different but equal", but works towards broadening possibilities and traits for both boys and girls by producing more complex, round, and non-stereotypical characters.

Similarity

- According to the principle of similarity, the script shall emphasize the shared aspects of girls and boys' lives, rather than dwell on the differences that can evolve into conflict, stereotyping, status-marking, and animosity.

The principle of similarity celebrates children who share the same challenges, aspirations, morality, dreams, and hopes; children who need love and friendships, have adventures and overcome difficulties; children who are curious and eager to explore their surroundings, and who struggle with their multiple identities; children who try to carve their place in the world. The principle advocates presenting children, both boys and girls, who are self-willed, positive, share their problems and accomplishments. In such cases, the issues are presented not as girls' issues or boys' issues, not as majority children or minority children, not abled children or disabled children, but as issues of children's lives.

Good programming, so the interviewees told me, brings children closer to each other and at the same time closer to themselves. This desire to see a shared world on television, where similarities between children override the differences between them, stands in striking contrast to the popularity of the gender segregation, for example, that highlights gender differences and construct two separate worlds for marketing purposes. As Matt (U.S.) put it to me, very simply:

> Appealing to every child is not a problem, because every child really wants the same things, you know. They want to be loved, they want to laugh, they want to cry, they want to learn, they want to celebrate their life, they want to feel like they can contribute in their local environment, they want all these things.

With so much in common, sticking to stereotypes "is just plain lazy", as they often said, while developing fun and smart characters who are true to themselves but also do unexpected things is difficult to create. As many of the conversations unfolded, it became clear that breaking stereotypes and opening up the screen to blurring gender and ethnic differences and offering children real choice that cuts across the gender divide is seen by interviewees as a way to foster a safer and more healthy environment for children's growth and development. They advocated presenting "strong" characters that are energetic, intelligent, active, trustworthy, cooperative, who work towards a goal, overcome difficulties and deal wisely with conflict. They are supported by good friends and caring adults. Abby (U.S.) said:

> [...] and I think that we as program-makers have a responsibility to those children, and we have to show them the good things in life. And the good things in life are not merchandizing and they're not television-to-sell things, they're embracing interesting characters, they're showing love, they're showing strength in individuals, morality, and when I say morality I mean individual morality, doing the right thing. And not all television does that.

Beatriz (Ecuador) wanted

> [....] to show the process how one can deal with weakness and convert disabilities into abilities

and Eric (Canada) suggested:

> It's not about role models (on television), it's about becoming who you are.

Unity

- Unity requires that friendships and relationships between girls and boys be constructed on equal terms.

The principle of unity refers to the possibility of presenting children as sharing life experiences together, collaborating with one another, united in their joint quest for happy growth and development. Discussions of similarities between children, applying the principle of unity will bridge existing gaps between gender and mutli-cultural relationships and assist in overcoming barriers by presenting narratives in which children manage cross-group friendships. Scripts seeking to achieve greater unity emphasize the basic qualities and aspirations that mark all children as human beings. In advancing unity, interviewees argued that demonstrating alternative relationships and encouraging cooperation would serve as an intervention in attempts to reform contemporary childhood segregation on television.

Most central to interviewees' claims was the desire to see boys and girls collaborating on terms that are not reduced to sexual tension and romance. Samora (South Africa) expressed it directly:

> I want to see boys and girls interact together, friendship without being sexual... we lost that... everything on TV that shows interaction patterns is sexualized. I want to see that they can go out and have fun together, share the same dance, share the same hobbies, and it will change the dynamics of life together.

Kasper (Denmark) shared an experience producing a more complex program and message to viewers:

> We tried to do something that shows relationships between the two genders... we have a game show right now called *Amigo* and there we tried to make boy and girl friends that help each other. They realize that they both have different skills that they can use, and sometimes it is the girls that are based on the physical things and sometimes the boys on the academic things, or vice versa. We are trying.

A very different example was demonstrated in the *Little Peace of Mine*, a documentary about a tense and complicated relationship between two teens – a Jewish-Israeli boy and a Palestinian girl – who try to collaborate in initiating a peace movement, and who challenge one another as they seek to understand their deeply engrained political differences.

Furthermore, such an approach argues for breaking the linkage between attractive appearance and experiencing satisfying relationships as well as exciting adventures. Eliminating such stereotypes suggests that boys and girls of all shapes, colors, and forms can be friends and enjoy good times together.

Family

- Family is the main social context of children's lives and, therefore, grounding children's experiences within a context of supportive, caring family life offers positive role models for human relationships, for parent-child as well as adult-child relations.

The centrality of family in children's programming was a major theme in interviewees' practice. Regardless of the kind of family structure accepted as desirable, there was agreement that children need to be seen growing up in nurturing and healthy family environments. Harsh criticism was expressed against the trend in many American situation comedies and films to present dysfunctional families, generally represented by incompetent parents, or to just ignore families altogether, as part of the "home alone" trend. The interviewees in this study resisted this trend whole-heartedly. In their family-centered view, childhood is a period requiring special care, in general, and adult-characters who embody a vision and model what children can, indeed, grow into being.

The centrality of parents to children's healthy development and as models of parenthood, albeit one that is changing, is expressed by Hanne (Norway):

> [...] parents are very important; parents are always behind the relationships and stories [...] there are also grandparents and I like to put them in roles of passing on traditions but highlighting more the ones that are more gender fair in their roles. And, there is something to be said about our commitment to promote our own local culture and to highlight certain aspects of it.

Locating stories within an inter-generational context is thus a way to encourage connectivity to a collective culture and heritance as well as to specific family arrangements that foster healthier childhoods.

The discussion of families was often translated more specifically into a discussion of fathers and new forms of masculinities. The desire to see positive role models of men who are neither dictators in their families nor stupid buffoons came up in many of the interviews, with professionals from all parts of the world, although it was particularly prevalent in interviews with Northern hemisphere interviewees. In her discussion of *Sesame Street* co-production in the Arab world, Caroline (U.S.) said:

> [...] to have very strong adult characters, both males and females; males that are integrated with females; males that are supporting women in their roles; males that are also very active with their kids. One of the things that came out with our Palestinian program was that men who were watching the show commented that they learned from the show about being more active with their own kids. [...].

The presentation of children growing up while being supported and cared for by responsible and loving adults is claimed, by many, to be one of the major contributions that television can make to assist children: These may be street children in huge urban centers whose life circumstances left them to fend for themselves or "latchkey" children of affluent families caught in the pressures of a competitive capitalist world who pamper their children with leisure technologies and accessories as replacement for real meaningful presence in their lives.

Authenticity

- Authenticity leads television programs to be constructed with depictions of true-to-life characters, narratives, and social contexts.

The principle of authenticity reflects producers' call for programs that present a social world that seems "true to life" with the potential to foster identification and attachment. This stance is particularly striking in the face of pressures exerted on producers by broadcasting authorities to conform to external, profit driven market values that produce higher rating scores; and to exceed to political and ideological pressures to refrain from dealing with sensitive topics that might alienate audiences or undermine the status quo (e.g., homosexuality; opposition to the ruling governments; fads and fashion in the industry to follow winning formulas and successful clichés, and the like).

The interviewees' focus, in regard to authenticity, was on the credibility of the characters themselves. Tina (U.S.) discussed characters' appearance:

> They are real kids and so, you know, they've got pimples, their hair looks bad some days, and they are not perfect looking. And, I actually think that this is just right, something as simple as that is very empowering to see. Just to see yourself reflected back on screen, particularly girls, because I think that it's been the standard and the ideal for young girls in the U.S. – skinny, being pretty, being perfect, in all the magazines they read nobody is real. I think this is really groundbreaking to present really just genuine authentic looking kids.

The relevancy of the TV characters to their audience's everyday experience was a central theme in relation to authenticity. Such, for example, was the discussion offered by Omar (Syria):

> When we adopt imported animation programs from China, Korea, Japan, we have to adjust them to fit Arab children. They need to make it familiar to the children, so it won't look strange to them; for example, in things like relationships between children and parents, or in schools, their treatment of authorities.

Disrespect to adults is foreign to Moslem cultures and perceived as undermining their mores and values. Alternative forms introduce unauthentic experiences of what social life is or should be like into the homes of children, in this case in Syrian society.

Thus, authenticity for the interviewees, in the sense of presenting a credible reality and being "true to life", offers not only a criteria for evaluating the quality of programs and its potential to resonate with their audiences, but perhaps more importantly, a criterion for introducing change in an effective and meaningful way. Authenticity in the context of producing television for children was only cited to mean a positive principle that can be stated colloquially as not "selling out"; meaning, not to surrender to external pressures to abandon one's inherit local culture and values and a desire to create a program which is true to one's social reality.

Voicing

- Voicing is achieved when television programs are organized in such a manner as to present the perspectives of children themselves as they are viewed and expressed by them.

The final principle is interviewees' call to "give voice" to children themselves. The notion of empowering under-represented and mis-represented groups by giving them a voice in the media has been discussed extensively by scholars with diverse interests from a variety of theoretical approaches. Children, in particular, lack space, a voice and hence agency in both the theorizing of childhood as well as in its representation, in all cultural and media forms. In the context of our discussion, "giving voice" refers, essentially, to enabling children's perspectives to be expressed in adult-produced media. It is the value of "children talking to children" that is highlighted in these calls for "giving voice" rather than "children talking to adults" or children "working out" their inner world for their own benefits.

Interviewees felt that creators of children's programs often talk about children rather than letting children talk for themselves. This was also expressed in the form of a distinction between programs that are *about* children versus those *for* children. This distinction suggests a program featuring children does not necessarily have children's well-being and needs as its goal. Casting children as program characters may be a necessary but certainly not a sufficient condition for consideration as a quality program for children. Several examples illustrate this argument. Emma (Bolivia) said:

> We made a series with the title *With Our Own Voices* where children talk about their lives, about their rights. They can speak, they can talk with their point of view; and I think it's very important that they do so in their language [...]. Margaret (Kenya) shared: We were watching a program from Asia about a girl who wants to go to school and it is very interesting because it was a story from a girl's point of view [...] so the issues are still the same but from different point of view. And Mpule (Botswana) recommended: I give them all voices so that they share how they feel, they share their success stories, their fears, their disappointments together. Let them have a face.

As in reference to the other principles of equality, there was the assumption behind the interviewees' call for "giving voice" that such a strategy will somehow contribute to social change by allowing children to be agents of change themselves, and that it will also benefit children, both on and off screen. It was believed that it somehow has the potential to empower children, girls and marginalized children in particular, who are still silenced to a great degree in many societies around the world.

In conclusion

The concept of "principle" is used here as an ideal, a vision to be achieved, and through which prescriptive statements for action by producers seeking social change in children's world are derived. Accordingly, they can based be framed as "working" principles that can serve as strategies for production practice and recommendations for advancing concrete change on television screens viewed by children and youth throughout the world. Concern of the principles of equality, diversity, complexity, similarity, unity, family, authenticity, and voicing seems to be shared by many of the interviewees – despite differences in cultural and geographical location, gender, education, conditions of employment, professional expertise – and thus can be claimed to be universal in large degree. However, clearly, the interpretation of how the principles presented could, or should, be translated into media productions, as well as their social implications, vary culturally. This having been noted, when most interviewees referred to each of these conceptual-ideals they did so with the intent of stating that these are issues that concern them and are part of their decision process in conceptualizing and executing a programmatic idea for children's TV whose general vision remains within the overriding goal of engaging young viewers in a humane, just world.

Note

1. This article is based with permission on an abbreviated form of chapter 6 in Lemish, D. (2010) *Screening Gender on Children's Television: The Views of Producers around the World*. NY: Routledge. Please see book for the extensive discussion of these and other issues.

What Underlies Children, Media and Democracy in the Middle East and North Africa (MENA)?

Ibrahim Saleh

> When all have access to the lights of knowledge, the time of democracy will have come. (Victor Hugo, circa 1840)

The daunting reality of the contemporary world is that autocracies and semi-authoritarian states lack the basic foundation for building a democracy. In these countries, the media are weak, fragile, and at risk of collapse, which means that the challenge is not to pressure media and media educators to surrender power, but rather to figure out how to regenerate legitimate power in the first place. The imperative is not just mediate empowerment of citizens but also make them interested in truth, in full and universal knowledge, rather than in improving society. This would be 'political thought', which instigates the achievement of knowledge, by making the civil society play a role in forming a collective view and a common mission to make the states serve the interests of their people instead of the current reverse situation that ended by strikes, violence and societal disintegration in Tunisia, Algeria, Jordan and Egypt.

At the same time, the media could be a powerful entertainment and educational tool for children, given the right programming. Media also play a crucial role in shaping a healthy democracy, because they simply make us aware of the various social, political and economical activities and developments taking place around the world. Moreover, a democratic system of governance is supposed to enable citizens to choose their rulers and live equally within a state of law and order, where the citizens are the key factor in the process.

In recent years, there has been an explosion of interest in the role of media in the lives of children. Much of this interest has been inspired by those who recognize the immense potential of the UN Convention on the Rights of Child (1989) – which contains many messages for media practitioners – to become a universal standard against which society's attitude towards children can be judged.

However, it is important to note that the media emerge as an independent institution with a certain logic to which other institutions have to accommodate. Besides, the media have simultaneously become an integrated part of other institutions, such as politics, work, family and religion, and media activities are increasingly performed through both interactive and mass media (Hjarvard, 2008: 105).

At this historical moment, we cannot ignore the inseparable roles of mediatization and social change, which the media could offer to societies, especially children, such as the extension of human communication abilities in both time and space, replacing social activities that previously took place face-to-face, instigating the amalgamation of activities, and combining face-to-face communication with mediated communication, thus causing the media to infiltrate everyday life. Moreover, different actors in different sectors must adapt their behaviour to accommodate the media's evaluations, formats and routines (Schulz, 2004).

In the Middle East and North Africa (MENA), governments are not subject to the will of the people, but instead dominate and control their subjects. However, the region is still suffering from internal disputes over different issues, such as wealth and power, which makes democracy an alien notion within the traditional political vocabulary.

The primary conditions for any media development include the availability of a potential audience, the development of symbolic language, technology, and the evolution of freedom of expression (Hick, 1977). Having said so, the attainment of the concept of "deliberation of democracy" requires not only the ability to offer independent acceptable reasons, but also to articulate the concept of justice that legitimizes such reasons. This situation sets a high bar that certainly excludes children (Cohen, 1997).

However, a proper media discourse and real advocacy of political and civil society activists, as well as schools, could still orient children to the fact that democratization expands into the political participation of citizens and provides for real and meaningful collective control over public policy. The key to democratization is inspiring younger generations to believe it is possible, even though the general picture is dim. This requires a complete reshuffling of the traditional political systems, even if the fierce resistance from factions with deeply rooted interests in maintaining the current status quo makes any development almost impossible (Al-Asaadi, 2007).

Having said this, the present article seeks not only to "include" the children of the Middle East and North Africa (MENA) in the media, and not only to ask how the media treat them as disenfranchised apprentices to adult society, but also to position them at the heart of human rights standards and empower them in a democratized society.

This is happening at a time when the region faces the challenge of having a very young population. As mentioned in the UNDP (United Nations Development Programme) Arab Knowledge Report 2009, the 10-24 age group accounts for 60 per cent of the population, and is expected to number between 125 and 150 million by 2025. Many of these young people are unemployed, and the data show that unemployment rates have risen continuously, from 10.6 per cent in the 1980s to 14.5 per cent in the 1990s.

The present article also attempts to find ways to equip children in MENA with the knowledge and tools needed for meaningful participation in civil society and democracy. Hence, the central question is: "How do we instil the values of citizenship and active participation in the youngest, and in many ways the most important, members of our society?"

Considering the current Middle Eastern political map, one can readily understand that democracy is a cause and effect for any possible development, and accordingly there must be a drastic change in the current setting before introducing any real democracy in MENA. At the same time as many scholars from the region describe it as having common dominators – such as religions, cultures and languages – they usually forget to include violence, instability and the dominance of authoritarian regimes that have created a real "culture of fear" and uncertainty. Having said so, these regimes everywhere in MENA both reject any democratic restructuring, and also block any possible change that might alter their status quo as the ultimate powerful actors in these troubled societies (Saleh, 2010).

In this kind of environment, it is quite rational to find that the majority of the public is not interested in learning or permitted to learn that they have certain freedoms and rights. According to Amr Hamzawi, a senior researcher at the Carnegie Endowment for International Peace, the concept of citizenship is new to our region. A situation that makes this progressive idea a cosmetic media reality and a privilege that some might marginally enjoy while the majority of the angry publics remain deprived of it for many reasons (Al-Asaadi, 2007). A sad reality that made young generations in the MENA states as in the case of Tunisia and in Algeria reach a point of burning themselves alive in public place as a last call for attention to their miserable lives.

School textbooks, government-controlled mass media and chauvinistic national celebrations tend to glorify the heads of state (regardless of whether the state is a monarchy or a republic), resonating with the idea of the Pharaoh in ancient Egypt as the ultimate sacred figure, who remained in power for decades. Those rulers behave like they own the country, and they commonly pass on that ownership to their sons, as if the country were a family heirloom.

It is thus possible to summarize the four main criticisms of media in the Middle East and North Africa: The first is that the media only half-heartedly endorse freedom of expression and of the press, while ignoring other basic human needs. The second is that the media take a superficial approach to freedom and democracy, something that marginalizes the interests of the majority to preserve the ruling minority's interests. The third problem is the media's overemphasis on major regional issues – such as the invasion of Iraq, Islamophobia, and the "resentment and tyranny" motivated by hatred for the Arab-Israeli conflict – while ignoring the vital local and national issues that affect the lives of the public directly and indirectly. The fourth problem is the simplistic official analysis of the multifaceted complexities that produce a perception of fear of the "other", and with that excessive use of force against the opposition.

There are numerous examples, including Syria, because when Hafez Al-Assad died, his power went directly to his son, Bashar, and the constitution was changed to satisfy the condition of age, as he was not yet forty. It is feared that the same thing will be repeated in Libya, Egypt and Yemen, although Egypt considers itself to belong to the "emerging democracies" (Saleh, 2007).

The MENA countries are still operating under authoritarian systems, so their roles are limited to advancing government policies, because they are at the mercy of their governments, through licensing, legal action and financial assistance (Saleh, 2003).

There is a growing phenomenon of either not carefully reading the statistics, or trying to project an inaccurate utopian reality, motivated by pride or lack of knowledge or even a clash of interests, such has presuming that every young man in the region wanders the streets carrying his laptop (!). For example, when there was an escalating threat of the influenza AN1H1 in 2009, the MENA states recommended use of the internet for distance education (!). This statement ignores the fact that millions of students can neither follow lessons on the Internet nor perform examinations over the network because they do not have Internet in their homes in the first place.

In 2009, The Egyptian Agency for Public Mobilization and Statistics revealed that the total number of TV sets in all households in the Egyptian governorates was about 16,580,832, which means that at least 750,000 households in Egypt do not have TV sets (some households have more than one television). Furthermore, the number of computers in the country was about 1,376,343, while approximately only 428,451 computers out of this number were connected to the Internet, which is equivalent to only 32.1 per cent of the total number of households owning computers in the country (Abd El-Wahab, 2009).

The UNDP Arab Knowledge Report 2009 points out that the Arab media operate under government control, exercised through many channels of official oversight anchored in multiple laws (pp. 65-66). In addition, there is an unlimited number of obstacles facing the media practice, which range from licenses to financing, including the infrastructure. Censorship is widespread in the pre-publication stage and may also take the form of removing books from the shelves, after a number of years of publication. Given these impediments, the Arab civil society is absent from the global scene (p. 78).

In this kind of socio-political setting, the media scene in MENA is one of the most contradictory models in the world, with almost no attention given to children or to democracy *per se*. In this context, societies are troubled and overwhelmed with the negative effects of imposed democracies and the internal tripled-edged syndromes of illness, poverty and illiteracy. In reports on global indicators, most of the traditional media reflect a taming media and journalism practice by the governments making their roles a more public relation apparatus than a real forum for ideas. This dim picture is not different from media aspects that relate to democracy for children.

For example, in the Democracy Index published by the Economic Investigations Unit of the London weekly *The Economist,* all of the MENA states, with the exception of Iraq, Lebanon, and the occupied Palestinian territories, were ranked low (DI, 2010). And Transparency International, based in Berlin and publishing the Corruption Perception Index, stated in its 2009 report that 17 of the 22 Arab countries scored less than 5 (on a scale from 0 to 10) (CPI, 2010). The rankings correlate with the decline in the levels of freedom and democracy, the spread of corruption, and the decline in government performance.

It is thus not in the mind-set of many scholars, officials and educators in the region to value the possible role of media education in creating this sense of need for orientation that can alter the current societal values and promote a sound democratic practice to function properly and to keep up with the complex whole, as well as the continuously changing environment for children.

Even among children of the elite, who can afford to have a computer, can speak more than two languages other than Arabic, and are computer literate, these indicators seem alarming. In a media and society project sponsored by the British Council in Cairo, statistics emphasized that "surfing/navigation on the Internet" comes fifth in the ranking (62 per cent) after "watching TV" (100 per cent), "reading newspapers" (100 per cent), "hanging out with friends" (74 per cent), and "listening to the radio" (73 per cent). When the sample was asked about their computer skills, only 8 per cent said they are comfortable using the computers, while 47 per cent said they only know the basic applications. And 11 per cent said they are "very poor" in their computer skills, 4 per cent that they are "poor", and 30 per cent that they need to learn the basic skills (Saleh, 2007). The age of the students range from 18-22 and they are defined as elite who belong to high-income families. Nevertheless, this represents a very marginal percentage in societies with very high rates of illiteracy, poverty and illness.

In sum, Internet penetration is a far-fetched dream for the majority of our deprived societies, with the exception of the oil-producing countries, which have very few locals with Internet penetration in comparison to the foreign expatriates living there as in the case of the United Arab Eremites, Qatar, etc.

In an explorative study conducted in a course on media ethics and responsibility at the American University in Cairo in collaboration with "Soliya's Connect Program" over a period of five years (2004-2009), an attempt was made to assess the role of e-learning in attaining four main goals in the context of democracy: understanding democracy, knowledge development concerning democracy, skills building needed for democracy, and how this media education can help students improve their intellectual and human freedom (Saleh, 2007). The programme allowed sophomore students (2nd year) to engage in active participation and discussion among students from 49 universities all over the world through a sustained dialogue of 1.5 hours/week. One result was that 90 per cent of the students agreed, or strongly agreed, that the "Connect Program" gave them a better understanding of why people in the U.S. think the way they do. One student said:

> I learned a lot of things but most importantly, I started reading more about other cultures and even my own culture. I started educating myself more on different issues. (female, Sudanese, American University in Cairo)

Prior to the programme, 21 per cent of the students rated their knowledge of history and politics as "high" or "very high", and after the programme, the corresponding figure was 50 per cent.

Discussion

There is a need to change the direction of the power flow of communication between the educators and children in MENA. There must be a priority to engage and educate educators in the first place, before empowering children through skills building and outreach to everyone with lower levels of education and everyone living in rural areas, who are less aware of their rights. Most of the children in MENA live in a lie and die in silence (Saleh, 2009), especially because they neither have access to the media nor are allowed to embrace diversity in all its aspects, leaving them entrapped in their daily problems without the chance to think about media as a new window of development.

There is certainly some legitimate explanation for the current dim picture, which may be the result of long years of prevailing media hegemony that has failed to appeal to children, or to alert educators to orient children towards any ideas of civil liberties. In this context, there is no room for the luxury rights, at the same time as the majority of the public (with the exception of the Gulf States United Arab Emirates, Kuwait, and the kingdom of Saudi Arabia) is affected by more urgent matters, such as poverty, illiteracy and unemployment. At the same time, the media are heavily coloured by censorship and opinionated reporting to justify their corrupt practices, and furthermore promote the common practice of self-censorship, creating a culture of fear for future generations (Saleh, 2009).

But most importantly, the tragedy really lies in the dysfunctional relationship between the public and the state, and the absence of vision and strategy to address it. The media's role has been converted into a platform for pseudo-patriotism and embedded discourse of acute fear based on external threat. For example, Egypt and Algeria had a serious diplomatic crisis as a result of typical fights between soccer fans, at the same time as the crucial issues were completely disregarded.

This clouded situation has created a state of dissonance and continuous fighting between the angry publics and the autocratic states on the one hand, which resulted in further signs of vulnerability of the structure of civil society, on the other, causing societal tension and setbacks in democracy and impoverishing children.

A cornerstone in the current situation relates to the educators themselves and the blurring difference between their self-interests and the welfare of societies, and the overwhelming red lights that make any progressive initiative directly threatened by the autocracies in all the MENA states. Hence, media education lacks the authority to maintain personnel and implement curricula, to deal with problems in a transparent manner, and to produce sufficiency well-trained educators who are accountable and have the potential to believe in democracy and develop its related aspects of skills building and effectiveness.

Hence, there is a growing phenomenon of disengaged students, increasing rates of dropouts, lack of reading habits in general and motivation for reading about other cultures. The media in MENA are overwhelmed with heavy entertainment, absence of investigative reporting, widespread artificial academic barriers that have caused "contentious politics", and an absence of critical thinking and analytical skills due to the political climate and educational policies (Saleh, 2008). In addition, the schooling system in MENA continuously copycats Western curricula without any localization of the model, including the UNESCO frame of reference.

Conclusion

In conclusion, the present article deals with the current phase of media, democracy and children in a hostile and confusing setting in MENA. Yet one would safely frame the setback in the process of democratization due to many factors, which are all hampered by the Arabic media's "linguistic isolation" in the area of information technology, which puts the media in a complete state of flux for developing appropriate tools for work and production. And the media contents, coloured by religious extremism and intolerance, have been further aggravated by the current spin and dissemination of radical religious discourses.

There are two levels at which to address the many concerns about what underlies media, children and democracy in MENA:

At the micro levels, the value of teaching to promote democracy should have been a crucial part of the students' lifelong education; yet it has rarely been given sustained attention, if any, in the formal curriculum or the school community. Children's media education in democracy has to begin in their primary years, when the learning foundations of children's skills, habits and knowledge are laid. Children must learn how to question the reliability and validity of decisions and to offer constructive criticism and alternatives, as well as to understand that there exist other viewpoints, solutions or perspectives in addition to their own. The skill of listening to others and accepting and respecting their points of view are valuable lessons that could be taught in a classroom or in a children's programme that values democracy. In the end, children should realize that the aim of a democracy is never to convert people to one view, but rather to seek common ground and learn ways to improve society as a whole.

At the macro level, the media systems in MENA should aim to codify and amalgamate in a positive way the enthusiasm of children, their creativity, emotions, frustrations, fears, and anger and to generate safety valves so as to consolidate the modes of democratic production that are found in the micro-actions of everyday life, but that are still too weak to content ourselves with. If we acknowledge the necessity of conceiving of democracy's progression in MENA as the realization of two parallel phenomena, rationalization of the operation of institutions and codification of the modes of informal resistance, the problem nevertheless remains and is difficult to solve – how to harmonize the various aspects of this dual approach.

Teaching children the skills, processes and values of democracy involves the serious process of reflecting upon how we want to live as a society. Indeed, children's participation in building up democracy in their community through media would engage them in an active learning process.

The goal is primarily based on how we can attain real "edutainment" in the schools, universities and the media in a concurrent and complimentary paradigm that rests upon modelling the way democracy works. Tolerance, respect, and a willingness to learn from one another are primary values that must be provided through active learning at school and through the media – acquiring the necessary media skills – and through educating the educators.

In the end, there must be immediate attention to the question of "why media should teach democracy to children". As media educators, we need to have a firm conviction that democracy is possible, and that the value of a democratic way of life can be lived through media in conjunction with integrating it into the media discourse, not just in the school curricula. Hence, we need to focus on developing children's skills. Moreover, there should be a gradual construction of media accountability to unite the centrifugal forces now competing in society and to transform these forces into constructive energies.

References

Abd El-Wahab, S. (2009) Human Development Reports: 14 million households do not have computers and only 430 thousand families connect to the Internet. And more than 750 thousand families do not own TV sets from the ground up, Newsroom, Issue 225, 26/10/2009, http://www.elfagr.org/index.aspx, retrieved on February 15, 2010

Al-Asaadi, M. (2007) Democracy in the Middle East: The Missing Link. Strategic Foresight, *Inclusive World Forum*. http://www.strategicforesight.com/iwforum/al_assadi.htm

Cohen, J. (1997) Deliberation and Democratic Legitimacy, in Bohman, J. & Rehg, W. (Eds.) *Deliberative Democracy*. Cambridge, MA: MIT Press, p. 67

Corruption Perception Index 2010 Results. Transparency International, *The Global Coalition Against Corruption*. http://www.transparency.org/policy_research/surveys_indices/cpi/2010/results

Democracy in Retreat: Democracy Index 2010, *The Economist Intelligence Unit*. http://www.eiu.com/public/democracy_index.aspx

Hick, R.G. (1977) *A Survey of Mass Communication*. Gretna: Pelican Publishing Company

Hjarvard, S. (2008) *The Mediatization of Religion in Northern Lights*. Bristol: Intellect Press

Saleh, I. (2003) *Unveiling the Truth About the Middle Eastern Media. Privatization in Egypt: Hope or Dope?* Cairo: Cairo Media Center

Saleh, I. (2007) The Arab Search for a Global Identity: Breaking Out from the Mainstream Media Cocoon, in Seib, P. (Ed.) *New Media and the New Middle East*. New York: Palgrave MacMillan, pp. 19-38

Saleh, I. (2007) Teaching by Assessment: JMC Initiative, *Fourteenth AUC Research Conference*, Cairo, Egypt.

Saleh, I. (2008) Sitting in the Shadows of Subsidization in Egypt: Revisiting the Notion of Street Politics, *Journal of Democracy and Security*, Vol. 4:1-24

Saleh, I. (2009) Living in a Lie and Dying in Silence: The Trauma of Civil Society in the Middle East and North Africa, *The International Journal of Not-For-Profit Law,* 11(4), pp. 30-38

Saleh, I. (2010) In the Foggy Middle East: Just Wars Remain the Name of the Game, in Power Shifts and Global Governance: Challenges from South and North, in Kumar, A. & Messner, D. (Eds.) *Managing Global Governance*. German Development Institute: Anthem Press India

Schulz, W. (2004) Reconstructing Mediatization as an Analytical Concept, *European Journal of Communication*, 19(1), pp. 87-101

UNDP (United Nations Development Programme) (2009) Arab Knowledge Report 2009. Towards Productive Intercommunication for Knowledge.

http://content.undp.org/go/newsroom/2009/october/the-arab-knowledge-report-2009-towards-productive-intercommunication-for-knowledge.en, retrieved on August 26, 2010

Panel Session on
Media Literacy and Education

Introduction

Jordi Torrent and Alton Grizzle

We would like to thank NORDICOM for their support in organizing the Research Forum series at the 6th World Summit on Media for Children and Youth (June 2010, Karlstad, Sweden). NORDICOM's vision and generosity has enabled in-depth seminars, where Media and Information Literacy (MIL) experts from around the world have gathered to present and discuss their latest research and findings. It is within this framework that UNESCO and the United Nations Alliance of Civilizations (UNAOC) have the opportunity to present the upcoming joint initiative, currently known as "UNESCO and UNAOC Chair on Media and Information Literacy and Intercultural Dialogue" (UAC-MILID).

UAC-MILID will be a network of universities collaborating on the research, advancement and implementation of MIL across the world, in general, and in their own communities, in particular. At this Summit, five representatives of the core universities and associated universities of UAC-MILID's network will submit their latest thoughts and findings for open discussion. The session is the first public occasion to see the scope, quality and high level of analysis that will be generated through UAC-MILID's activities.

The eminent representatives and universities participating in this Research Forum session are the following:

- Dr. Renee Hobbs, Temple University, USA
- Dr. C.K. Cheung, Hong Kong University, China
- Researcher Mireia Pi with Dr. José Manuel Pérez Tornero, Universitat Autònoma de Barcelona, Spain
- Dr. Esther Hamburger, University of São Paulo, Brazil
- Dr. Samy Tayie, Cairo University, Egypt.

We are looking forward to continuing our collaboration with NORDICOM and all the partner universities of UAC-MILID, with the firm belief that the development and integration of Media and Information Literacy initiatives, within educational systems and in society at large, will support advancement towards more peaceful, just, and socially inclusive societies.

Views on the News

Media Literacy Empowerment Competencies in the Elementary Grades

Renee Hobbs, Henry Cohn-Geltner and John Landis

Few topics are more marginalized in the scholarly literature of mass communication, education and human development than the topic of children, current events, and news. For all the discourse circulating in scholarly journals about the importance of democracy, agency, critical practice, and the building of citizenship skills, there has been little exploration in the United States of the practice of helping children make sense of and engage with current events, news and journalism. Unlike England and several other European and Asian nations, the United States has no public television programming that offers national news targeted to children. In the U.S., private companies like Scholastic, Time and Channel One do provide news content to children, but there is scant little evidence about its value and relevance for children and youth.

By contrast, in Britain, children's news is a part of contemporary culture. A digital channel, CBBC, available nationwide, offers news and information programs to children aged 6-12, including the celebrated program *Newsround*. Other BBC networks focus on young children (CBeebies) and teens (BBC Switch). In Europe, there is some evidence that when it is available, children's news finds a receptive audience. In Northern Ireland, Messenger-Davies (2008) found that nearly one-third of children watched news frequently and 60 percent watched sometimes. In addition, children who watched children's TV news were more knowledgeable about news and current affairs and had more pronounced opinions on the representation of children than did a control group of children in the study. However, when news producers aim directly to reach child audiences, they may tend to "dumb down" the content, leading children to find it "boring" and "patronizing" (Messenger-Davies, 2008, p. 305). Matthews (2009) shows how news professionals' limited views of childhood may shape the audience's access to news content. Journalists who create news specifically for children may question the relevance of serious adult news topics and feature this less frequently within the news agenda as a result.

Children struggle "to connect the 'political' dimensions of their everyday experience with the official discourse of politics encountered through the media" (Buckingham, 2000, p. 203). Children and young people are affected by the news, especially when it depicts the harsh and painful aspects of contemporary life, including crime, war and injustice (Huston, Pfefferbaum & Ryes, 2008). There is a value to providing children with emotional consolation as they respond to news and current events, acknowledging the emotional vulnerability of children, who may be upset by representations of suffering depicted in news coverage of wars, conflict, terrorism and natural disasters like hurricanes and earthquakes. Exposure to television news can intensify children's anxiety and fear (Cantor, 1998). Experimental research on children, parents and terrorism news has shown that media literacy education for parents can reduce threat perceptions and anxiety, for both children and their parents, which may result from watching news about terrorism (Comer, Weiner, Furr, Bedias & Kendall, 2008).

But exposure to disaster news may also support the development of children's empathy with others. Adult intervention is required to activate this potential positive influence. As Huston, Pfefferbaum & Ryes (2008, p. 18) explain: "Parents, educators, and clinicians cannot leave it to the media to provide the clarifications that are necessary for young people to learn from a disaster. In times of disasters the media is focused on providing as much information as is possible to a largely adult audience. For something to come of this content that is of positive benefit for youth will require adults who moderate young people's media use by clarifying misconceptions, addressing reactions and concerns, and providing appropriate reassurance." Adults must provide some context and explanation of the content of what is presented, but they must also help children understand why news is structured the way it is, and how it is produced.

Unfortunately, when elementary educators bring newspapers into the classroom, it is simply used to model a writing format that combines pictures, words and snippets of unrelated information (Sahn & Reichek, 2008). Current events discussions may involve bringing in examples of daily news stories, but rarely move beyond a simple recitation of the information provided. In many schools, news and journalism is often treated simply for its value in developing vocabulary skills (Newspapers in Education, 2010). When social studies educators address the topic of current events, news and journalism at all, they often do so with notions that news is a "window on the world", simply providing information about "what happened". Walker's (2010) careful observation of six high school social studies teachers showed that although print and media texts are used in the classroom, teachers summarize media texts both before and after students were asked to interact with the material, eliminating the need for students to actually engage with the texts themselves. In this study, only 1 percent of classroom activities in social studies classrooms included media literacy activities that required students to analyze the content and format of media texts. Social studies teachers generally rely on lecturing, explanation, and recitation, which can be conceptualized as 'defensive teaching strategies' in which teachers control knowledge and classroom interaction, summarizing texts to guarantee a particular interpretation (Kinchloe, 2001).

These approaches to the use of news and journalism are problematic in the context of elementary education. When it comes to news, "children want understanding and explanation; they don't only want to see dramatic and violent explosions, they want to know why these explosions are happening, and what the underlying conflict is about" (Messenger-Davies, 2008, p. 308). If children and young people are to grow up as citizens in a democracy, then it is important that they understand how news is constructed, the economic context in which news is produced, how it aims to represent the world, and how it shapes our sense of ourselves and our community, nation and world.

Although learning about news has long been identified as a key part of the argument for media literacy education (Masterman, 1985), "it has proved difficult to support, develop and sustain teaching about broadcast news because of the ephemerality of the subject matter and the effort involved in bringing current TV, radio or Internet news into the classroom" (Bazalgette, Harland & James, 2008, p. 81). It's also difficult to conduct research on children's interpretations of the news because of the epistemological issues raised: researchers must "steer a course between the objectivist view that meaning is simply inherent in the text and the subjectivist view that the text can mean whatever the reader wants it to mean" (Buckingham, 2000, p. 215). Media literacy pedagogy is grounded in an inquiry-based model of teaching and learning which combines message analysis and creative production skills generally in relationship to mass media, popular culture and digital media. Although these practices are more likely to be found at the high school level (Hobbs, 2007), a number of elementary schools are beginning to introduce media literacy into the curriculum. In one elementary school in Silver Spring, Maryland, a communication arts focus is embedded into the Grade 4 and 5 program, students learn about journalism by comparing and contrasting the differences between newspaper and television news, analyzing patterns in news coverage, and interviewing and writing news articles and television reports (Hobbs, 2004).

Media literacy education is potentially "a very significant site in defining future possibilities for citizenship" (Buckingham, 2000, p. 221) especially as it is able to connect the fundamental practices of accessing, analyzing messages, and engaging in participation and social action. Educators generally acknowledge a cycle of empowerment, often defined as access, analyze, evaluate and communicate messages in a wide variety of forms (Thoman & Jolls, 2004). Media literacy education emphasizes that while education may begin in the classroom, it culminates with meaningful creative participation in the larger culture, leading to a personal and political transformation from spectator to citizenship.

Examining informal learning through an expanded empowerment model

In developing a media literacy program for urban elementary children, we wanted to explore some of the nuances of teaching about news and journalism, by combining activities that involve reading, viewing and discussing news and current events, with media analysis activities as well as composition and creative production. In the summer of 2009, a month-long educational program entitled Powerful Voices for Kids was offered as an intensive, summer enrichment program. In this university-school partnership program, 77 urban elementary children strengthened media literacy competencies by exploring issues in mass media and popular culture. The children enrolled in the program were primarily African-American children, from 41 different neighborhoods in the city of Philadelphia in the USA. The children enrolled in the program during the summer of 2009 were children who were attending a morning summer school designed to remediate reading, writing and math skills. More than 70 percent of children in the school were eligible for the free and reduced lunch program and only 50 percent of children in Grade 4 were reading at grade level.

The Powerful Voices for Kids program took advantage of the flexible nature of an informal learning environment, which supports opportunities to explore children's own interests and concerns in ways that are often not possible in the context of the academic school year. When children demonstrated an interest in news and current events, instructors opened up a space for conversation. Learning activities were the result of children's lived experience, interests, questions and concerns. While the instructors brought to the table the key concepts and core principles of media literacy education, the content and activities of the lessons emerged from the students themselves. Student interest and feedback was taken into account at each stage.

To capture the learning experience in these case studies, we conducted interviews with instructors, made classroom observations, reviewed samples of student writing and video production, and examined field notes produced by instructors during the learning process. Three case studies from this program illustrate some instructional practices of media literacy in relation to news and journalism. These practices emerged from an active process of dialogue and refinement between the instructors and students. Each of these case studies is then examined by considering its relative focus on seven processes that represent an expanded conceptualization of the media literacy empowerment model. It is important to note that this work is part of a process of discovering a model of learning progression in media literacy education that is developmentally sensitive to the needs of young children.

By looking at some examples of media literacy practice in the context of work with urban elementary children through the lens of these seven competencies, we seek to better understand the relationship between communication skills development, critical thinking and social action, in relation to the development capacities of young children. In this article, we identify some gaps and challenges in media literacy learning that are evident when looking at the three case studies in relationship to each other.

Grade 2/3: Comprehending news and creating a news broadcast

The instructor for this group worked with a group of children ages 7 and 8 over the course of four weeks for a period of about twelve hours per week, working in the afternoon after children had participated in an academic remediation program. The instructor framed student learning through a focus on vocabulary development and promoting comprehension of the content, structure and function of news, culminating in a student-produced television news program.

This class first learned the names of different types of television programs, moving from using the term "show" to genre-specific terms like comedy, drama, reality TV, talk show, game show, music video, news, advertising and sports. They then watched examples of local and national news programs to determine the structural features of a newscast, looking at the relationship between taped and live elements, the "happy talk" between anchors and the functions of local news, nation and international news, sports and weather. They learned the occupational names of the members of the production team, discussed the types of stories being reported, and overall use of time within the structure of the news program. Additionally, there was a meta-level of media literacy analysis when students created their own logo for their news program. This led to a discussion of branding and advertising of news organizations and their corporate news logos, including the use of terms like "Action News".

Children were motivated to analyze the news as a first step in the process of replicating this structure for their very own news production. In examining the structure of television news, it was possible to open up questions about the relationship between message form and content. Even young children were able to explain the visual bias of television news, for example, noting that fires and other visually intense news content received more attention than news about the economy and city politics. But the instructor discovered that children lacked a level of prior knowledge needed for much of television news to be comprehensible. The instructor observed children miscomprehending ideas from television news, often as a result of their limited life experience and prior knowledge. Viewing and discussion of TV news revolved around the instructor's checking for comprehension, asking students to summarize and responding to children's questions about what they had viewed. There was much filling in of gaps in children's understanding of local and national events since local and national television news is simply not targeted to children who are 7 and 8 years old. Some high-quality discussion emerged from these viewing activities when the focus was on comprehension of news and current events, and some evidence from parent feedback suggests that some children felt empowered to talk about news and current events with family members when they went home after class. Scaffolded exercises that build comprehension skills may be vital for children to be able to conduct critical analysis in later grades. But it is also the case that sometimes children focused on the structure and production elements of television news because the informational content of news was simply not accessible or relevant to them.

In making their own newscast, children approached the challenge from a decidedly local vantage point: they chose to discover what was happening in the other classrooms where older and younger children were also participating in the Powerful Voices for Children program. The instructor encouraged children to assume production roles, including interviewer, anchor, set design, graphic design, camera operator, etc. Two children worked as interviewer and camera operator and moved through the building, interviewing children and teachers about the projects and activities they were developing. To conduct interviews, they used a list of questions co-created by the members of the class. After class, this video was edited by the teacher. Students reviewed and critiqued what their teacher had edited the following day. This created opportunities to discuss framing, shot composition, and the quality of questions and responses received in the practice of interviewing. Coaching of interviewer-cameraperson teams by peers supported the development of teamwork and group collaboration. Lessons exploring the type of music used in news broadcasts created opportunities for discussion about how rhythm and tone help convey feelings about immediacy, seriousness and importance.

After the pre-packaged interview segments were created, the whole class participated in shooting the newscast itself. Children demonstrated leadership in directing the 10-minute newscast, with anchors using a simple script created by the instructor, practicing their oral reading skills using a simple teleprompter, and exercising teamwork in completing a collaborative project. Parents, family members and peers viewed the newscast during a final screening on the last day of class.

The highly scaffolded media production activity put the teacher in the center of the action. As a teacher-directed activity, opportunities for student involvement and participation were simplified and structured as a result of the developmental needs of young children. How many instructors would be comfortable or confident in personally taking responsibility for so many aspects of the production process? We suspect that the construction of the news program provided as much educational value for the instructor as to the children themselves.

Overall, substantial teacher scaffolding supports children's vocabulary development and comprehension of news content, key competencies of "access". There is some focus on identifying production processes of television news, which might be framed as "analysis". This approach may build children's interest as news consumers. But the instructor's curriculum choices to have children "communicate" by making a newscast produced a rather superficial imitation of a professional news broadcast, which was merely performed by children. It is possible that focus on the structural features of the broadcast may have actually diminished the focus on careful attention to message content.

Grade 4: Exploring pop-culture controversy through a mock trial

The instructor for this group worked with a group of children ages 9 and 10 over the course of four weeks for a period of about twelve hours per week, working in the afternoon after children had participated in an academic remediation program. This instructor used an ongoing controversy in contemporary popular culture to open up issues of celebrity representation in news media. Children studied the case of Chris Brown, the chart-topping pop singer who made headlines in the summer of 2009 when he was accused of beating his girlfriend, fellow pop star Rhianna.

After analyzing the news event, and working from some of his students' earlier request to "play judge and jury", this lesson culminated with a student-produced mock trial. Ultimately, the purpose of the trial was not to determine Chris Brown's guilt or innocence with regards to the assault charges, since Brown had already plead guilty and posted an apology video on YouTube. Rather, the instructor challenged his class to understand and analyze the event as a series of media phenomena, each with its own stake in informing, entertaining or persuading an audience. With this understanding, the mock trial functioned as opportunity for the students to evaluate some of the ethical and rhetorical dimensions of this event.

To develop their own mock trial, after discussion of the Chris Brown case, children investigated the genre of the courtroom drama. In order to compare and contrast fictional depictions of courtrooms with actual courtrooms, the instructor showed examples from episodes of Judge Brown and Judge Judy, inviting a law student to offer basic information about the practice of law. Students learned about the differences between civil and criminal court, and the federal and state constitutions. As part of this work, children discussed the differences and similarities between fictional and real courtrooms. As a type of research activity, this instructional practice encouraged children to strive for authenticity to their own mock-trial, but it also allowed the class to understand how the entertainment function of courtroom drama shapes and informs creative choices which affect how courtrooms are represented.

The next stage of the process involved research on the facts of the domestic violence case, a topic that was widely being discussed in the community in the summer of 2009. Although every student in the class had some familiarity with the details of the news event, knowledge among students was naturally divergent, with different students having awareness of different aspects of the case. Students also drew their knowledge from different sources, including media, family and peers. The instructor used class discussion, with a particular emphasis on listening skills, to promote the sharing of knowledge about the case. The class then watched Chris Brown's YouTube apology. The instructor led the class in a discussion of the clip, asking the class to identify Chris Brown's purpose in posting this video, and whether or not Brown's words and choice of setting served that purpose.

The power of performance as an instructional strategy to support the development of critical analysis skills is evident in this case. The instructor chose to use a student performance as the "communicate" phase of the media literacy cycle. Students energetically performed the roles of judge, prosecutor, defense attorney and jury. The scripting and performance of the mock-trial certainly qualifies as a creative act, and one that offers a very real critique of the situation being studied. Yet, the performance was one which never left the classroom, and therefore cannot be said to truly contribute to the larger public debate about Chris Brown.

However, this limitation did not seem to affect the success of the lesson from the students' point of view. While the students had not been enthusiastic about other writing activities, they were eager to work hard on the script for their trial. Although the trial had no audience outside the classroom, the performative nature of the activity served as a powerful motivator at each stage of the process. This suggests the possibility that these students were able to successfully view their peers as a meaningful audience, and did not require a large set of onlookers to motivate their activity.

This lesson placed its greatest emphasis on "analyze" and "evaluate" components of media literacy pedagogy. By choosing a mock-trial as the lesson's product, the instructor encouraged his students to see themselves, quite literally, as judges, evaluating a case of ethics in the media. This focus came at no small expense to both the "access" and "communicate" phases of the media literacy process. Rather than having his students conduct their own research into the Chris Brown domestic violence case, the teacher supplied students with a handful of print and video resources, selected from entertainment news magazines and prominent celebrity blogs. But students were not directly involved in the research process themselves. This decision also sidestepped some potentially important learning opportunities.

By Grade 4, children are beginning to develop "access" skills involving finding and using sources, evaluating their authority, relevance and credibility. These skills may be at an early stage, a matter which may be complicated by the pop-culture nature of the subject matter, where the sharing of personal opinions about such topics are a normal part of family life. Perhaps such access skills are relatively unimportant in this case, given the pop culture subject matter where the differences between the credibility of *People magazine*, TMZ.com, and PerezHilton.com may be negligible. In any case, for children of this age to do research on a controversial topic like this would have required individualized scaffolding and support. By pre-selecting research materials, the instructor was able to dedicate greater time and energy to discussion to promote analysis and communication skills involved in the production of the mock-trial itself. By choosing to select a range of informational materials himself, the instructor was able to lead by example, modeling good access skills and introducing analysis to explore perceived differences in source credibility among the resources used for the project.

Grade 5: Talking back to the news media

The instructor for this group worked with a group of children ages 10 and 11 over the course of four weeks for a period of about twelve hours per week, working in the afternoon after children had participated in an academic remediation program. This instructor's lesson on news began with an informal conversation, where children articulated their frustration with the representation of their local community on television news. From nearly the first week of class, children in this class were comfortable expressing their frustration with the stories that mainstream news was producing, such as exploitative and sensationalistic stories about celebrities and violence that may scare and frighten children. Instead, children discussed their wish to see stories about the new president, Barack Obama. They did not want to see "bad" news about crime and violence. They wanted to learn more about humanitarian and social causes such as ailing the sick (health care reform), "democracy, good deeds, and nutrition" and stories about events in Philadelphia.

These children were demonstrating their growing desire to see stories that reflect their personal interests and the issues that are important to them. As we learned from the research on British news aimed at children, children are beginning to feel like stakeholders in the world and want explanations for the problems and crises that are part of daily life. This is significant because children in Philadelphia frequently encounter television news broadcasts that showcase high levels of interpersonal violence in local neighborhoods. For example, during the summer of 2009, there were more than 100 homicides, averaging one per day! (Philadelphia Police Department, 2010). For many children who participated in our program, exposure to such tragic news coverage is a part of daily family life.

Evidence from the teacher's field notes and interviews with the students as well as a review of work samples suggests that learning about the news began with sharing complex and genuinely emotional responses about the news. This activity ultimately culminated in taking action to collaboratively compose a letter to the local television news organizations, asking broadcasters to make changes in their representation of social reality to more accurately reflect their community. The students visited a television news studio to watch the making of the noon news, hand-delivering their message about the news media to the broadcasters themselves.

The instructor was surprised to find that the children entered the program already cynical in their outlook of the news. Was this outlook acquired from exposure to family members who were critical of mainstream news? The instructor chose to accept students' cynicism at face value and then construct lessons that would deepen their understanding of the institutional structures that are involved in news production. Children learned that news organizations are complicated organizations, controlled by large corporations that are private, non-transparent organizations.

Children learned how writing is used as a means for social action when they decided to write a letter to send to news outlets. The goal was to address broadcasters who were in a position to make real change. In the process, they discovered the challenge of transforming thoughts and feelings into words that would have rhetorical power with their target audience. Children began to see new ways of communicating and that there were multiple ways and methods to be able to communicate ideas, thoughts, feelings, and information to reach particular audiences. They also created videos about the letter-writing process and recorded a staged reading of the letter that would be put on the class website, with the intention and understanding that they would be reaching a different audience of their family members and peers. Children practiced collaboration and teamwork in order to complete these projects, utilizing a collaborative writing process that resulted in the letter. By deciding to contact the news station, the instructor wanted to provide children with an actual change to have their letter finally heard, after many failed attempts to make contact with a news producer. Upon this visit, they were able to see how a television news program was produced.

However, this instructional practice, because it started with students' existing beliefs and attitudes and moved directly to communication and action, may have limited children's abilities to access new information about the news media. For example, children offered their own critique of the news based on their frustration with "bad news" without learning about the newsmaking process to understand how news values shape editorial decision-making. Did children gain new knowledge and points of view about the practice of broadcast journalism? Children may have merely developed more elaborate ways to "communicate" their existing cynical views without deepening skills of "locate, comprehend, access and analyze".

Empowerment competencies

Each of these lessons activates some of the seven competencies that we identify as an expanded conceptualization of the empowerment cycle. These processes relate specifically to the development of media literacy competencies for children: engaging, locating, comprehending, analyzing, evaluating, communicating, and taking action. Table 1 provides an overview of our analysis. We saw evidence of *engagement* when Grade 4's instructor capitalized on children's interest in pop star Chris Brown's domestic violence case, which was certainly a controversial and relevant current event in the summer of 2009. Similarly, Grade 5 students activated their existing opinions and beliefs in discussing their complaints about "bad news" on television. However, none of the case studies engaged children in *locating* information. Instead, children were presented with information that the teacher had previously selected. This may have been a consequence of perceived time pressures, lack of confidence in children's search skills or in the ability to scaffold a process that may require individualized attention. In addition, the practices involved in finding and accessing information from a variety of media sources, including print, electronic and digital resources require access to physical resources, like a school library or computer lab, which were not available to the Powerful Voices for Kids program during the summer of 2009.

Table 1. Evidence of the expanded empowerment model in three case studies

Competency	Grade 3	Grade 4	Grade 5
Engaging: connecting to lived experience and stimulating curiosity and motivation		X	X
Locating: finding and selecting information			
Comprehending: constructing meaning through active interpretation	X		
Analyzing: identifying author, audience, purpose and point of view and examining the relationship between form and content	X	X	
Evaluating: making judgments about the value and worth of a particular message		X	X
Communicating: composing or creating a message using the processes of brainstorming, composition and revision.	X	X	X
Taking Action: disseminating a message to an authentic audience for the purpose of making a difference in the world outside the classroom			X

Teachers activated student *comprehension*, as in the example where the Grade 3 instructor used samples of TV news and asked children to summarize what they had learned in the broadcast. Similarly, we see some evidence of children activating *analysis* when Grade 4 children considered the purpose, target audience, and point of view of Chris Brown's YouTube message to his fans. Grade 3 children explicitly looked at the relationship between the message form and content by identifying the parts of a TV newscast and considering how content is shaped by the broadcast formulas. Students *evaluated* Chris Brown's communication strategy and ultimately served as "judge and jury" regarding his decision to talk back to his fans about the accusation of domestic violence. Grade 5 children also evaluated the decisions made by broadcast journalists to focus on crime and violence instead of focusing on issues of public health and wellness, clearly forming judgments about the worth and value of the local news media in relation to social values.

Students in all three grades strengthened *communication* competencies through oral communication, writing, and dramatic expression. All cases involve substantial levels of small group collaboration, teamwork and problem-solving and included the iterative processes of brainstorming, drafting, and revision. Only children in Grade 5 can be seen as *taking action*, by actively disseminating their complaints about the news media in a real-world context, where the message is explicitly designed to make some kind of difference in the world outside the classroom.

By looking at some examples of media literacy practice in the context of work with urban elementary children through the lens of these seven competencies, we may be able to better understand the relationship between communication skills development, critical thinking, and social action in work with pre-adolescent children, identifying some gaps and challenges in media literacy learning that are evident when looking at the three case studies in relationship to each other.

These case studies illustrate both the opportunities and pitfalls in exploring news and journalism with elementary-aged school children. Clearly, children strengthened communication and collaborative skills through engaging, high-interest activities that drew upon connections between children's exposure to news, popular culture, connecting journalism to their own lives and their own interests. In each case, learning progressed through a sequence of activities that were based on children's own interests and talents.

However, when we compare and contrast the case studies, some challenges underscore how instructional choices may shape learning outcomes. In Grade 3, we see how an emphasis on comprehending the content of news and recognizing the structural formula used in producing may have led to uncritical reproduction of news genres. In Grade 4, we see that a focus on analyzing messages may limit students' opportunity to access, comprehend and find new information that builds children's independent learning skills. In Grade 5, we see that a lack of emphasis on accessing information and analyzing news and journalism may lead to communication projects that simply reinforce knee-jerk media bashing, potentially deepening children's sense of alienation and cynicism.

This model encourages educators to more deeply consider *how* exploration of current events, news and journalism may activate various competencies. Lessons that more explicitly use each of these phases of the model may help children understand the depth and vitality of communicative power in the world outside the classroom. As Buckingham (2000, p. 223) notes, a media literacy "curriculum must seek to socialize students for the experience of social change". In our view, media literacy education must also help children cultivate their curiosity, appreciate complexity, acknowledge diversity, and be optimistic about the future.

This work is not easy. It is important to note that contextual factors influenced instructors' decisions about the scope of learning. Instructors in this program faced time constraints, the need to focus on student interests, and other constraints resulting from their perceptions of the developmental abilities of the children in their classrooms. All these factors played a role in the design and implementation of learning activities. Fortunately, these examples also show the importance of flexible instructors and a curriculum that puts emphasis on students' interests and lived experience with mass media and popular culture. Instructors must actively and constantly gauge their students' learning and engagement and modify the next lesson appropriately.

This article has offered three case studies to document some instructional practices designed to help children develop media literacy empowerment competencies in relation to current events, news and journalism. Current events, news and journalism offer a vitally important function: they help people understand and make sense of our neighborhoods, our communities, our country and the world around us. They offer information that helps people make practical decisions and perform their roles as citizens in a democracy. But like all media messages, news does not offer a "window on the world", but instead provides a highly constructed set of messages that are constrained by the historical, economic and political contexts of news organizations and the institutions they interface with. The case studies presented in this article demonstrate that even very young children have the ability to understand some key ideas about how news media messages are constructed and how they shape our understanding of the world. The expanded empowerment model, because it moves through the phases of engagement, finding and using information, analyzing and evaluating it, then communicating ideas and taking social action, offers a systematic framework to help educators to develop children's knowledge and understanding about current events, news and journalism.

Acknowledgements

We acknowledge grant support from the Verizon Foundation and the Wyncote Foundation. We thank Aggie Bazaz Ebrahimi and Rachel Hobbs for the development of instructional practices presented in this article.

References

Bazalgette, C., Harland, J. & James, C. 2008. *Lifeblood of democracy? Learning about broadcast news*. London: British Film Institute.

Buckingham, D. 2003. *Media education: Literacy, learning and contemporary culture*. Cambridge: Polity Press.

Buckingham, D. 2000. *The making of citizens: Young people, news and politics*. London: Routledge.

Cantor, J. 1998. *Mommy, I'm scared: How TV and movies frighten children and what we can do about it*. New York: Harcourt Brace.

Comer, J., Weiner, C., Furr, J., Bedias, R. & Kendall, P. 2008. Children and terrorism-related news: training parents in coping and media literacy. *Journal of Consulting and Clinical Psychology 76*(4), 568-578.

Hobbs, R. 2007. *Reading the Media: Media literacy in high school English*. New York: Teachers College Press.

Hobbs, R. 2004. A review of school-based initiatives in media literacy education. *American Behavioral Scientist, 48*(1), 42-59.

Huston, J.B., Pfefferbaum, B. & Ryes, G. 2008. Experiencing disasters indirectly: How traditional and new media disaster coverage impacts youth. *Prevention Researcher 15*(3), 14-17.

Kincheloe, J. 2001. *Getting beyond the facts: Teaching social studies/social sciences in the twenty-first century*. New York: Peter Lang.

Masterman, L. 1985. *Teaching the media*. London: Comedia.

Matthews, J. 2009. Negotiating news childhoods. *Journal of Children & Media 3*(1), 2-18.

Messenger-Davies, M. 2008. Fair and balanced reporting. *Journal of Children & Media 2*(3), 305-310.

NAMLE (National Association for Media Literacy Education). 2008. Core principles of media literacy education. http://namle.net/core-principles.

Newspapers in Education 2010. The Forum. http://www.nieonline.com/theforum/index.cfm

Philadelphia Police Department. 2010. Crime maps and statistics. http://www.phillypolice.com

Sahn, L. & Reichek, A. 2008. Read all about it: A classroom newspaper integrates the curriculum *Young Children 63*(2), 12-18.

Thoman, E. & Jolls, T. 2004. Media literacy: A national priority for a changing world. *American Behaviorial Scientist 48*(1), 18-29.

Walker, T. (2010). The red pill: social studies, media texts, and literacies. *Learning, Media and Technology 35*(1), 1-14.

A Study of the Impact of Media Education on Students' Media Analysis Skills

An Interim Report

Chi-Kim Cheung

Today's children and adolescents spend an enormous amount of time with the media. For many, this is a major cause of concern. There is a substantial body of literature that shows correlations between media exposure and obesity (Robinson, 1999), violent behavior (Federman, 1998), early sexual activity (Pardun et al., 2005), drug use (Pierce et al., 1998), endorsement of stereotypes (Herrett-Skjellum & Allen, 1996), and reduced sociability (Nie & Erbring, 2000). The ever-increasing exposure of students to potentially harmful media contents influences needs to be matched by an appropriate level of media literacy, fostered through media education. Defined as the ability "to access, analyze, evaluate and communicate messages in a wide variety of forms" (Aufderheide & Firestone, 1993: 8), media literacy develops in children an informed and critical understanding of the nature, techniques, and impact of media. With media literacy, children learn to deconstruct the value-laden meanings of media images and messages, thereby developing the necessary critical distance towards the media-saturated environment in which they live.

Unfortunately, the importance of media education has not been recognized everywhere, and is almost non-existent in the formal curricula of many countries. Where media education exists at all, it frequently suffers from a lack of funding, status, recognition, teacher training, and basic equipment and resources (Cheung, 2009). Even in countries in which media education is more firmly established, such as Canada and England, there are "signs of weariness among its most prominent advocates" (Buckingham & Domaille, 2001: 11), and many policy-makers "do not really appreciate the importance and urgency of media education – or indeed, even seem to understand what it might involve" (Buckingham & Domaille, 2001: 20).

In response to the indifference on the part of many parents, principals and policy-makers, media teachers and practitioners worldwide have formed networks and associations which collectively argue the case for media education. Too often, however, their arguments simply take for granted the effectiveness of media education and fail to "move beyond implicit assumptions about the benefits such efforts can achieve and toward their explicit definition and measurement" (Scharrer, 2002: 355). In the absence of basic research on whether and how media education succeeds in its stated goals, the proposals of media educators are likely to meet with suspicion from the educational establishments, which tend to be inherently conservative and resistant to change. Unfortunately, research into the effectiveness of media education is still in a relatively embryonic state. The present study, part of a bigger study granted by the General Research Fund, the most prestigious research grant in Hong Kong, is guided by the following three research questions:

Q1: Is media education effective in improving Hong Kong secondary school students' media analysis skills?

Q2: If it is, what are the factors that determine how effective it is?

Q3: What impact, if any, does media education have on students' media use habits?

This article is an interim report focused on the first question.

Methodology

Multiple methods

A multi-method, multi-source data collection strategy is used, including documentary analysis, field notes, questionnaires, interviews, classroom observation, and diary writing in the form of reflection sheets. Triangulation between the evidence produced by different research methods is used to analyze the different sources of data.

Questionnaires

Pre-test: All students were asked to complete a questionnaire exploring their views on media education lessons as well as their own evaluation of their knowledge, skills, and values before the implementation of media education lessons.

Post-test: All students were given the same test at the end of the academic year to see if any changes had occurred during the year after media education lessons had been adopted.

The questionnaires were coded so the pre-test and post-test questionnaires were given to the same student

Interviews

The media education teachers were interviewed. They were asked questions related to the impact of the new implementation of media education lessons on the attitude and learning outcomes of students. Ten students from each of the participating schools were randomly chosen and invited for two interviews, one before the beginning of media education lessons and one towards the end of the academic year to see the impact of the new implementation of media education on the media consumption habits and learning outcomes of students.

Observations

During this data collection period, the researcher visited the schools frequently (at least 5 times) to observe lessons, conduct interviews, and write field notes. Each observation session lasted for 40 minutes (the normal length for a single period). During the observation, a checklist was used to assess the quality of questions (whether they appealed to high order thinking or whether they were just close-ended questions) and quantity of questions asked by the teachers and students, the quality of answers provided by the students, the kind of activities used and the responses of students. Notes were also written to give an overall impression of the lesson observed.

Data analysis

For the questionnaire survey, quantitative analysis was used to analyze the Likert scale questions to obtain a general picture of the reasons, means and impact of the implementation of media education in the curriculum. The statistical program SPSS was used to analyze questionnaire data. As the acquisition of media education skills has not been theoretically conceptualized or widely measured by previous researchers, the multivariate analysis procedure (MANOVA) was not used in this study. ANOVA and ANCOVA were used instead.

For the interview data, the researcher used two methods of analysis. One was computerized highlighting to find out key concepts. The other was transposing the data and using the qualitative data analysis software program to take note of emerging concepts. The trustworthiness of the data was enhanced by using these two different methods. Field notes made for interviews and classroom observations were used to confirm the information obtained from qualitative analysis.

Sample and design

Selection of schools

In Hong Kong, at the end of primary school, students are allocated Form one places in junior secondary schools. Three "bands" in order of merit are formed based on the scaled internal assessment of students in the same school net. The top one-third of students in the same school area goes into the first band in the school area, the next into the second band, and so on. The main part of secondary education lasts for five years, and is made up of a junior cycle of three years, which is compulsory, and a senior cycle of two years, which is not compulsory but nearly universal. Students have to take an examination in S.5 (i.e., 5th grade in secondary school), and those who obtain sufficient marks can continue their studies in S.6, preparing them for university entrance examination.

1. Three schools were selected. One school from each band was chosen, as this allowed investigation of the differences (if any) between students of different academic levels in their outcomes from media education. The researcher had carefully chosen each selected school based on the socio-economic status of the students' family backgrounds, the school size, age of school, and staff profiles so that it could be a good representation of other schools in the same band.
2. The selected schools taught at least 10 media education lessons in the regular timetable of S.3. Furthermore, the areas to be covered in the media education lessons were to be similar. S.3 students were chosen for the following reasons:
   i. Students at senior level have to face the pressure of public examination, and it would be difficult for schools to have media education lessons implemented.
   ii. It is appropriate to have S.3 students as the subjects of this study as they will have already completed two years of education in the same school, where certain learning habits have been formed and records of their previous results can be checked.

Every S.3 student in the selected schools participated in the questionnaire survey.

The pilot

A pilot study was carried out. Fifty students were recruited from different schools of different bands to come to the University of Hong Kong on a Saturday morning. A questionnaire survey was conducted and parts of the media education lessons were taught. As a result of the pilot study, slight revisions were made to the questionnaire survey, but no revisions were needed for the media education lessons.

The research

The sample consisted of 164 Secondary 3 students in School C (a band 3 school), 153 Secondary 3 students in School B (a band 2 school) and 151 Secondary 3 students in School A (a band 1 school).

A pretest questionnaire was administered immediately before the media education lessons. The same questionnaire was administered approximately six months after the intervention.

The ten 40 minute media education lessons were conducted in over three months, dealing with five types of media messages: advertisements, songs, TV game shows, movies, and comics. Although a longitudinal study such as the one by Hobbs and Frost (2003) would have been more desirable, the present research design was necessary both because of budget constraints and because we agree with Scharrer (2002) that "in the short term, and in response to participation in as few as only one media-literacy unit in the curriculum, outcomes in the realm of cognition and affect are [...] immensely important in their own right" and "should not be underestimated".

After the 10 media education lessons, the data from movies and comics were not used for the following reasons. Surprisingly, although movies and comics used to be very popular among students, they had lost their appeal tremendously. Many students said that they watched very few movies compared to their instant media consumption behaviour because the time needed to watch a movie was too long and it was difficult for them to sit still to enjoy the movie. Even if they did watch movies, they tended to watch them from the internet or DVD, which could be stopped anytime they wished, and their viewing was affected by their surroundings as well as their lack of concentration due to their multitasking behaviour. With respect to comics, it is difficult to find a common one which appeals to both boys and girls as boys prefer contents loaded with sex and violence, where girls prefer love stories.

The lessons on advertisements

In the media education lessons on advertisements, students viewed a necklace commercial that shows a dozen or so women carrying out various activities in a bathroom. One is putting on make-up, one is shaving her legs, two are having a dispute, two are cuddling and kissing, etc. Towards the end of the commercial a woman is seen gazing into the mirror while adjusting her necklace, and a female's voice can be heard in the background saying: "There are many reasons women go to the bathroom; for men there are just two." The tagline "True women, XY (the brand name)" is then repeated.

After the first viewing, students were asked to fill out an answer sheet designed to assess their skills in analyzing the commercial. Students were asked to write down what they had seen and heard and any thought they had about the commercial. This was followed by an interactive lesson of questions, brainstorming, and media analysis. After this, students viewed the same commercial again and filled out the same answer sheet for a second time. Both the pretest and posttest answer sheets were scored and compared to see if there was any improvement in media analysis skills.

Measures

The answer sheets administered during the first and second sessions measured students' media analysis skills in response to the necklace commercial, both before and after the lectures. Partly following Hobbs and Frost (2003), analysis skills were divided into three broad categories: the ability to identify techniques used, the ability to identify values, and the ability to identify target audience and purposes. Unlike Hobbs and Frost, however, students were not asked three separate questions, each designed to measure one particular skill. Rather, students were given much latitude as to what they wrote, and each answer sheet was looked at holistically for evidence of each of the three categories of skills. The idea was that such a format would more accurately capture students' ability to analyze media messages in actual contexts. After all, in everyday contexts, no one would be there to remind the students of the questions to ask from a media literate perspective; it would be up to students themselves to come up with the questions. The very ability to come up with appropriate and relevant questions is an achievement in and of itself and should be considered part of the media literacy skill set.

Accordingly, each answer sheet was examined holistically and given a score for each of the three kinds of skills (which were then added up to obtain the overall score). The score ranged from 0 (little or no evidence) to 1 (moderate evidence) to 2 (ample evidence). For example, trying to identify the implicit values in the necklace commercial, a student received 2 points for writing this:

> When a girl turns into a woman, they become materialistic and trivial. Only if you wear XY are you considered a "true woman" and sexy enough to attract men.

Another student received 1 point for writing this:

> Jewelry is very important to women.

Zero was given to responses like the following:

> Women are the best.

While trying to identify the target audience in the necklace commercial, a student received 2 points for writing this:

> From the age of the many women in the bathroom you can tell it is aimed at women between 20 to 40. But it is also aimed at men because it is often men who buy jewelries for women.

A 1-point response would be like:

> It attracts women to buy jewelries.

Finally, a zero would typically be given to responses that did not attempt to identify the audience at all.

Results

Q1: Is media education effective in improving Hong Kong secondary school students' media analysis skills?

On average, students of school B, a band 2 school, received significantly higher overall scores after the media education lessons than beforehand (0.76 vs. 4.0, $p < .01$), with a significant improvement in media analysis skills (in all cases $p < .01$). The same was true of students of school A, a band 1 school, who had moved from an average score of 0.32 to 2.08 ($p < .01$). For students of school C, a band 3 school, there was a slight improvement. This suggests that actual learning had indeed taken place among students.

An interesting fact revealed by a survey of the responses was that in the first trial, many students focused primarily on criticizing both the commercial and the game show; it was as though they were keen to show that they were immune to media influences. However, when they did it the second time after some discussion, students began to take note of the more subtle aspects of technique, values and audience, as required in media analysis. For example, in response to the necklace commercial, a student wrote before the media education lessons:

> ...This is the archetypal bad ad, and is completely meaningless...

and received a zero overall score. The same student wrote the following after the media education lessons:

> ... If you want to appear more feminine, you should wear jewelries...

and received 1 point for identifying values. As another example, in response to the game show, a student wrote before the media education lessons:

> This is disgusting and absurd.

Her response after the media education lesson, however, was substantially more reflective:

> ... It is fun to see celebrities being made fun of, and this helps improve the show's popularity, which helps attract advertisers. Celebrities also can take this opportunity to boost their own popularity.

From the researcher's observation and field notes, the following points were written that deserved attention:

> I observed the same class in different subjects. In general, students were quiet and passive, very typical of Hong Kong students, but they tended to behave a little differently during media education lessons. Some students took the initiative to respond, and after a period of time, students seem to go beyond questions and answers that required simple observation and understanding. Some of their questions and answers were quite in-depth. In a few cases, some students had moved into the critical discussion of values behind the media messages.

The teachers' reflection sheets shared similar sentiments. Mr. Chan, a teacher of school B wrote:

> I have been teaching this class for two years in Geography and Civic Education and they did very well in examinations. They liked to copy notes from the blackboard and relied on teacher's explanation. When I first taught media education, students did not know what was expected of them. Then I adopted the method of observation – interpretation – analysis – and students were able to list out what they could observe. Under a bit of guidance, they were able to discuss freely, other than giving you the 'model answers'. Quite interestingly, their learning mode has a positive effect on the learning and teaching of Geography as students started to take the initiative to raise questions.

Ms Lee, a teacher of school C noted:

> My class was split. Half of them did not bother to listen, while another half just fooled around and spoke nonsense during class. Media education lessons do make a difference, though not very significantly. I could see that those who did not pay attention were more motivated and could answer some questions. A few students even took the initiative to ask questions, and the quality of some questions was not bad.

Follow-up interviews with students confirmed the above observations. Shannon, a student from school A, remarked:

> I am an A student, and the trick in scoring high marks is you have to pay attention during lessons and study hard at home. Media education is different. There does not seem to be a model answer and the teacher makes us think a lot. I found it hard at first as we were not used to this kind of teaching but because the materials used are familiar, it is easier for me to follow, and as the lessons move on, I enjoy the lessons very much.

Ping, a boy from school C, noted:

> Many teachers do not think that our class could perform. The truth is I want to, but I could not. First, the teachers are boring. Then, the tests are difficult. We have to memorize so many things in order to score high marks. Media education is different. We are allowed to express our opinion freely. Then the teacher leads us to think more deeply, and suddenly I realize that I could learn.

Discussion

Hong Kong schools are criticized for their outdated curricula, failure to keep abreast of the latest knowledge and boring teaching methods (Cheung, 2006, 2007), and the general observation of secondary students in Hong Kong is that they are passive and quiet, not willing to participate in classroom discussion, and are satisfied with notes provided by the teacher. This is especially the case in senior forms and students with better academic results. For the three experimental schools in this research, the above description was generally true, with the slight exception that students from school C were relatively restless, not because they wanted to participate in classroom discussion, but rather they found most of the lessons boring. This was the observation the researcher had from attending several regular lessons in the experimental schools and confirmed by teachers and students in later interviews. However, when media education lessons were conducted, the differences were apparent. Students seemed to respond more, and the average frequency of responses and initiation increased tremendously. Table 1 shows the average number of responses and initiations from students per lesson observed in the six media education lessons and two non-media education lessons during the same period and the result suggested that media education can transform young people from passive receivers to active practitioners.

Table 1. The average number of responses from students per lesson from observing the six media education lessons (MEL) and two non-media education lessons (NML)

	Frequency of responses		Initiation	
	MEL	NML	MEL	NML
School A	18.5	6.7	7.6	2.8
School B	16.3	6.9	7.3	3.1
School C	17.4	6.1	6.6	3.4

Follow-up interviews agreed with the above analysis as well. Mr. Cheung, a teacher from school A commented:

> My students are afraid to respond or ask questions during lessons. Actually, it is a common phenomenon in Hong Kong schools. Students are afraid that if they come up with the wrong answer, or if they ask a stupid question, it will cause them embarrassment. Media education lessons are different. It is like friends taking a causal chat after watching a movie, and ideas and questions come so naturally.

Q2: If it is (i.e., if media education is effective according to Q1), what are the factors that determine how effective it is?

We were interested in the question of whether learning is enhanced when the media example used bears personal relevance to the student, or is previously known to the student. Given that the necklace commercial explicitly concerns women, it should be more relevant to girls than boys, and so it was hypothesized that female students would have more interest in the material and therefore gain more out of the media education lesson than would male students. The results confirmed this hypothesis. Although pretest overall scores for both female and male students' were roughly the same (0.95 vs. 0.9, respectively), paired sample t tests showed a significant difference in scores between the groups after the media education lessons. Female students scored significantly higher (4.3 vs. 2.57, $p < .01$) and demonstrated significantly greater improvement in overall skills than did male students ($p < .01$).

Conclusion

In line with previous research, the present study confirms the effectiveness of media education in improving students' media analysis skills. The value of media analysis skills *per se*, however, are not universally recognized, and media educators have often sought to justify media education on other grounds, for example, by arguing that it minimizes harmful media influence, or (as Hobbs & Frost, 2003, showed) that it improves students' traditional print literacies. This study confirms that though media education might not reduce the time students spend on media consumption, the beneficial effect on students of media education is that they are more prone to choose the programmes suitable for them in a more critical manner.

Finally, we only measured impact on analysis skills in the short-term (i.e., immediately after the media education lessons). As Worth (2004) argues, "a key issue in behavior-focused media literacy education … is whether the post test survey results will actually translate into changes in attitudes and behavior, particularly over time". The present study cannot rule out the possibility that the observed growth in analysis skills is merely a short burst of reflection that will not ultimately be sustained in the long run. As Worth (2004) remarks, "If the goal is to create attitudinal changes in students and motivate them to think critically about their real life media use beyond the classroom, then longitudinal studies which actually measure that media use are required". Future studies that are better-funded should therefore attempt to measure the impact of media education in the long run.

Acknowledgement

This article originated from a research funded by the RGC CERG Grant: HKU7441/06H and the author wishes to thank his research assistant Guo Yu.

References

Aufderheide. P., & Firestone, C. (1993). *Media literacy: A report of the national leadership conference on media literacy*. Queenstown, MD: Aspen Institute.

Buckingham, David & Domaille, Kate. (2001). UNESCO Youth Media Education Survey, http://www.unesco.ru/rus/pages/bythemes/stasya27012005181243.php

Cheung, Chi-Kim (2006). Media Education as a Vehicle for Teaching Religion – A Hong Kong Case, *Religious Education,* 101(4), 504-515.

Cheung, Chi-Kim (2007). The Teaching of Moral Education through Media Education, *The Asia-Pacific Education Researcher* International, 16(1), 61-72

Cheung Chi-Kim (2009). The significance of media education: current realities and future possibilities, in Cheung C.K. (Ed.) *Media Education in Asia*, 217-232, Dordrecht, Heidelberg, London, New York: Springer

Federman J (1998). *National Television Violence Study III.* Thousand Oaks, CA: Sage

Herrett-Skjellum, J. & Allen, M. (1996). Television programming and sex stereotyping: A meta-analysis. *Communication Yearbook*, 19, 157-185

Hobbs, R. & Frost, R. (2003). Measuring the acquisition of media literacy skills. *Reading Research Quarterly*, 38(3), 330-355.

Nie, N., & Erbring, L. (2000). *Internet and Society: A Preliminary Report.* Stanford, CA: Stanford Institute for the Quantitative Study of Society.

Pardun, Carol J. et.al. (2005). Linking Exposure to Outcomes: Early Adolescents Consumption of Sexual Content in Six Media, *Mass Communication and Society*, 8:2, 75-91

Pierce JP, et. al. (1998). Tobacco industry promotion of cigarettes and adolescent smoking, *JAMA,* 279: 511–515

Robinson TN. (1999). Reducing children's television viewing to prevent obesity: a randomized controlled trial, *JAMA,* 282: 1561–1567

Scharrer, E. (2002). Making a case for media literacy in the curriculum: outcomes and assessment. *Journal of Adolescent and Adult Literacy*, 46, 354-357

Worth, P. L. (2004). Evaluating the Effectiveness of School-Based Media Literacy Curricula. Retrieved on May 24, 2009 from http://ldt.stanford.edu/~pworth/papers/effectiveness_medialit.doc

A New Horizon

Media Literacy Assessment and Children in Europe

José Manuel Pérez Tornero and Mireia Pi

The recognition of media literacy in the *European Audiovisual Services Directive* (Art. 37) and the consequent development of media literacy indicators – applied to all people, even youth and children – are the result of a long process in which organizations such as UNESCO and the European Commission have played an important role, not only in development of the public dimension of media literacy, but also in acceptance of the importance of media education in the political genda.

The UNESCO International Congress on Media Education that took place in Germany in 1982 released the *Grünwald Declaration* on Media Education, ratified by the 19 participating countries, which became the benchmark of why media education should be a central topic in the public debate. The Grünwald Declaration was the first to claim the need for educational and political systems to promote critical understanding and awareness on the part of citizens to allow them to face the media. Seventeen years after the Grünwald Declaration, the rapid technological development in the late 90s caused the congress in 1999, organized by UNESCO in Vienna, *Educating for the Media and the Digital Age*, to establish: "Media Education is part of the basic entitlement of every citizen, in every country in the world, to freedom of expression and the right to information, and is instrumental in building and sustaining democracy [...]." In 2002, UNESCO held the *Youth Media Education Seminar* in Seville, which reaffirmed the creative and critical component of media literacy, highlighting that media education should be included in both formal and informal education on the individual as well as the community level.

Europe: Creating conditions to assess media literacy

For over a decade, both the European Parliament and the European Commission have recognized the importance of media literacy as a central component in national agendas and in the European agenda itself. These institutions have played an important and active role in the development of media literacy in Europe, and have defined the concept as including two dimensions: the protection and promotion of human rights, mainly regarding the protection of minors, and the social and economical *raison d'être*. The permanent *Safer Internet Programme*,[1] the first step in such protection politics, was created in 1999 to empower parents, teachers and children with Internet security tools. However, the programme also covers other media, such as videos. The *Safer Internet Action Plan*[2] ran from 1999 to 2004.[3] The objective of the action plan is to promote safer Internet use and to encourage, at the European level, an environment favourable to the development of the Internet industry.

In order to achieve this objective, the following actions have been taken:

- promotion of industry self-regulation and content-monitoring schemes (for example, dealing with content such as child pornography or content that incites hatred on the grounds of race, sex, religion, nationality or ethnic origin)
- encouraging industry to provide filtering tools and rating systems, which allow parents or teachers to select content appropriate for children in their care while allowing adults to decide what legal content they wish to access, and which take account of linguistic and cultural diversity
- increasing awareness among users of the services provided by industry, in particular parents, teachers and children, so they can better understand and take advantage of the opportunities of the Internet
- support actions, such as assessment of legal implications
- activities fostering international cooperation in the areas enumerated above
- other actions furthering the objective set out in Article 2.

The basic Safer Internet Program hypothesis was that "Today, young people and children are some of Europe's biggest users of online and mobile technologies". As a consequence, "together with the raising popularity of these new technologies, risks that the numbers of young people and children may face when they are also surfing online, are growing".

On a legislative level, in 2006 the European Council also developed the *Recommendation on Empowering Children in the New Information and Communications Environment,* [4] adopted by the Committee of Ministers at the 974th meeting of the Ministers' Deputies. The recommendation called on EU Member States to familiarize children with the new ICT (information and communication technology) environment.[5] A new *Recommendation of the European Parliament and of the Council of 18 December 2006 on key competences for lifelong learning*[6] identified the abilities that should be developed: digital competence (critical use of technology), social and civic competence (provide individuals with the tools to play an active and democratic role in society), critical awareness and creative competence (individuals should be capable of assessing the creative expression of ideas and emotions spread by the media). The same year, the European Parliament issued *Recommendation 2006/952/EC of the European Parliament and of the Council of 20 December 2006 on the protection of minors and human dignity,*[7] which emphasized the need for teacher training in the field of media literacy, as well as the inclusion of media literacy in the curriculum in order to protect children and, at the same time, to promote responsible attitudes among all users. All of these initiatives fostered the media education (and literacy) policy.

In parallel, from 2000 to 2008, the European Commission have launched several initiatives to promote digital and media literacy among the EU Member States: a high-level expert group advised on the development of these actions; studies were carried out; and, gradually, the outcomes were reflected in changing the Commission's strategy from the promotion of Digital Literacy[8] to "Public policies and stakeholders initiatives in support of Digital Literacy".[9]

Promoting Digital Literacy

The European Commission requested the implementation of a course of action: to promote Digital Literacy within the *eLearning Programme*. In order to do so, the EU commissioned a study "to identify and analyse a limited number of successful and innovative experiences for promoting Digital and media literacy and identifying strengths and weaknesses..." The report, called *Promoting Digital Literacy. Understanding Digital Literacy* (2006), carried out by the Autonomous University of Barcelona (UAB), focused on these aspects: a) the identification and analysis of a limited number of successful and innovative experiences that have helped promote digital and media literacy, b) the strengths and weaknesses of these experiences, and c) the drawing up of recommendations for the implementation of promoting a digital literacy course of action.

Digital Literacy High-level Experts Group

As part of the *i2010 initiative on e-Inclusion,*[10] the European Commission set up a *Digital Literacy High-Level Experts Group*[11] to provide expertise and guidance on digital literacy policies in preparation for the *Commission Communication on e-Inclusion*. The experts, representing industry, academia and civil society, were invited to comment on the findings of the *Digital Literacy Review* the Commission had produced as part of its commitments resulting from the Riga Declaration in 2006.[12]

In parallel, focusing exclusively on media literacy, the European Commission set up the *EU Media Literacy Expert Group,*[13] which included experts representing both the role of the media industry in media literacy and that of academic research, in order to analyse and define media literacy objectives and trends and therefore highlight and promote the best practices at the European level and propose actions to follow in promoting media literacy.

Based on the findings of the Media Literacy Expert Group, the European Commission launched in 2006 a *Public Consultation,*[14] a questionnaire that sought the public's views on media literacy in relation to digital technologies and information about initiatives in commercial communications, as well as in the cinema and online world. The replies showed that the correct way to speed up progress in this field would be to spread regional and national good practices in media literacy. "It also emerged that criteria or standards for assessing media literacy are lacking and that good practices are not available for all aspects of media literacy."[15]

In the second half of 2007, a study entitled *Current Trends and Approaches to Media Literacy in Europe*[16] was commissioned by the European Commission to the Autonomous University of Barcelona. The study maps current practices in implementing media literacy in Europe, confirms the results of the aforementioned consultation, and recommends measures to be implemented in Europe to increase the level of media literacy. It also outlines the possible economic and social impact of an EU intervention in this field.

In 2008, the European Parliament adopted the resolution on the *Report of Media Literacy in a Digital World,*[17] which had been scheduled (November 24th) for consideration in a plenary session by Christa Prets on behalf of the Committee on Culture and Education. It required EU Member States to pay systematic attention to the development of media literacy. The Parliament urged the European Commission to develop an action plan on media literacy and organize a meeting with the Committee on Audio-Visual Media Services in order to facilitate information exchange and cooperation on a regular basis.

European Audiovisual Media Services Directive

As mentioned, efforts to make digital and media literacy a key element of the development of the information society in Europe were concluded in the enactment of the *European Audiovisual Media Services Directive,*[18] which was incorporated (in December 2009) into legislation in all Member States of the European Union, introducing for the first time the need to promote media literacy into a regulation of the media system.

During the past ten years, the initiatives have changed from protection to promotion of active policies aimed at improving citizens' media competences. The European Commission has set the philosophical and legal bases for media literacy development, both in Europe and in its member countries. Thus, it is expected that in the coming years we will see increasing participation of more – new and traditional – actors in media literacy issues: NGOs (non-governmental organizations), families, municipalities, the media, authorities, teachers' associations, journalists, lawyers, etc. The communication and education policies of each country will be designed to properly promote the development of media literacy in their population and, thus, stimulate universal media literacy.

The central point of the above-mentioned Directive is the proposal to measure media literacy competences using new media literacy indicators. To meet this objective, in 2009 the European Commission commissioned a European consortium led by EAVI (European Association for Viewers' Interests) to perform a *Study on Assessment Criteria for Medial Literacy Levels,* directed by José Manuel Pérez Tornero and Paolo Celot.

The study proposes a new framework of media literacy in order to find criteria or assessment for media literacy levels. The starting point of the framework is the concept of media literacy developed by international organizations, such as UNESCO and the EU. Emphasis is placed on the themes that emerge from the latest Communications and Recommendations of the European Commission (*Communication on Media Literacy, Report on Media Literacy in a Digital World*, etc.). Thus, in the study, the definition of media literacy is in accordance with the one formulated by the European Commission: "Media literacy is the ability to access the media, to understand and critically evaluate different aspects of the media and media contents and to create communications in a variety of contexts. Media literacy relates to all media, including television and film, radio and recorded music, print media, the Internet and other new digital communication technologies."[19]

Conceptual map of media literacy

Using the European Commission definition as a basis, our study integrates different concepts of media literacy in a systemic way in order to highlight explicitly the media literacy skills that should be acquired and measured, where possible, at both individual and country levels. Therefore, the study distinguishes between two fundamental dimensions, individual competences and environmental factors.

Individual competences

Individual competences refers to the personal, individual ability to exercise certain skills (access, use, analyse, understand and create in relation to the media). These skills are found within a broader set of abilities that allow for increasing levels of awareness, the capacity for critical analysis, a creative problem-solving capacity and the ability to create and communicate content, i.a., when participating in public life.

Among the individual skills relating to media literacy, we can identify the following components:

a. Use skills: a component centred on the relationship between the individual and the media as a platform; it refers to the technical dimension (instrumental and operative abilities required to access and effectively use media communication tools).

b. Critical Understanding competences: a component centred on the relationship between the individual and the content (information – attribute of the message; or comprehension – attribute of the individual), that is, a cognitive dimension.

c. Communicative and participative abilities: a component related to the technical and cognitive abilities in different fields – social relations, creation and production of content, and civic and social participation – which involves personal responsibility.

These abilities allow for processes that range from a simple contact to the creation of complex cooperation and collaboration strategies that use media tools as their base.

Environmental factors

Environmental factors are a set of contextual factors that affect individuals and are related to: media education, media policy, cultural environment, citizens' rights, the roles that the media industry and civil society play, etc.

It is important to highlight that media literacy is the result of media education and an environment that stimulates creative participation in and through the media. However, how can we secure this enabling environment? The aforementioned study *Current Trends and Approaches to Media Literacy in Europe* developed aims to do this by focusing on the following aspects:

1. Educational activity for school systems and families
2. The active role of laws and regulatory authorities
3. The role of media industry
4. The tasks of civil society

Why? Because all of these aspects influence media literacy levels; therefore all of them must be taken into account when thinking about promoting media literacy.

The conceptual map (Table 1) enables further elaboration of the media literacy criteria and the key environmental factors, which hamper or facilitate the development of media literacy in the EU countries.

Children's media literacy

Literacy in relation to children includes the following strategies in the context of new values: a) critical understanding; b) appropriation of media; c) autonomy and responsibility; d) creativity; and e) social relations and participation.

Based on the above-mentioned conceptual framework – which considers the dynamism and complexity of the phenomenon of media literacy – the assessment criteria consider some indicators that measure not only the use of media,

Table 1. Framework of Basic Criteria to Assess Media Literacy Levels

DIMENSIONS	CRITERIA	OBJECTIVES
INDIVIDUAL COMPETENCES	• Use skills (technical) • Critical Understanding (Cognitive competences) • Communicative abilities	• To increase awareness about how media messages influence perceptions, popular culture and personal choices; • To provide the skill for critical analysis; • To provide the creative skill to solve problems; • To develop the capacity of production; • To consolidate communicative rights; • To develop intercultural dialogue; • To consolidate democracy; and • To develop active and participatory citizenship. (Among others)
KEY ENVIRONMENTAL FACTORS	**MEDIA AVAILABILITY** • Supply of media **MEDIA LITERACY CONTEXT** • Media Education as a process to develop Media Literacy capacities. • Media Literacy policies and regulatory authorities. • Media industry role and activity in relation to media literacy. • Civil society role and activity in relation to media literacy.	

but also the critical competencies and creative and communicative abilities, such as citizen participation skills.

The following pyramid (Figure 1) illustrates the dimensions and criteria for measuring media literacy levels and the ways in which they are reliant on each other.

The base of the pyramid illustrates the pre-conditions of the Individual competences: media availability, that is, the availability of media technology or services; and the media literacy context, which is the activities and initiatives of institutions and organizations aimed at fostering media literacy capacities. Without these two criteria, media literacy development is either precluded or unsupported. They share the same level because, although they are autonomous components, they are, to a degree, interrelated; media literacy policy is carried out in the context of availability, and certain aspects of availability are conditioned or influenced by the context.

Thus, media literacy does not exist in a bubble. It is affected by a variety of dynamic factors and facilitates interdependent skills and competences to allow individuals complete participation in the new digital world. As a consequence, it is assumed that environmental influences (education, institutions, industry, etc.) affect the way in which individual skills develop: educational opportunities and favourable environmental factors produce better educated and developed

Figure 1. Structure of the Media Literacy Assessment Criteria

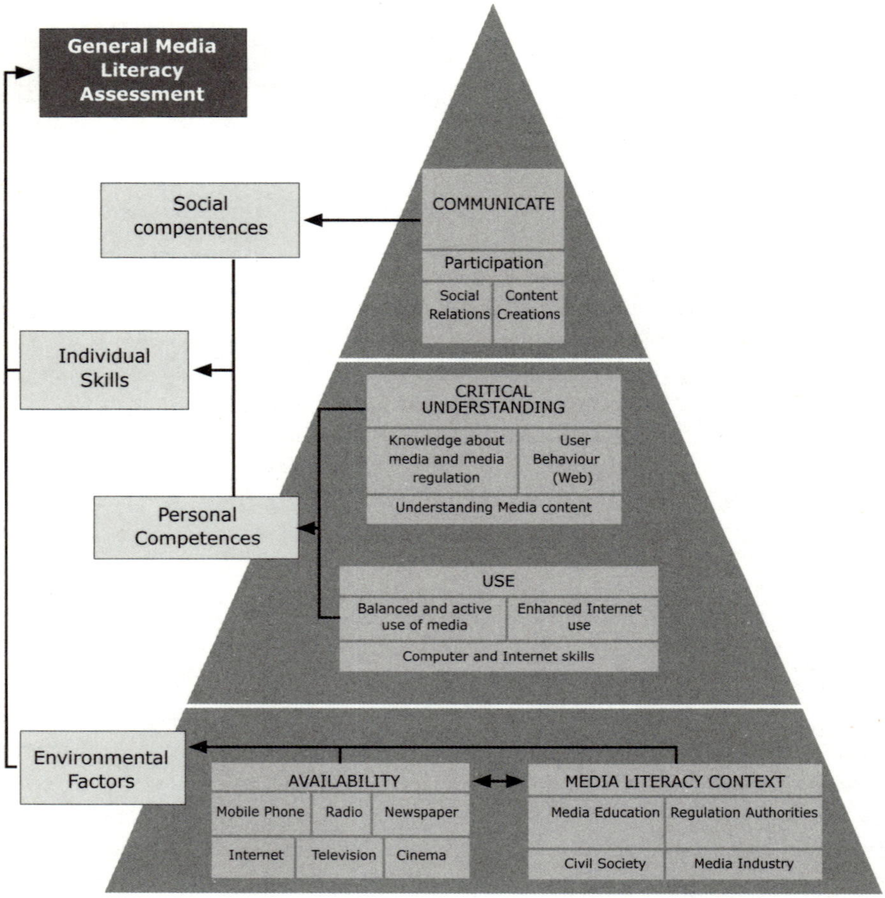

Source: Celot, Paolo and Pérez Tornero, José Manuel, 2009, p. 8.

individuals. However, these factors do not guarantee a specific result. Research cannot encompass all the variables that may potentially affect a particular process.

The Individual competences are illustrated by the second level of the pyramid, which begins with Use, a secondary prerequisite of media literacy development. Use is the intersection between availability and operational skills, which are practical skills involving a low degree of self-conscious awareness.

Then follows Critical Understanding, which is the knowledge, behaviour and understanding of media contexts and contents, and how it manifests itself in behaviour. It includes all the cognitive processes that influence the user's practices (effectiveness of actions, degree of freedom or restriction, regulation and norms, etc.). Use requires knowledge; this factor requires meta-knowledge (knowledge about knowledge). This allows the user to evaluate aspects of the media, by way of comparing different types and sources of information, arriving at conclusions about its veracity and appropriateness, and making informed choices.

The apex of the pyramid represents Communicative Abilities, which are the manifestation of media literacy levels, the quality of which rests on the success or failure of the lower levels. These are skills that manifest themselves in communication and participation with social groups via the media and in content creation. This is the highest degree of media literacy.

As can be seen, media literacy is the result of dynamic processes between the base (Availability and Context) and the apex (Communicative Abilities). The route from the base to the peak is Individual media competence (Media Use and Critical Understanding).

However, because media literacy refers to the individual's relationship with the media, the type of individual referred to in the study cannot be found in reality. The individual in focus in the study represents the average of the attributes of the individuals surveyed in each country, or an average individual who represents the average condition of the individuals in his or her country.

New horizons, new challenges

Referring to the contextual factors, the above-mentioned study *Current Trends...* has identified the emerging orientations related to the role of actors in the field of media literacy, namely:

a. media convergence as a pervasive reality in Europe;

b. the growing concern for the protection of users, mainly children;

c. the general public's critical awareness;

d. the growing presence of media literacy in curricula;

e. a more attentive and responsive media industry;

f. the active participation of civil associations (of parents and teachers);

g. the participation of European institutions and the emergence of regulatory authorities.

The study also focused on the importance of the basic participation of active stakeholders – European institutions (EC, EP, CoE, UNESCO), regulatory authorities, educational systems, civil society (citizens, consumers, families) as well as the media industry – for the development of media literacy, and discerned the following aspects:

- sharing responsibilities (emissary and receptor)
- shift from protection to promotion focus

- combining interpretative (critical thinking) and productive elements (media production skills)
- combining formal and informal education
- combining civil actors and educational actors

On the other hand, one of the conclusions of the *Study on Assessment Criteria for Medial Literacy Levels* was that it is not possible to build a purely mathematical model to measure the exact media literacy level of every country, because there is a partial lack of information of the context or the individual (attitudinal) relations to the media. Some components are more difficult to measure than others, and media literacy needs to be approached as a dynamic phenomenon. It should be clarified that, considered individually, the indicators can highlight no more than the sum of their data, but when considered holistically, the results generate an aggregate measure that allows us to draw workable conclusions.

In 2010, the Danish Institute of Technology (DIT) and the Oxford Institute of Technology have become responsible for testing and refining the development of these indicators.[20] This assures an emergent paradigm of research, namely:

- It will be necessary to transfer the principles and system of indicators to micro-collective situations, institutions, etc.
- On the other hand, it is necessary to develop more qualitative and precise indicators with the objective of applying them to specific individuals and at different stages of development.
- Finally, these indicators must be improved to be applied to measuring development in relation to children and the media environment.

We are therefore facing a new horizon of research, the perspectives of which can be very helpful in the following respects:

- The study of cognitive abilities of children in relation to the media (and the conditions of sociability that the media open), analysing the development from purely technical and operational capabilities to higher capabilities that contain a certain degree of consciousness and critical sense.
- Analysis of how these indicators can help to promote the child's own psychological development and the educational stimuli that s/he receives.
- The specific analysis of the media conditions conducive to the development and environment of children.

More research for practical objectives

Thus, there is a need to develop new indicators for achieving the following practical objectives:

1. Available forms of assessment and diagnosis of the impact and consequences of certain cultural settings, media, social and institutional development of skills and communicative behaviours, and the need to compare them.
2. To establish and evaluate frameworks for the development of media education programmes and target special audiences with both general – to increase the basic media literacy – and specific "how to" purposes, such as the dissolution of cultural barriers.
3. Establish guidelines to promote the creation of content and media sharing situations conducive to the development of children's media literacy skills.

In summary, the on-going *Study Assessment Criteria for Media Literacy Levels* opens a new horizon of opportunities in relation to children and media and for building a new style of media education based on new competences, critical understanding, creativity and participation. It is a long road that must be developed during the next decade.

New paradigm

It is no exaggeration to say that we find that the new paradigm of research, from the framework developed, gives us the opportunity to establish policies for international cooperation in the field.

This will require strong and renewed efforts of interdisciplinary groups and different cultures and nationalities, who will share the idea that in science, measuring instruments, diagnostics and evaluation are necessary. They are in the base of the development of appropriate policies.

Notes

1. The Safer Internet Programme. Retrieved at: http://ec.europa.eu/information_society/activities/sip/policy/programme/index_en.htm
2. Decision No 276/1999/EC of the European Parliament and of the Council of 25 January 1999 adopting a multiannual Community action plan on promoting safer use of the Internet by combating illegal and harmful content on global networks. Retrieved at: http://eur-lex.europa.eu/LexUriServ/LexUriServ.do?uri=CELEX:31999D0276:EN:NOT
3. The successor programme is The Safer Internet Plus Programme 2005-2008.
4. Council of Europe. *Recommendation Rec (2006)12 of the Committee of Ministers to Member states on empowering children in the new information and communications environment.* 27th September, 2006. Retrieved at: http://portal.unesco.org/ci/en/files/25152/11861425271Recommendation_Rec%282006%2912.pdf/Recommendation%2BRec%282006%2912.pdf
5. The European Council published the *Internet Literacy Handbook*, a guide for parents, teachers and young people.
6. European Commission. *Recommendation of the European Parliament and of the Council of 18 December 2006 on key competences for lifelong learning.* (2006/962/EC) Retrieved at: http://eur-lex.europa.eu/LexUriServ/LexUriServ.do?uri=OJ:L:2006:394:0010:0018:en:PDF
7. European Parliament. *Recommendation 2006/952/EC of the European Parliament and of the Council of 20 December 2006 on the protection of minors and human dignity and on the right*

of reply in relation to the competitiveness of the European audiovisual and on-line information services industry (Official Journal L 378 of 27.12.2006). Retrieved at: http://europa.eu/legislation_summaries/audiovisual_and_media/l24030a_en.htm

8. Pérez Tornero, J.M. (2004) *Promoting Digital Literacy. Understanding Digital Literacy.* Final Report EAC/76/03. Retrieved at: http://ec.europa.eu/education/archive/elearning/doc/studies/dig_lit_en.pdf
9. European Commission and DTI (2009). *EU Digital Literacy Review. Public policies and stakeholder initiatives* (This is a comparative analysis of different Digital Literacy initiatives around the world. The study focused on initiatives and policies targeted at disadvantaged groups.)
10. The Commission adopted on 8.11.2007 the Communication *European i2010 initiative on e-Inclusion – to be part of the information society.* Retrieved at: http://ec.europa.eu/information_society/activities/einclusion/policy/i2010_initiative/index_en.htm
11. Digital Literacy: High-Level Expert Group Recommendations. Retrieved at: http://ec.europa.eu/information_society/eeurope/i2010/docs/digital_literacy/digital_literacy_hlg_recommendations.pdf
12. European Commission. *Digital Literacy. European Commission Working Paper and Recommendations from Digital Literacy High-Level Expert Group.* e-Inclusion Ministerial Conference & Expo. 30th November-2nd December, 2008. Retrieved at: http://ec.europa.eu/information_society/eeurope/i2010/docs/digital_literacy/digital_literacy_review.pdf
13. See http://ec.europa.eu/culture/media/literacy/expert_group/index_en.htm
14. European Commission. *Making sense of today's media content: Commission begins public media literacy consultation.* Brussels, 6 October 2006. Available at: http://ec.europa.eu/culture/media/literacy/consultation/index_en.htm. See also the "Report on the results on the public consultation on Media Literacy: http://ec.europa.eu/avpolicy/media_literacy/docs/report_on_ml_2007.pdf
15. Ibid, p. 5
16. Pérez Tornero, J.M. & Celot, P. (2007). *Current trends and approaches to media literacy in Europe,* EC. Retrieved at http://ec.europa.eu/culture/media/literacy/studies/index_en.htm
17. European Commission. *Report on media literacy in a digital world (2008/2129(INI)).* Committee on Culture and Education. (Session Document) November 24th, 2008. Retrieved at: http://www.europarl.europa.eu/sides/getDoc.do?type=REPORT&mode=XML&reference=A6-2008-0461&language=EN
18. *Audiovisual Media Service Directive* 2007/65/EC of the European Parliament and the Council of Europe, December 11, 2007. Retrieved at http://ec.europa.eu/avpolicy/reg/avms/index_en.htm (This Directive replaces the European Directive on Television without Frontiers (DTVSF 89/552/EC.)
19. http://ec.europa.eu/culture/media/literacy/index_en.htm (December 2010)
20. EC requested the Study *Testing and refining criteria to assess media literacy levels in all Member States* (2010)

References

Audiovisual Media Service Directive 2007/65/EC of the European Parliament and the Council of December 11th 2007. Retrieved at http://ec.europa.eu/avpolicy/reg/avms/index_en.htm

Celot, Paolo & Pérez Tornero, José Manuel (2009) *Media Literacy in Europa. Leggere, scrivere, e partecipare nell'era mediatica.* Roma, Eurilink. Prólogo de Gian Maria Fara

Council of Europe. *Recommendation Rec (2006)12 of the Committee of Ministers to Member States on Empowering Children in the New Information and Communications Environment.* 27th September, 2006. Retrieved at: http://portal.unesco.org/ci/en/files/25152/11861425271Recommendation_Rec%282006%2912.pdf/Recommendation%2BRec%282006%2912.pdf

Decision No. 276/1999/EC of the European Parliament and of the Council of 25 January 1999 adopting a multiannual Community action plan on promoting safer use of the Internet by combating illegal and harmful content on global networks. Retrieved at http://eur-lex.europa.eu/LexUriServ/LexUriServ.do?uri=CELEX:31999D0276:EN:NOT

Digital Literacy: High-Level Expert Group Recommendations. Retrieved at: http://ec.europa.eu/information_society/eeurope/i2010/docs/digital_literacy/digital_literacy_hlg_recommendations.pdf

European Commission. *Recommendation of the European Parliament and of the Council of 18 December 2006 on key competences for lifelong learning*. (2006/962/EC) Retrieved at: http://eur-lex.europa.eu/LexUriServ/LexUriServ.do?uri=OJ:L:2006:394:0010:0018:en:PDF

European Parliament. *Recommendation 2006/952/EC of the European Parliament and of the Council of 20 December 2006 on the protection of minors and human dignity and on the right of reply in relation to the competitiveness of the European audiovisual and on-line information services industry* [Official Journal L 378 of 27.12.2006]. Retrieved at http://europa.eu/legislation_summaries/audiovisual_and_media/l24030a_en.htm

European Commission. *Digital Literacy. European Commission working paper and Recommendations from Digital Literacy High-Level Expert Group*. e-Inclusion Ministerial Conference & Expo. 30th November-2nd December, 2008. Retrieved at http://ec.europa.eu/information_society/eeurope/i2010/docs/digital_literacy/digital_literacy_review.pdf

European Commission. The Commission adopted on 8.11.2007 the Communication *European i2010 Initiative on e-Inclusion* – to be part of the Information Society. Retrieved at http://ec.europa.eu/information_society/activities/einclusion/policy/i2010_initiative/index_en.htm

European Commission. *Making Sense of Today's Media Content: Commission begins public Media Literacy consultation*. Brussels, 6 October 2006. Available at http://ec.europa.eu/culture/media/literacy/consultation/index_en.htm. See also the "Report on the results on the public consultation on Media Literacy", http://ec.europa.eu/avpolicy/media_literacy/docs/report_on_ml_2007.pdf

European Commission. *Report on Media Literacy in a Digital World (2008/2129(INI))*. Committee on Culture and Education (Session Document) November 24th, 2008. Retrieved at http://www.europarl.europa.eu/sides/getDoc.do?type=REPORT&mode=XML&reference=A6-2008-0461&language=EN

Pérez Tornero, J.M. (2004). *Promoting Digital Literacy. Understanding Digital Literacy*, Final Report EAC/76/03. Retrieved at http://ec.europa.eu/education/archive/elearning/doc/studies/dig_lit_en.pdf

Pérez Tornero, J.M. & Celot, P. (2007). *Current Trends and Approaches to Media Literacy in Europe*, EC. Retrieved at http://ec.europa.eu/culture/media/literacy/studies/index_en.htm

The Safer Internet Programme. Retrieved at: http://ec.europa.eu/information_society/activities/sip/policy/programme/index_en.htm

Youth and Children in Contemporary Brazilian Film and Television – and Film and Television by Youth and Children

Esther Hamburger

It is a pleasure to participate in this Research Forum at the World Summit on Media for Children and Adolescents with other universities engaged in research on and intervention in media literacy. This is a great opportunity to learn about the specific configurations of media and diverse approaches to media literacy found in different countries around the world. My presentation considers the research on media literacy conducted at the Department of Film, Radio and Television, School of Arts and Communications, University of São Paulo.

We hope that the information gathered in this Forum will help foster new forms of collaboration between our universities, as we are dealing here with very different contexts, but also with many points of intersection, which contain a potential for collaborative efforts to promote a creative and empowering media environment.

Our own work approaches media literacy from a dynamic perspective, which involves discussions on the history and aesthetics of audiovisual forms, but also the production of film, video and digital media. Among the different media, we concentrated on film, television and the internet. Professors and graduate students develop different components of our project, each dealing with short and feature-length films, but also with TV and IPTV (Internet Protocol television) programs, made both by children and youngsters who live in underprivileged areas, and for youngsters and children living in these neighborhoods. Our goal is to associate the different branches of our project with other groups inside and outside the university, including public and community television stations.

Our work departs from a diagnosis of the ways in which, in Brazil, the cartography of film and television relates to social, gender and race discrimination, in order to propose different and specific interventions. In short, while film only reaches spectators who live in urban upper middle-class neighborhoods, television has grown to become the main national means of communication and one of the largest television industries in the world. Because access to film has been so restricted, there is a popular demand both to view and to make films. Relatively cheap new technologies have favored community audiovisual workshops in peripheral areas. Film has an especially symbolic appeal. In general, communities welcome projects of social inclusion that deal with film.

Since in order to define specific approaches, each component of our project relies in this same analysis of the ways in which film and television relate to each other, and to different forms of discrimination, and since the specificities of the Brazilian case may be useful in informing a transnational comparative framework, I start this contribution with a short description of the structure of film and television in this Portuguese-speaking Latin American country. I then move on to describe different components of our work, each geared to foster one aspect of media literacy. Our project endeavors to further develop creative writing, production and criticism of film and television. Our work involves interaction between artists, university students and professors, students and teachers in the public schools and participants in community audiovisual workshops in peripheral areas.

Overall view of the structure of film and television in Brazil

The first element to be taken into account in understanding the particular relevance of audiovisual media in everyday life in Brazil is that although the Brazilian economy is among the 10 largest in the world, and even though inequality has decreased over the past 15 years, Brazil remains among the 5 percent most unequal nations in the world.[1] One component of social inequality is poor education. Although Brazilian illiteracy rates have consistently decreased throughout the 20th century, large portions of the population still cannot read.

In a country of few readers, audiovisual media, especially television has been particularly present in everyday life. In 1950 when television was introduced, 50 percent of the national population older than 15 could not read or write.

Brazilian television started early, but grew slowly. It was only under the military government, which took over in 1964, that television became a significant industry. The military considered television an important tool in their policy of "national integration". Indeed, from the late 60s on, under strong censorship, state investment in technology rapidly turned television into perhaps the first, and certainly the main, national source of information. Even though it relied on government financial and political control, Brazilian television has adopted a hybrid structure that combines various sorts of state interference with commercial networks. Public television is small by comparison.

In some senses, the Brazilian television model mirrors Hollywood's 1930s and 40s classic "vertical" mode of production: networks both produce and broadcast. There is a "star system" that attaches actors and actresses to networks. Costumes sell fashion and meanings. Television has played the role of a national window to the segregated world of "modern" urban-white-upper-middle-class Brazilians.

It is under that axe that television helped to build a *sui generis* sense of national community in Benedict Anderson's sense.[2] Since the late 60s, one popular grid made up of what is called a "sandwich" of *telenovelas* (daily primetime soaps) and news programs has become conventional. Under censorship, broadcast news favored official and corporate stories. Both television news and fictional programs broadcast images of affluent white Brazil. Furniture, electronic devices, cars, planes, and other signs of glamour transmitted a sense of abundance. Tele-fiction has been mainly set in contemporary times and well-known landscapes. There is thus a sense of continuity in time and space between the universe of television narrative and viewers' everyday life. Television diffused a certain lifestyle – which was inspired by a small segment of the population – as a model for the nation.

Television drama revolved around the conflict between "modern" and "traditional" forms of behavior. The meanings associated with being modern have been continuously updated. Together with intense migrations from the Northeast to urban Southeastern centers, critiques of family structure function to deconstruct patriarchal authority. Increasingly, liberal family and romantic relations have combined with consumerism to signify social change. It was as if inclusion in this "country of the future" were only available to those who were able to buy – fashion, electronic devices, cars, and so on.

During the 70s and 80s, television expressed what Brazilians would like to become. It is as if television gave shape to the "country of the future" Brazilians have dreamed of for centuries. Consumerism played a key role in this imaginary land. Television has been key in developing an internal market for electronic devices, means of communication and of transportation. Indeed, television programs taught viewers both how to behave in certain circumstances, and what to buy in order to look like accomplished upper-middle-class viewers. In times of high inflation, Brazilians could hardly save any money at all. Of the many recently available industrial products, television sets were among the most popular. Brazilians got used to spending all they had, sometimes buying the best brand or the most expensive type of TV set. Sometimes a *favela* shack would have more than one television set.

In the early 80s when television was about to reach 99 percent of the national territory, 25.9 percent of the population over 15 was still illiterate. In 2000, 13.6 percent of the population over 15 continued to be illiterate.[3] Nonetheless, an average of 50 million viewers daily watched the same primetime grid, aired by the main commercial network: Globo. In the early 2000s, with the advent of cable television, DVD, and the web, audience concentration has decreased. But still, from 24 to 32 million viewers watch the same primetime programs every night.

Advertising supports networks in a country where until 1997 audience ratings excluded the D and E segments (those with the lowest socio-economic status) of the population, due to their assumed incapacity to consume. Indeed, the afore-mentioned social inequality is responsible for an interesting twist: while television is usually known for undervaluing its audience, Brazilian television might be thought of as having overestimated its audience. During the 70s and 80s, television produced high quality drama. First leftist writers with theater and film backgrounds, and afterwards a new generation of television directors with experience in video art, were responsible for the distinguished aesthetic quality of local programming. Perversely, in the late 90s, when poverty decreased and large segments of the population were included in the ratings, the quality of television programming decreased.

While television in Brazil has become part of the culture industry, film has remained a very restricted elite medium. Indeed, while television is present in almost every Brazilian household, the number of movie theaters has decreased since the 1970s, when the country had 3,300 cinemas, to the current 2,000.

With a population of 180 million, only rare film blockbusters are seen by over 5 million viewers, while television, again, reaches 50 million viewers daily. Foreign films are more popular, but as they are subtitled and not dubbed (with the exception of children's films), their potential number of viewers remains low. In the past couple of years, with rare exceptions, Brazilian films have hardly ever reached more than 100 thousand viewers. Film has not constituted a self-sustained industry. Brazilian cinema is state funded. Television in turn has become a profitable industry. Although Brazilian television has produced a broad range of quality programs, which have even been exported worldwide, quality has recently decreased. Perversely, commercially oriented, sensationalist low quality programming has increased since the late 1990s, when marketing and audience research institutes incorporated large portions of the population that had previously been excluded from the ratings (owing to their low consumer potential).

While Brazilian social inequality has been a key point in the history of cinema, it has been practically absent from television. *Rio 40 Degrees* (1955) and *Rio North Zone* (1957) by Nelson Pereira dos Santos mark the rise of modern cinema in Brazil.[4] Five "cinema novo" directors – Joaquim Pedro, Leon Hirzman, Cacá Diegues, Miguel Borges and Marcos Farias – produced *Five Times Favela* (1962). It is an ensemble of shorts, four of them produced by the Students' Union as part of the activities of its Center for Popular Culture (CPC), an organization that aimed to foster students' political engagement with working class movements. Both Cinema Novo and CPC concentrated on northeastern rural settings.[5] With few exceptions, such as *A Margem* (Ozualdo Candeias, 1967) or *Pixote* (Hector Babenco, 1981), up until 1999 when the documentary *News from a Private War* by João Moreira Salles brought the everyday drug-related violence found in Rio de Janeiro's *favelas* to the media, urban poverty was invisible. Salles' documentary started a still-ongoing controversial trend in Brazilian filmmaking that brings poor urban cityscapes and their inhabitants to the screens.

Indeed, up until recently, poverty has been almost invisible in the whole Brazilian public sphere. This invisibility has raised resentment and reproduced social discrimination. Recently, the invisibility was broken, first in film, and later on television. As a result, an intense dispute over who represents whom, where, and how has fed the audiovisual media scene. The question is both political and poetic as – and this is our point here – even though those who were excluded from media production might at first believe that this stereotyped form of portraying their universe on film is dependent on the fact that the filmmakers do not "belong" to those places, things are more complicated than that. Even when local underprivileged black youngsters have been given the chance to make their own films, they many times reproduce the same stereotypes they have criticized. To some extent this happened, for instance, in *Falcon, Boys of the Traffic* (2006), a documentary film by rapper M.V. Bill and his manager, Celso Athayde.[6] Engendering new esthetic forms to express old forms of discrimination has become a challenge for Brazilian filmmakers, social movements, and critics. The struggle over *appropriation* of the means of producing and distributing audiovisual content became a strategic issue in the public debate.[7] In this context, work on media literacy becomes particularly relevant.

Falcon, Boys of the Traffic can be understood as a response coming from within the City of God itself to the film *City of God* (Fernando Meirelles, 2002). M.V. Bill participated in the project of Meirelles' film, composing for instance the main song for the short *Palace II* Meirelles directed in 2001 as part of the preparation for the feature film, which won the Berlin Golden Bear for shorts, and which originated the TV series *City of Men*. Nonetheless, Bill is not only absent from the feature film, but also criticized the film exactly for reproducing stereotypes. According to Bill, after the release of the movie, it became difficult for people living in the neighborhood to go on with their jobs and/or other kinds of relations in the outside world. He stated that, for locals, living in the City of God after the film was synonymous with being a violent bandit. In order to counteract the idea that the whole *favela* could be reduced to a segment of the national population that can be found almost anywhere in Brazil, Bill and Athayde did their own research and then made their own film. In so doing, they opened up a realm that was previously very restricted. But the images and reports they presented were as terrible as the ones Salles had shown in his film. The two documentary films also echo words and gestures performed in *City of God*. If *Falcon* can be read as a voice from within the favela, *Elite Squad* might be taken as representing the voice of the police, or at least that of the BOPE, a police corps that supposedly is not involved in political corruption or in cahoots with drug dealers.

It is possible to list a series of films from 1999 onwards that deal with the problem from different perspectives. Films such as *A Wave in the Air* (Helvécio Ratton, 2002), *Bus 174* (José Padilha, 2002), *O Invasor* (Beto Brandt, 2002) can be thought of as expressions of different perspectives on the same subject. But it is not the aim of my presentation to delve into this long and diverse filmography.[8] The point I wish to make here is that there is a "multilogue" revolving around the interplay of image, inequality and violence taking place in films.

Undeniably, the geography of film and television media has become more complex thanks to the recent wave of *favela situation* films. Within the "new wave of Brazilian film"[9] these films have raised a whole new debate concerning visual form, legitimate authorship, and directors' social belonging.[10] Films made by and for elite audiences emphasize poor neighborhoods and favela settings, whereas television programs are geared towards general national audiences but offer little room for issues dealing with race or social discrimination.

Recent improvements in wealth distribution and poverty reduction have brought to the forefront a popular demand for films, among other forms of expression. Access to television production and programming has also become a popular demand. Use of the internet as an alternative to television has rapidly increased amidst what can be called cultural and artistic exuberance. Indeed, as literacy increases specific literary forms arise in peripheral neighborhoods. Rap expresses some of this writing flurry, but a number of periodic *saraus* such as Co-perifa's popular Wednesday's night poetry performance, or a number of peripheral publishing houses and papers, suggest a certain wealth of co-existing contemporary forms. Audiovisual workshops and production groups include exhibition and discussion of films that avoid conventional associations of violence, gender, race, and poverty to experiment with new forms of narrative. Poor black young men, as well as women, engage in what can be seen as both a political and esthetic challenge: to find modes of expression that not only do not reproduce usual stereotypes, but also help do away with conventional forms of audiovisual discrimination.

Common sense notions of belonging many times legitimatize rhetorical discourses that distinguish those who somehow pertain to universes that constitute the subject of certain debates, and therefore would be more prepared to create texts, images or sound expressions hailing from their own neighborhoods, from those who do not belong to those places and therefore have no right or knowledge to speculate about them. In this "identity politics" debate, it is as if only those who "belong" to the places or groups to be portrayed have the legitimacy to speak, or to film.

In our approach, we make an issue of the idea of "belonging" in order to unpack the essentialist bias that most often accompanies identity politics. The idea here is to stimulate the construction of new, innovative, relational senses of belonging. Assuming that communities are constructed according to certain interlocutions at certain moments in time and places in space, the idea here is to propose that senses of belonging might be constructed together with new senses of community.

Moreover, most of the time, films that express relations between professionals with "incomplete" or "partial" forms of belonging somehow suggest original takes on certain problems. Indeed, different forms of creating and reproducing "otherness" have recently been criticized in favor of ideal discourses constructed by these "others" themselves. Nonetheless, rather than an essential and objective thing, "otherness" is, by definition, a relative concept. "Otherness" is constructed in different ways, by different people, in different places and at different moments in time. "Otherness" is an intrinsically relational concept that necessarily supposes interlocutions at least between two people or groups of people. To a great extent, "one" is one only in relation to an "other", which is different from this "one" (or from the "self"). In relation to a third party, one would perhaps be a different "other". In this sense, the idea of "belonging" is far from descriptive of well-defined geographical domains. Borders tend to move as interlocutors move. In this sense, rather than looking for "authentic" representatives of certain identity groups, we value instead the process of construction of selves, always understood in relation to others. In this sense, sometimes distance, rather than proximity, inspires creative approaches. Although this proposition is often criticized by those who find in identity politics the strength and language to fight discrimination, from many different perspectives we find that disrupting stereotypes demands dialectic relations between distance and proximity.

Media literacy: strategies to foster film, television and the internet

In Brazil, audiovisual literacy could play a strategic role in the consolidation of democracy and in developing inclusive forms of citizenship. We have developed different lines of research in order to increase the potential of debates and alternative filmmaking.

In the first place, we have promoted screenings and debates at the university, but also at different peripheral settings, such as public screenings outdoors, screenings in community organizations, and screenings in public schools. The idea here is to bridge the gap that usually separates filmmakers and viewers who live in places where there are no movie theaters. The idea is that these encounters should stimulate a dialogue, although dialogue is sometimes based on tension. Indeed this project deals with what Shoat and Stam (1994)[11] have called the "burden of representation", meaning the intrinsically sensitive nature of representations that deal with people who resent being invisible or discriminated against through the reproduction of stereotyped representations, such as the conventional portrait of poor young black Brazilian men as violent outlaws.

We have arranged encounters between peripheral audiences, peripheral filmmakers and elite filmmakers, professors and students in order to foster debates on the politics and aesthetics of representation. The idea here is to research poetic and political forms to disarticulate conventional video narratives that reinforce discrimination. These encounters have proved to be intense and productive. As I stated earlier, in Brazil, visual discrimination is aggravated by the fact that invisibility has been broken in a medium made and viewed by filmmakers and with viewers who do not live in the places dealt with in the films. Therefore, this discussion becomes particularly tense. Many audiences find *favela situation films* offensive. Their first reaction is to debate about who belongs and who does not belong to the universe portrayed in the films. This debate may be written or oral, or pursued through film, television and other media.

Our screenings involved enacting this debate and confronting the often simple-minded ideas that could frame two possible poles of this debate: on the one hand, the idea that film form derives from social belonging, and on the other, the idea that form has nothing to do with social forces. In the encounters we promoted, filmic constructions of peripheral settings and characters were discussed. These situations provided rare contact between university graduate and undergraduate film students and viewers whom they rarely encounter, even though they live in the same city. We confronted the ways in which contemporary *favela situation films* both offend and fascinate peripheral viewers – the ways in which audiovisual workshops inspire peripheral viewers to themselves become filmmakers and to invent new forms for visually constructing their neighborhoods and their portraits of local inhabitants. This line of inquiry will continue in the form of proposed exhibits of films on the subject, followed by a closing international seminar. This component of the project has been financed by FAPESP, State of S. Paulo Finance Agency, as well as by a fellowship from CNPq, Federal Government.

This line of inquiry continues as well in the form of a series of proposed workshops on the history, theory and practice of audiovisual production with teachers from the São Paulo public school system. A pilot project involving the Film, Radio and TV Department of the School of Arts and Communications, the School of Education and the CINUSP (Cinema da Universidade de São Paulo) "Paulo Emílio" has just received funding from CAPES, Federal Government. Besides myself, professors Agnaldo Arroyo and Rogério de Almeida, Patricia Moran and Almir Almas are involved in this proposal. Breno Benedyct, an Education student, has been working on the intersection of Film Studies and Education.

Patrícia Moran, video artist, film director, professor of the Film, Radio and Television Department, and Vice-director of the CINUSP "Paulo Emílio" has had some of her work exhibited in electronic art and film festivals in several countries such as Hungary, Italy, Cuba, France and the U.S. Her recent debut in feature-length films, *Dot.org,* deals with the experiences of a group of children from the outskirts of São Paulo with a camera in hand as they both document life in the city and play with potential urban dangers. As filmed by them, the city itself becomes a character, acquiring images, projections and delicate movements that personify the dreams, secrets, and fears of those whose home is the streets.

Our team also includes video artist Milena Szafir, whose Master's thesis consists of a video essay that reflects not only on the debates we have promoted, but also on the different media references viewers relate to in their critical assessments of the ways in which the media treat poor urban cityscapes in relation to violence. Milena has also worked with the university IPTV, a medium that we intend to further explore in our work. Milena has researched YouTube excerpts from the film *Elite Squad* (José Padilha, 2006). She made a "remix film" with various clips she cut from the internet. Her work reflects her feelings of fear about the fascination that violence and militarist solutions portrayed in the film elicit in viewers from all over the world.

Inspired by an event that occurred during one of our screenings, Milena, using both the written word and images, revealed her fear of a society in which people value belligerent policemen but do not seem to care about vigilance. Unlike teachers, educational advisors, and directors, who constituted our first group of interlocutors with whom we discussed what to show in each school and who dislike films that portray peripheral settings in violent terms, one teenager declared his admiration for *Elite Squad*. For him, this controversial thriller, classified by many as fascist, was "more real" than the documentary *News From a Private War* (João Moreira Salles, 1999).

Our team also includes dramatist Renato Cândido de Lima who comes from a neighborhood on the outskirts of São Paulo. Renato's M.A. project involves researching how to publicly give visual expression to his experience, first as a mulatto undergraduate and now as a graduate student. Besides improving his skills as a playwright and director, Renato's proposal involves a series of workshops in peripheral schools and neighborhoods aimed at training new actors and actresses.

Dr. Moira Toledo has worked for over 15 years in the field of democratic cinema education. Her work is part of the rich body of audiovisual workshops that have been changing the landscape of the field. She has just defended her Doctoral Dissertation on the multiple experiences of Audiovisual Popular Education. The dissertation presents a mapping of the experience of cost-free media workshops and courses in Brazil, between 1990 and 2009, based on the shared educational challenges, practices and histories of the entities that provide them. The aim was to establish major intents, systemize common strategies and, especially, to reflect on the major results obtained, with a view to identifying how and when they achieve their best potential. With that purpose in mind, she has designed and employed 198 questionnaires and interviews with professionals from 70 entities around the country.

The collected data and the analyses carried out have shown that the professionals from such entities revisit – and to some extent recreate – theories, practices and philosophical principles from correlated fields of education, especially from the subfield we have identified as pertaining to alternative and democratic education. These entities have been achieving excellent results by many standards, which suggests that such theories, practices and philosophical principles – when integrated into the promotion of literacies, such as media literacy – have the potential to encourage solutions to the chronic challenges faced by formal schools and to bring about the development of public policies.

As a television and film critic, I have been tuned into the esthetic and programming shifts in the main networks, but also on cable (pay) and satellite television. Canal Futura and Sesc TV are two rare examples of channels that sometimes broadcast community productions resulting from the workshops. The public television channels TV Cultura (São Paulo) and TV Brasil (Federal) are another two rare examples of channels that broadcast these kinds of productions. As our UNESCO enterprise moves further, we will have more input with which to develop this kind of application. This operation also welcomes and aims to start collaborations with researchers working with other media, such as radio and newspapers.

Notes

1. See Paes de Barros, R. et al. (2006) A queda recente da desigualdade no Brasil, in Paes de Barros, R. et al. *Desigualdade de Renda no Brasil: uma análise da queda recente*. Brasília: IPEA, pp. 107-126
2. Anderson, B. (1983) *Imagined Communities*. London: Verso
3. See *Mapa do Analfabetismo no Brasil*. Brasília: INEP, National Education Research Institute. Available for download on October 20, 2010, at http://www.inep.gov.br/estatisticas/analfabetismo
4. See Xavier, I. (2005) *Modern Brazilian Cinema*. São Paulo: Paz e Terra
5. For more on the Cinema Novo's emphasis on rural topics and places, see Bernardet, J.C. ([1967] 2007) *Brasil em tempo de cinema*. São Paulo: Cia das Letras
6. For a close analysis of this film, see Hamburger, E. (2008) Wired Up to the World: Performance and Media in Contemporary Brazil, in Birle, P., Costa, S. & Nitschack, H. (Eds.) *Brazil and the Americas*. 1 ed. Frankfurt: Vervuert, pp. 199-222
7. For more on breaking the invisibility of the poor in Brazilian cinema, see Hamburger, E. (2008) Wired Up to the World: Performance and Media in Contemporary Brazil, in Birle,P., Costa, S. & Nitschack, H. (Eds.) *Brazil and the Americas*. 1 ed. Frankfurt: Vervuert, pp. 199-222
8. This is an ongoing work with partial results presented in Hamburger, E. (2008) (see notes above)
9. For more on this see Nagib, L. (2003) *New Brazilian Cinema*. London: Taurus
10. Kornis, M. (2006) Aventuras Urbanas em Cidade dos Homens: estratégias narrativas de inclusão social em seriados ficcionais, *Revista de Estudos Históricos,* Rio de Janeiro: FGV, and (2007) Cidade dos Homens e Falcão, meninos do tráfico: sobre as representações televisivas da realidade brasileira, in Castro Gomes, A. (Ed.) *Direitos e Cidadania*. Rio de Janeiro: FGV
11. Shohat, E. & Stam, R. (1994) *Unthinking Eurocentrism. Multiculturalism and the media*. Routledge: New York

Children and New Media Literacy

An Egyptian Case Study

Samy Tayie

Children's use of new media has become wide-spread in the world. For example, more than one quarter of the world's population (1.2 billion) uses the internet (Tayie, 2009). Due to the new media, the world is also becoming smaller. Increasingly, we are able to gain access to cultures and knowledge that used to be beyond our horizon. The information society of today has a great potential, especially for young people (Carlsson, 2009, p. 10).

The present article reports on findings of a qualitative pilot study on children's use of new media carried out among Egyptian children from one urban and one rural area. The study is part of a comparative project (2009-2011) on Youth Media Participation, funded by the Finnish Academy and including primarily Finland, Egypt, Argentine and India. The main objective of the project is to find out about children's use of new media, i.e., the internet and mobile phones, their media literacy, and their media participation. More about the comparative project is told in the article "Youngsters' Expressions of Responsible Citizenship through Media Diaries" by Sirkku Kotilainen et al., in this volume.

The research project started by collecting data in the form of one-day diaries and focus interviews, which were analysed as background material for forthcoming interviews, and quantitative data collected through questionnaires beginning in late 2010 in the four countries. In the present article, findings from the Egyptian focus interviews are presented.

The media situation in Egypt

Egypt is the largest country in the Arab World with respect to population, which exceeds 80 million. The people mainly live around the river Nile; it is estimated that 95 per cent of the population live on only three per cent of the land. The capital Cairo has a population of 18 million.

Education in Egypt is compulsory for all children from 6 to 12 years of age. There are mainly two types of schools: governmental (with low fees that are affordable to everyone) and private schools (some of them very expensive and following the American, French, British or German educational system and curricula). Children have to spend twelve years at school if they wish to enter a university, after having received the General Secondary School Certificate.

There are a wide range of governmental and private media in the country. The Egyptian Radio and Television Union, which is a part of the Ministry of Information, supervises radio and television. There are three national state-run TV channels and six local state channels. The national Channel Two broadcasts mainly in English and French and is meant to serve expatriates living in Egypt. There are also quite a few private TV channels.

Generally speaking, the viewer in the Arab world is exposed to a great number of TV channels. In addition to the terrestrial TV channels, there are 696 satellite channels, of which 97 are owned by governments and 599 are privately owned. They broadcast through 17 satellites working in the Arab World (Media Committee, 2010).

Among the governmental channels, 49 are generalist channels and 48 are specialized niche channels, whereas of the private satellite channels, 161 are generalist and 438 specialized. Most channels broadcast in Arabic (76%) and English (20%). They also broadcast in other languages, such as French, Persian, Spanish, Indian, Hebron, and Urdu. Moreover, children in Egypt and other Arab countries are exposed to satellite channels from Europe, North America and other parts of the world.

Regarding the Internet and mobile phones, it is estimated that nearly 75 per cent of the population in Egypt have mobile phone services. The Internet is available in 65 per cent of homes in Cairo and 40 per cent of homes in other areas. Moreover, Internet cafés are found in the big cities.

There are seven national radio networks. One of them broadcasts in more than 40 languages, i.e., the Overseas Radio. Furthermore, there are local radio stations in all parts of the country. There are also private radio stations (FM) that broadcast mainly light musical programmes, mostly listened to by young people.

With respect to print media, there are three important governmental publishing houses that publish newspapers and magazines in Arabic, English, French and German. Private and partially private newspapers are also numerous. It is estimated that there are more than 600 newspapers and magazines in total in Egypt (Higher Press Council, 2009). Issuance of private and partially private newspapers is subject to the approval of the Higher Press Council, which is the regulatory organization for the print media.

The film industry in Egypt is well advanced, and plays in the Arab World the same role Hollywood plays in the West. Egyptian films and TV programmes are very popular all over the Arab World. Arab TV channels rely a great deal on Egyptian programmes.

The study sample

In the present preliminary study, we decided to interview children from two different geographical areas, i.e., Cairo as the urban area and Fayoum (100 kilometres south of Cairo) as the rural area. Life conditions in Fayoum are different from those in Cairo; Fayoum can be seen as a typical rural area, where agriculture predominates.

All interviews were carried out with boys and girls in their homes, with the knowledge of their parents. The parents were assured that the data collected were only for research purposes, and that the names of their children would not appear.

In total, 36 interviews were carried out in Cairo and Fayoum with children aged 12 to 14 and 16 to 18 (however, one boy was 9 years old). The interviews were individual, except for two interviews that included two children each. Therefore, the total number of interviewed children was 38 – 19 boys (10 from Cairo and 9 from Fayoum) and 19 girls (10 from Cairo and 9 from Fayoum).

Method

Focus interviews have been used successfully for collecting qualitative data on everyday practices and have also been beneficial for studying the ideas and values of individuals and groups (Merton, Fiske & Kendall, 1990). The focus interview was initially developed to provide some basis for interpreting statistically significant effects of mass communication (ibid., p. 5). The focused interview is also useful both for the interviewer and the interviewee, as certain specified themes may be used to keep up the conversation and focus on its content. The conversation can be kept flexible, thus leaving room for unexpected themes or issues. This also offers possibilities to reach deeper structures in the conversation, as well as meaning making processes, including values, identity, feelings and attitudes, etc. Moreover, it gives the interviewee an active role in the interview. Based on these qualities, focused interviews have mostly been used as a tool for gathering information about people's intimate or difficult experiences.

The study's point of departure was "grounded theory" (Glaser & Strauss, 1967; Glaser & Holton, 2004). Using a grounded theory approach, one does not have a predetermined set of questions or themes. Our goal in conducting these interviews was to obtain a "thick description" (Geerz, 1973) that would give us useful insights for designing more specific questions for the questionnaire in 2010.

In the interview situation, the children were given the status of the expert. This was not difficult, as most children were able to talk about new media or applications for using them – whether they used them for games, drawing programs or web pages.

The approach in our analysis was multi-sited (Marcus, 1995, p. 117). Using the term "multi-sited ethnography", anthropologist Marcus describes research in which spaces and landscapes are analysed simultaneously in a larger social context.

Thus, the multi-sited approach is useful in comparative research like ours, when people from different economic classes, of different gender, age groups and social contexts are interviewed. Marcus (1995, pp. 105-106) stresses the ability of multi-sited research to bring into light the complex chains, paths, relations, positions as well as processes (Appadurai, 1990, pp. 21-24), in our case as regards personal, social, global and local media participation and its meaning-making processes.

The interviews were carried out from November 2009 to March 2010 with the help of two Ph.D. students from Cairo University. All interviews were recorded. On average, each interview lasted for an hour.

In addition to the interviews, 100 diaries were filled in by children from Cairo and Fayoum on April 21, 2010. In these diaries, children were asked in the classrooms about their media use the day before and to write down what their media activities were that day. The diaries were very short but useful in supporting findings from the interviews.

Before carrying out the data collection, the necessary official approval was obtained from the General Authority for Population and Statistics.

Findings

The interviews, which are given special attention here, dealt mainly with the children's use of the Internet and mobile phone and – indirectly – with their media literacy, i.e., the children's sources of information about the media, their interests in them, and their acquired skills.

Generally speaking, we have learnt a great deal from the interviews about children's insights, the world of children, and the way they use and deal with media, especially the new media.

Data collected were classified into four main categories:

- access to the new media
- socioscape
- genderscape
- children's media budget
- access to the new media

It was found that the children from Cairo had access to all media, except the young boy (9 years old) who mainly had access to television and the internet. He said that he used his mother's mobile phone sometimes to call a friend or his grandmother. All the children from Cairo had access to the internet in their homes. The children's parents subscribed to the net through DSL and the subscription fees were mainly paid by the parents.

In Fayoum, the rural area, only one girl (13 years old) mentioned not having a mobile phone. She added: "My father promised me a mobile phone when I pass the exams this year, and I think I'll need it then so that my parents can contact me and know where I am." Among these rural girls, one did not have a computer at home. However, she indicated that sometimes she used the net at either her friends' or relatives' homes. The other interviewed girls mentioned that they had access to the net in their homes.

The rural children used traditional media, i.e., newspapers, magazines, television and the radio, more than the children in Cairo did. This is in accordance with findings from a previous study (Asran,1998). Television was more important than any other medium for the rural children, a finding also supported by previous studies carried out among Egyptian children (Kamel, 1995; El Semary, 1995; El Sayed, 1996). The rural children's heavier use of traditional media is related to the fact that they do not engage in as many outdoor activities as the children in Cairo do (see also Tayie, 2008).

Age emerged as an important factor with respect to the children's use of new media. The younger children were more interested in games and being visible online. They saw this as a kind of prestige and showing off. They even created more things online than the older children did. The older children were mainly interested in listening to music, watching films and downloading them.

Socioscape

Social background was also a factor in the Egyptian children's access to and dealings with the media. The children from high-income families had access to all media, especially the new ones. Some of the children from low-income families, as in the case of some girls in Fayoum, did not have access to the new media. These children used television and newspapers more than the children from high-income families did. The low-income children also used television more than newspapers or magazines. Their preferred TV programmes were mainly religious and educational programmes.

Parents of the children from low-income families (for instance, girls from Fayoum) were more involved in their children's media use than parents in high-income families were. The low-income children also mentioned that they discussed some contents of newspapers and magazines with their parents, mainly with their fathers.

It was also noted that the children from high-income families were more open to talking about many things, including private and personal things, they were doing, for instance, with the mobile phone or the internet. However, it took the interviewers a bit of time to encourage the interviewees to talk about more intimate things and the things the children were doing behind their parents' back. The children did not talk about sex, but about, e.g., having boy friends or girl friends. Children from low-income families were less open, and sometimes very conservative.

Genderscape

Gender emerged as an important factor in the children's use of new media, as did geographical area. Although the number of interviewed children was small, the variation was especially remarkable between girls from the urban and rural areas. In Cairo, the girls did not differ a great deal from the boys with respect to their access to and use of new media. The girls were also heavy users of the net, iPod and mobile phones. Only one girl mentioned not having a mobile phone because she thought she did not need it now. It was a matter of principle rather than lack of money, as she was from a high-income family. All girls mentioned that they mainly used the mobile phone to stay in touch with their parents and to contact relatives and friends. The father paid the costs of the phones in all cases.

All the boys from Cairo had internet access at home, which was paid for by their parents. The net was mainly used for playing or chatting with friends, and Facebook and YouTube were their most commonly used sites. All girls reported having had e-mail addresses for a few years. They also mentioned having used the internet to download music and movies. When asked about their sources of information about the net sites, friends were mentioned as the main source.

As indicated, television was the most mentioned medium among the traditional media, a finding supported by previous studies (Reda, 1994; El Shal,1997; El Abd, 1988). All girls had satellite receivers and dishes at home. The most preferred TV programmes were films and serials. One girl also reported liking programmes that encourage viewer participation. She added that she would like to see more programmes with viewer participation, not only through mobile phones but also through normal land telephone lines. This girl did have a mobile phone, but it was clear she had an anti-mobile phone attitude. Another girl mentioned liking religious programmes, which taught people the correct basics of religion. Radio and newspapers were hardly used by this group of girls.

When asked about their hopes or expectations regarding the media, the girls said they would like to see TV programmes tailored for each age category and not only two categories of programmes, for children and adults.

Though the girls were free in terms of their use of the new media, they were sometimes controlled by their parents regarding what they should or should not see on television at home. One girl said she exercised self-control regarding what programmes she should not see – programmes that do not match the culture and traditions. (Apparently she meant pornographic programmes.)

The girls from Cairo talked openly, to a great extent. At the beginning of the interviews they were conservative, but this attitude changed towards the end of the interviews.

The girls from the rural area were considerably different; they were more conservative than those from Cairo. None of the rural girls said a single word about private and personal matters. Their use of media was mainly said to be for education and informative purposes, bearing in mind that they were mainly using the traditional media, especially television. Only one girl did not have access to the internet. Two girls had mobile phones they said they had recently received.

As mentioned, the girls from the rural area used the traditional media more than the girls from Cairo did. The rural girls also said they talked frequently about media contents with their parents. This was not the case for the Cairo girls, who said they never talked with their parents about media contents. The rural girls also mentioned mostly watching television with other members of the family.

When asked about their hopes and expectations regarding the media, the girls from Fayoum indicated that they expected more serious and educational programming. They also hoped to see more programmes that reflect the reality of their own geographical area.

The boys were generally heavy users of the new media, especially the boys in Cairo. All the boys had access to the internet. One boy from the rural area had had an internet connection for only three months. Before that, he said, he used the net occasionally at friends' or relatives' homes.

The internet was mainly used for chatting. Only one boy indicated that he used the net for educational purposes to do his school assignments. The boys also indicated that they used the internet to download programmes and films. For the younger boys, it was mainly used for chatting with peers. One boy indicated that he combined the net with television, so that he could watch films downloaded from the net on the TV set. Facebook was the most visited internet site. All boys pointed out that they had learned about this and other websites from their friends.

All boys except the young boy (9 years old) had mobile phones. The boys from Cairo had owned and used mobile phones for many years, whereas in the rural area, a few boys said they had started using them recently (less than one or two years).

The boys from Cairo had state-of-the-art mobile phones, i.e., the latest models, whereas the rural boys had older models. All the boys from Cairo reported using the mobile phone heavily on a daily basis and at any time of the day. The exception was the 9-year-old boy who did not have a mobile phone, who said he would get one when he grows older. As mentioned, he sometimes called some of his friends or his grandmother using his mother's mobile phone, underlining that he knew how to use one. Generally speaking, the boys used the mobile phone more than the girls did.

The boys from the rural area were more likely to abide by the school rules than the boys from Cairo were. Although using mobile phones at school was not allowed, all children in Cairo said they hid the phones and used them during breaks, putting the phones on the silent mode while at school so the teachers would not find out about them. However, the rural boys said they never took their mobile phone to the school, because it was not allowed.

The boys from Cairo also mentioned having used the mobile phone to access the internet. One boy even indicated that he often watched films on his mobile phone. The girls were less frequent users of the mobile phone; they used the internet more. The boys in the rural area used the mobile phone only to make calls. One boy said: "I use it only in cases of emergency; the mobile phone was meant to be used only for such cases."

It was clear that the boys from Cairo frequently used the mobile phone for messaging friends – SMS-ing was common among the children. The Cairo boys said they used the SMS function to agree on meetings and outgoings. Surprisingly, even when they were at home, they never used the land lines, only their mobile phones. The boys from Fayoum used SMS less often, and they used the land phones when they were at home.

Though the boys from Cairo hardly mentioned newspapers, magazines and even television, these media were frequently mentioned in the rural area. Two boys from Fayoum also said they usually watched television together with other members of the family. That was also the case for the rural girls. The boys from Cairo usually watched TV alone, as all of them had TV sets in their own rooms.

All the boys indicated that they listened to the radio. For the boys from Cairo, musical programmes were also listened to through their mobile phones, which all had radio and musical services. Boys from the rural area listened to the radio, too, but at home and not on their mobile phones. They liked to listen to religious, educational and news programmes.

All the boys from Cairo knew and used the iPod, whereas the boys from the rural area had never used an iPod or even heard about it.

In sum, it was found that especially social background and geographical area were important factors influencing children's use of new media and the new media literacy.

Budget for the media

Talking with the children about the budget for media use, all the girls from Cairo were allowed to use mobile phones, which were paid for by their parents. The situation for the boys from Cairo was a bit different. Three of them were given certain air time (paid by their fathers) and then they bought more air time (prepaid cards) out of their pocket money. It was also evident that these children spent most of their pocket money on buying credit for their mobile phones as well as on going out with friends during the weekends. Two boys from Cairo were given free mobile phone use, paid for by their fathers. (The 9-year-old boy who did not have a mobile phone did not have any money to buy media.)

The boys and girls from the rural area were only given limited time to talk on the mobile (paid by their fathers). They had what they called "controlled lines", meaning that they could use them to speak for a limited number of minutes per month. They did not bother about buying any credit when the allowed number of minutes was used up. Newspapers and magazines were mainly purchased by the parents.

Conclusion

Clearly, the present pilot study showed that media, especially the internet, set the agenda for the children. The internet provided them with topics to talk about with peers and friends and was mainly used for chatting and entertainment, hardly for educational purposes. The younger children were more active than the older children in creating materials and uploading them on the internet. In this respect, we did notice a kind of addiction to the new media among the children, an addiction that was rationalized and used for their own sakes. It is here the value and importance of media literacy education comes in.

It seems that the internet has created a kind of popular culture among children in parts of the world where it is available. We have seen children in Egypt as well as in Finland and other countries doing the same thing with the new media.

We look forward to the second part of this comparative study, among other things, the quantitative research that will be conducted at the end of 2010, with the aim of providing more information on the world of children and their dealings with the media.

In sum, the new media are becoming a crucial and vital factor in children's processes of meaning making. This is why more attention needs to be paid to media literacy education. It also justifies the hard work being done in this respect by scholars and with the support of international organizations, such as UNESCO, the United Nations' Alliance of Civilizations, the Finnish Academy, The International Clearinghouse on Children, Youth and Media at Nordicom, and Mentor International Association for Media Education. It is worth mentioning that there is an urgent need for more data from different parts of the world. More joint and comparative studies are also needed.

References

Appadurai, A. (1990) "Disjuncture and difference in the global cultural economy", *Public Cult*, 1(2), pp. 21-24.

Asran, S.S. (1998) *The Role of Television Drama in Providing School Leavers with Social Values: A Study on a Sample of Egyptian Children Who Have Left Education*. Egypt, Zagazeeg: Faculty of Arts (published in Arabic).

Carlsson, U. (2009) "Young People in the Digital Media Culture", in Carlsson, U. (Ed.) *Children and Youth in the Digital Media Culture from a Nordic Horizon*. Yearbook 2010. University of Gothenburg, Nordicom, The International Clearinghouse on Children, Youth and Media, pp. 9-22.

El Adb, A. (1988) *Children's Programmes on Television*. Dar El Fekr El Arabi (published in Arabic).

El Sayed, L.H. (1996) *Children's Realization of Televised Reality*. Cairo: Childhood Studies Center, Ein Shams University (published in Arabic).

El Semary, H.B. (1995) *Influence of Watching Television on Egyptian Children's Habits of Reading*. Cairo: Childhood Studies Centre, Ein Shams University (published in Arabic).

El Shal, I. (1997) *Relationship of the Child with Print and Electronic Media*. Dar Nahdet El Shark (published in Arabic).

Glaser, Barney G. & Holton, J. (2004) "Remodeling Grounded Theory", *Forum: Qualitative Social Research*, 5(2) May.

Glaser, B. & Strauss, A. L. (1967) *The Discovery of Grounded Theory. Strategies for Qualitative Research*. Chicago: Aldine publishing company.

Geertz, C. (1973) "Thick Description: Toward an Interpretative Theory of Culture", in Geertz, C. *The Interpretation of Cultures*. New York: Basic Books.

Higher Press Council (2009) Statistics. Cairo: Higher Press Council.

Kamel, O.M. (1995) *Children's Perception of Personality Characteristics which Are Portrayed in Children's Programmes*. Cario: Childhood Studies Center, Ein Shams University (published in Arabic).

Marcus, G. (1995) "Ethnography in/of the world system: the emergence of multi-sited ethnography", *Annual Review of Anthropology*, 24, pp. 95–117.

Media Committee of the Arab League (2010) Statistics. Cairo: Arab League.

Merton, R.K, Fiske, M. & Kendall P.L. (1990) *The Focused Interview. A Manual of Problems and Procedures*. Illinois: The Free Press.

Reda, A. (1994) "Impact from Television Violence on Children's Behaviour. Cairo", *Journal of Communication Research*, July 1994.

Tayie, S. (2008) "Children and Mass Media in the Arab World: A Second Level Analysis", in Carlsson, U., Tayie, S., Jacquinot, G. & Peres Tornero, J.M. (Eds.) *Empowerment Through Media Education: An Intercultural Dialogue*. University of Gothenburg, Nordicom, The International Clearinghouse on Children, Youth and Media, pp. 67-87.

Tayie, S. (2009) "The Internet and Our Young People", paper presented to the Internet Governance Forum (IGF), Sharm El Shiekh, Egypt.

Panel Session on
Children, Media, Consumption and Health

Introduction

Dafna Lemish

This panel will explore a number of key issues of concern in the area of children, media, consumption, and health by problematizing our thinking about them as well as the methods most often employed in studying them. The panel brings diverse international perspectives to debates about the implications of media for children's health and highlights the ways they can also be used for public and policy advocacy. Ground in research and intervention experiences accumulated in Hong Kong (Kara Chan), Northern Africa (Ibrahim Saleh), and the U.S. (Kathryn Montgomery), as well as overviews of cross cultural research (Arvind Singhal), the articles in this section deal with several overriding themes.

What do we mean by media?

Current research trends require that we expand the range of media studied from traditional mass media and their influence on consumption and health (e.g., television and obesity; advertising and consumerism; early media exposure and cognitive skills) to the whole range of new and emerging media – including internet, mobile media and gaming consoles – as well as to the more complex ways they are integrated in children's everyday lives. The definition we often use of "old", "new", and even "emerging", seems, increasingly, to be meaningless, as children are growing up in a landscape where all media exist, converge, and constantly develop and change. As a result, we have to consider expanding and dealing with increasingly complex media-related topics of study: for example, blurring of genres and contents (e.g., advergames; edutainment; social marketing); a need to redefine audience/producer distinctions (e.g., interactive media; youth made media; blogging); and accounting for the expanse of media-institutions across a continuum from global corporations to local community efforts. All of these changes require a much more holistic and grounded understanding of the ways media make a difference in children's lives.

What do we mean by children?

As the studies presented in this session demonstrate, our understanding of childhood as a socially constructed and culturally contextualized period of human development has become, gradually, more commonplace. While earlier media studies focused specifically on the very young and their unique characteristics and abilities (e.g., their ability to distinguish between advertising and content; understanding the persuasive intent of commercials), the research illustrated here broadens our agenda to wider and more complex concerns of adolescents with gender and sexuality, where the influences of consumerism indirectly infiltrate every aspect of their coming of age. Furthermore, these contributors raise important questions that relate to our definition of children as both future consumers as well as citizens, and the ability to perceive both as not distinctively unique, but wholly integrated.

What do we mean by health and consumerism?

While employing seemingly clear concepts, I submit that the studies presented here, like many others in this area, employ a very open-ended understanding of health; one that encompasses the general well-being of children and adolescents, including the physical, social, emotional, mental, cognitive, behavioral aspects of their lives. Such a broad approach renders research limitless and, as a result, studies and findings can appear to be somewhat vague. Similarly, the concept of consumerism seems to incorporate all forms of cultural and materialistic consumption. Thus, both the health and consumer foci are areas in which we need clearer, more focused theorizing.

The importance of cultural relevance is a central aspect of each of these studies, as individually and collectively they demonstrate how compromises as well as benefits of media for healthy child development have to be contextualized locally. Thus, it is very informative to see how sexualization of youth culture in Hong Kong, for example, raises very different concerns and carries different risks than those in Egypt, U.S., or Latin America.

How do we study all of that?

The studies included in this session demonstrate the need for use of multiple methods of investigation in order to produce deeper, grounded, and nuanced understandings of the complexities involved in studying the role of media and consumption in children's healthy development and well-being. Cross cultural comparisons allow us to identify themes, aspects, or concerns that cut across different nations and life circumstances. These may be more universal in nature versus those that are unique to particular cultural contexts; or they may be characterized by national, social class, religion, ethnicity, or other human groupings. The recurring concern for gender differences that cuts across several of the contributions in this section demonstrates not only the need to contextualize our studies, but also to incorporate possibilities for the voices of the children and youth studied to express their own perspectives and understandings of the phenomena we are studying. All these crucial challenges require creative and innovative methodologies that move away from a strict adherence to one specific methodological tradition or another. Thus, it is the triangulation of methods, the comparative dimensions, the multi-disciplinary approaches, and the incorporation of different perspectives, that seem to be the recommended approach to fulfill the potential for more meaningful studies of the role media and consumption play in children's well-being around the world.

How does research contribute to social change?

Finally, the studies presented in this session are unique in the way they employ social science research for the purpose of advancing social change aimed at bettering the lives of children and adolescents. The examples in this session include a study on girls' developing sexual identity in Hong Kong, as well as, promoting sexual and reproductive health among adolescents in Northern Africa; development of principles of fair marketing to children and public interventions in order to foster better media interaction that will foster healthier life styles; as well as development of public policy advocacy that enhance the health of children worldwide. All of these examples illustrate the strong linkage that research and social change can have in the pursuit of children's well-being.

Tween Girls' Sexuality and a Media Scandal in Hong Kong

Kara Chan

Adolescents today are more confused about their sexuality than they were in the past. With the development of birth control measures and the rise of the feminist movement, adolescents have moved from viewing sex as forbidden to viewing sex as accessible and interesting, yet terrifying (Rice & Dolgin, 2005). Researchers have found that youths around the globe are more likely than previously to have pre-marital intercourse, and the age of their initial sex experience has been declining (Michael et al., 1994). Unfortunately, many adolescents are not prepared to deal with intimate relationship with the opposite sex and have difficulties handling relationship problems. They have insufficient knowledge about sexually transmitted diseases and birth control. As a result, early sexual behaviors often turn out to be unsatisfying (Rice & Dolgin, 2005).

As society becomes more open to sexual topics, there are more opportunities for people to abuse that freedom. Children and youth are increasingly exposed to sexual images. Sexually explicit materials are present in newspapers, youth magazines, television, music videos, and movies. Scholars in the United States have expressed concerns about the sexualization of young girls, as demonstrated through the marketing of scantily clad dolls to 6-year-olds, or teens turning to heiress Paris Hilton and pop star Britney Spears as role models. The Task Force on the Sexualization of Girls of the American Psychological Association concluded that sexualization has negative effects on various aspects, including cognitive functioning, as well as physical and mental health. According to the Task Force, sexualization occurs when people value a woman or girl predominantly for her sexual appeal or behavior; hold her to a narrow standard of beauty; equate her physical beauty with sexiness; view her as an object for sexual use; or inappropriately impose sexuality on her. The Association called for the development of media literacy programs in the current school curricula to promote healthy activities for girls, and of a more comprehensive sex education program for boys and girls (American Psychological Association, 2007).

Hong Kong provides an interesting example of a society in which youths are equally exposed to both Western and Chinese cultures, which may have implications for their attitudes toward sex and sexuality (Woo & Twinn, 2004). Over 95 percent of the Hong Kong population is Chinese. In the traditional Chinese culture, premarital sexual activity is considered a deviation from the societal norm (Goodwin & Tang, 1996). There is evidence from higher rates of pregnancy termination that adolescent pregnancy in Hong Kong is increasing (The Family Planning Association Hong Kong, 2000).

Hong Kong is a media rich society. Televised messages are seen in homes, on public transportation, in public areas such as shopping centers, and on the Internet. Outdoor posters and advertisements fill the busy streets, the subway stations, and public vehicles. Over 700 titles of newspapers and magazines are published. Free newspapers are distributed in major business areas, housing estates, and subway stations. Over 70 percent of the households in Hong Kong have personal computers connected to the Internet (Census and Statistics Department, 2009a). Mass mediated messages are considered important socializing agents with regard to values, beliefs and attitudes (Comstock, 1991; Strasburger and Wilson, 2002). Media and communications are a central element in our society, while gender and sexuality are at the core of how we construct our identities (Gauntlett, 2008). Because the media are filled with messages about images of males and females, there is a need to study how the young female audience consumes and interprets these images. Specifically, the study focuses on how tween girls define sexiness and the evaluation of sexiness, how they see intimate relationship with the opposite sex, and their attitudes toward sex as well as sexual behaviors.

Literature review

The "Tween" market segment

"Tweens" is a sub-teen consumer segment (Lindstrom & Seybold, 2003; Siegel et al., 2004). The segment is defined by age and the concept is based on the idea that these children are "in-be-tween" childhood and teen-hood (Cook & Kaiser, 2004; Siegel et al., 2004). Tweens are typically defined as 8- to 12-year-olds (Siegel et al., 2004). In the present article, we focus on 10- to 12-year-olds, which we consider to be the older part of the tween segment. This phase of life is of particular interest because of the salience of sexuality during it, not just for the young people themselves, but for adults who impose all sorts of disciplinary practices on them (Ho & Tsang, 2002). Tweens are also considered to be powerful influencers of their parents' consumption as well as consumers with a considerable direct consumption of their own (Andersen et al., 2008). Lindstrom (2004) proposed that the global direct – and indirect – tweens' consumption was no less than 1.18 trillion U.S. dollars in 2003. Although some scholars consider tweens a global market segment, recent empirical studies found that tween consumption and responses to marketing communication were motivated differently in cultures of individualism and collectivism (Andersen et al., 2008).

Sexuality in Hong Kong

As a former British colony, Hong Kong has laws protecting women from gender bias in terms of education, employment and pay packet (Chan, 2000). Free education is provided to all children, both males and females, between the ages of six and sixteen. The proportion of females with tertiary education is similar to that of males (Census and Statistics Department, 2009b). Because of improvements in education, economic development, and the influence of the Western feminist movement, the status of women in Hong Kong has achieved significant improvements during the past two decades (Lee & Collins, 2008). The Hong Kong government takes an active role in promoting gender equality. The Equal Opportunities Commission was established in 1996 and introduced the Sex Discrimination Ordinance. The Women's Commission was set up in 2001 to promote the well-being and interests of women in Hong Kong (Lee & Collins, 2008).

As a Chinese society, Hong Kong is influenced by the Chinese paternal oriented culture that discourages gender equality. Confucianism influences a majority of the population. The Chinese tradition favors males as they are responsible for passing down their family names. Chinese culture accords greater esteem, privileges, and status to males, and there are more restrictive prescriptions for the role of women. The virtues of a woman are defined narrowly in her role as wife and mother (Cheung, 1996).

Since 1981, The Family Planning Association of Hong Kong has conducted a territory-wide survey entitled "Youth Sexuality Study" every five years in Hong Kong. The findings of the latest "Youth Sexuality Study" in 2006 showed that the percentage of students in secondary forms 3-7 (equivalent to U.S. system grade 9 to first year of university) who had sexual intercourse experience was 13 percent for boys and 9 percent for girls. Both percentages were higher than that reported in 2001. Among these sexually active respondents, 52 percent of males and 57 percent of females experienced their first sexual intercourse at age 15 or below. However, the rate of contraceptive practice was low. Trend analysis revealed that "public intimacy between two sexes", "premarital sex" and "cohabitation" were more acceptable among respondents. The acceptance of other people having "multiple dating partners", "multiple sexual partners" and "induced abortion" demonstrated a decline. Similarly, "premarital sex" and "cohabitation" were also the most commonly accepted behaviors of other people among youths aged 18-27 (The Family Planning Association of Hong Kong, 2007). The spokesperson of The Family Planning Association of Hong Kong commented that Hong Kong youths' attitudes toward sex and sexual intercourse behavior were still relatively conservative when compared to most Western developed countries. The Association expressed worries that the trend toward increased openness in sexual attitudes and activity among Hong Kong youth was not supported by an improvement in sexual knowledge (The Family Planning Association of Hong Kong, 2007).

A survey of 178 secondary school students in Hong Kong indicated positive attitudes toward the importance of family and the importance of birth control. Male respondents reported a higher level of acceptance of pre-marital intercourse and the use of pressure and force in sexual activity than female respondents did (Ip et al., 2001). The cultural values of female pre-marital chastity and martial fidelity in Chinese Confucian traditions discourage sexual promiscuity among females (Tang, Wong & Lee, 2001). With the recent improvement in education of females, and the social environment promoting a more gender-equal society, attitudes toward sex and sexual behaviors may be changing in Hong Kong and across greater-China. The current study attempts to update our knowledge on Chinese tween girls' perception of and attitudes toward sexuality.

Methodology

A qualitative research methodology was adopted. The data for the study were collected in March 2009 in Hong Kong. Sixteen interviewees participated. All interviewees were female Hong Kong girls between the ages of 10 and 12 recruited through personal networks. Ten interviewees were studying at local Chinese speaking schools and the remaining six interviewees were studying at international schools that use English as the langauge of instruction. Two interviewees were Caucasians and the remaining were Chinese.

Prior to the face-to-face interview, each interviewee was asked to take 7 to 10 digital photographs each day for a week. The instruction was: "Please take images from any media that are about *what girls or women should be or should not be,* and *what girls or women should do or should not do*. These images can come from all kinds of media, including newspapers, magazines, outdoor posters, television programs, MTR (Mass Transit Railway) posters, websites, books, and so on. The media should be those you sometimes use in your daily lives. The media can be directed at people like you or at people who are different from you."

The image collection week was followed by an interview, which involved a review of the photos and a discussion of how the images may help to elaborate the interviewee's perspective on the sexuality of males and females. In the current article, sexuality is operationally defined as contents related to any of the following issues:

1. attitudes toward sexiness
2. the definition and meaning of sexiness
3. attitudes toward sex and sexual behaviors
4. perception of intimate relationships, including heterosexuality and homosexuality
5. pregnancy, birth, and birth control

Although the interview questions (see Appendix) do not mention sexuality explicitly, the issues related to sexuality and sexual behaviors were often brought up by the interviewees when they commented on what girls should be or should do. The interviews lasted from 20 to 36 minutes and took place at public and private venues including sports centers, schools, and interviewees' homes. The photos taken by each interviewee were downloaded to the researcher's computer. Some of the interviews were attended by the interviewees' parents, who were asked to remain silent during the interview. The interviews were conducted by the author in the language that the interviewees felt most comfortable with. All interviews were recorded and later transcribed or translated into English by a female graduate research assistant.

All the contents related with the above five issues on sexuality were listed and entered into an Excel file. Marshall and Rossman's (1999) comparison analysis method was used throughout the data analysis process to link data by constantly comparing and contrasting them (Strauss, 1987). For each item of the content, we analyzed the dominant theme of sexuality. Representative quotes and photos are presented in the following section.

Findings

Analysis of the interviews generated three dominant themes on sexuality: attitudes toward sexy clothes, attitudes toward pre-marital sex and pregnancy, and lessons learned from a media scandal. The following sections elaborate on the three themes in details.

Attitudes toward sexy clothes

When the interviewees were asked what girls or women should do or should not do, six out of 16 reported that girls or women should not wear sexy clothes. Another interviewee said that girls or women should wear proper clothing and not something that resembles underwear. To the interviewed girls, sexy clothes are clothes that expose too much of a female's body. When this issue was brought up, the researcher asked them to select pictures from their photo collections to illustrate "sexy" clothes. Results found great diversity in the categorization of sexy clothes. One interviewee commented that an outfit that exposes the shoulders and the belly (see Image 1) was sexy. She suggested that these girls should wear something on top. Another interviewee commented that a seductive outfit was sexy (see Image 2). In particular, clothes that reveal most of the breasts and the buttocks were classified as sexy clothes. The images of women wearing sexy clothes originated mainly from two sources: advertisements of slimming services or beauty products and entertainment news on fashion models or media celebrities.

Image 1. Sexy clothes I

Image 2. Sexy clothes II

Sexy clothes were often described as inappropriate, not courteous, or simply not good; the tween girls in Hong Kong generally did not approve of sexy clothes. While most of the interviewees did not explain why sexy clothes are not acceptable, one interviewee provided a functional reason. She thought that sexy clothes do not adequately serve their purpose. Showing a girl in a bikini, she commented:

> If she goes swimming, she should wear proper swimming suits. I mean those normal ones. I don't think she can swim in this apparel. It's very weird. (age 12, international school student)

Only one interviewee showed a slight approval of sexy clothes. She thought that sexy clothes can show the identities of females:

> Some girls and women wear sexy clothes because they want to catch the attention of men. This is needed in some situations. If women wear high-neck or long sleeve clothes, their figures cannot be shown. They may not look that pretty. So photographers will create photos that allow others to see the full figures of women. Then their photos will be much more beautiful. I think the figure is important to women. For example, if a woman is flat-breasted, then she will look like a man. The figure shows the identity of females. (age 12, local school student)

Attitudes toward intimate relationship with the opposite sex and pre-marital pregnancy

The interviewees demonstrated conservative and cautious attitudes toward intimate relationships with the opposite sex. Sexual relationships at a young age and pre-marital sexual relationships were disapproved of. The girls showed a great deal of concern about pre-marital pregnancy. Three interviewees captured images with the caption "a 14-year-old mother" (Image 3). They thought that pre-marital pregnancy was bad both for the mothers and for the babies. The following quotes demonstrated the disapproval of underage pregnancy:

> If she's gonna give birth to kids, she should be ready. She should be older than 18. If you're like 14, you are still in middle school and you cannot look after the kid. The kid is not going to have a good life. The kid may need to be sent to a foster home and you don't know what may happen to the kid. (age 12, international school student)

> This is a photo of a 14-year-old mom. I think girls should not get pregnant before marriage or have sex before marriage. The risk is too great. Nowadays people don't want to take responsibility and prefer to have an abortion. This will cause great harm to the girls. (age 12, local school student)

From these two quotes, we can see that the interviewees had negative attitudes toward pre-marital sexual behaviors and pre-marital pregnancy. Disapproval of pre-marital sex seems to originate from fear and disapproval of pre-marital

Image 3. "A 14-year-old mother"

pregnancy. The girls were concerned about the harmful effect of pre-marital pregnancy on the mothers and the babies. They felt that the mother shoulders much responsibility in child care. Personal maturity is a prerequisite of motherhood. If a girl is not mature enough, she cannot handle it. The interviewees disapproved of pre-marital pregnancy to such a great extent that one of them even thought courtship at a young age was unacceptable.

Despite the worry about pre-marital pregnancy, the interviewees generally supported the notion that girls should marry and have babies. Establishing a family was considered fulfilling and meaningful. Here is one quote:

> Girls should get married and have babies. It will bring her life to a new stage and it is meaningful. She can have her next generation. When she takes care of the baby, she can develop intimacy with the baby. The relationship with

the children will leave her with many happy or unhappy memories. (age 12, local school student)

Intimate relationships with the opposite sex were perceived to be risky because of the possible bad consequences, such as date-rape and violence. Other than pre-martial pregnancy, the interviewees showed disapproval of all forms of sex trade, including compensated dating and engagement of prostitutions. The following is an illustrative quote:

This is a photo of a group of prostitutes (Image 4). I think it is bad for a woman to become a prostitute. Why do they work as prostitutes when they could do some proper work? (age 12, local school student)

Image 4. A group of prostitutes

One interviewee took two pornographic photos of female prostitutes in indecent postures from the newspapers. She commented that these photos are disgusting because the prostitutes are engaged in an improper business. She thought that these girls should be arrested by the police.

The interviewees did not specifically mention whether they supported heterosexuality or homosexuality. We think that heterosexuality was assumed to be normal, as they often mentioned not having sex with a guy. One interviewee took a photo of two female singers kissing on the stage. She commented that they should not do this. This indicates that homosexuality was not quite acceptable among the interviewees.

Lessons learned from a sex scandal in the media

Altogether seven out of 16 interviewees commented on a sex scandal in the media that occurred in February 2008. They reported that girls should not allow their boy friends to take nude pictures of them. The sex scandal involved Edison Chen, a popular Hong Kong singer, and at least six female singers. Among these female singers, one was very popular among children and young girls. Nude photos of Edison Chen's sexual partners were released through the Internet after he took his computer for repair. The female popular singers involved in the scandal suffered immediate damage to their careers, as advertisers pulled out product endorsement and performance contracts. At the time of the data collection, the scandal had been revitalized with the news of the court testimony given by Edison Chen and the press conferences of two of the female singers involved. Five interviewees took pictures of the female singers and one took pictures of the male singer.

The scandal appeared to be a real-life social learning experience for the tweens. Several interviewees reported that females should not be involved in taking nude pictures and another interviewee said you should never put 100 percent trust in your boyfriend. Three interviewees used strong emotional words such as regret, silly, and stupid. Four interviewees blamed the female singers for being careless and too casual in their relationships with the opposite sex. One interviewee thought that a female singer was promiscuous. Here is an illustrative quote:

> The girls should not have taken those kinds of photos with him. Originally they didn't think others would see these photos and they took them just for fun. But in the end, a lot of people can see these photos. Because of this, Gillian Chung had to step down from show business. She admitted that she was stupid to have loved Edison Chan. She regretted a lot and she scolded him. I think she should have thought it through early on. (age 12, local school student)

Six out of the seven interviewees who commented on the scandal felt the female celebrities involved were victims of the event. The interviewees commented that these girls suffered in their reputation and career because they had made a bad decision. None of the interviewees saw Edison Chen, the male character, as a victim. The interviewees seemed to feel that the female characters in the media scandal suffered more damage and hurt than the male character.

Discussion

Based on this qualitative study, we have made the following four observations about tween girls' perceptions about their own sexuality and the sexuality of other girls and women.

First, our interviewees aged 10 to 12 adopted a conservative attitude toward sex. This can be seen from their disapproval of sexy images as well as pre-marital sex relationships. The conservative attitude toward sex is consistent with the dominant discourses on parenting and education in Hong Kong, which emphasize female chastity. Young women are not supposed to have sex before they get married (Ho & Tsang, 2002). Adolescent sexual expression is constructed as "deviant" and is usually associated with danger, moral problems, crime and psychological disorder (Ng, 1998; Wong, 2000). However, the finding was in sharp contrast to previous studies showing that youth in Hong Kong endorsed rather liberal attitudes toward sex. In 2001, 36 percent of youth aged 15 to 39 considered pre-marital sexual relations wrong. Fifty percent of the respondents found abortions acceptable and 16 percent reported that having more than one sexual partner at the same time was acceptable (Hong Kong Federation of Youth Group, 2001). The evidence therefore suggests that attitudes toward sex and sexual relationship change a great deal between 10-12 years of age and 15 and above. There is need for further research to examine the factors accounting for the change and the role played by various socializing agents in such change.

Second, the interviewees of similar age showed a wide range of standards with regard to the definition of sexiness. Some interviewees perceived that sexually seductive and revealing clothes were sexy, while others felt that clothes simply exposing the shoulder or the belly were sexy. According to Bandura's (1986) social learning theory, girls learn about the standard of acceptable and unacceptable clothing from socializing agents. The wide range of standards in sexiness may reflect the differences in standards of sexiness among parents (especially mothers), school teachers, and friends.

Third, the study showed that the girls had access to a variety of sexy or even indecent images of females. A few interviewees took photos of explicit sexual materials that they had come across. Even though they condemned the images for their indecency, the fact that they took these photos with them indicated that they had an interest in and curiosity to know more about their own sexual identity and sexual life-world.

Sexually explicit media, including magazines, books, and VCD/DVD, are readily available in Hong Kong. Popular newspapers and magazines contain advertisements for commercial sex. The new Internet and media technology give plenty of opportunities for people, including children and youth, to get access to sexual materials (Janghorbani & Lam, 2003). Our study indicated that advertisements of slimming services providers and entertainment news are a major source of sexy images of females. The finding is consistent with American media critic Kilbourne's accusation that "advertisers are the real pornographers of our time" (Kilbourne, 2000). It seems that the prevalence of these images may convey a controversial message to the tween girls in Hong Kong. If girls should not wear sexy clothes, why are all these media celebrities wearing them on glamorous occasions? Is it because females above a certain age have the privilege to dress themselves in a sexy way? Does society have a double standard on sexuality for media celebrities and for ordinary people? Scholars have expressed concern about the effects of sexy images and explicit sexual contexts on adolescents and young adults in many countries, including Hong Kong and other Chinese communities where sexual media are considered immoral (Janghorbani & Lam, 2003). Because of the easy access to explicitly sexual images among the tween girls found in our study, there is a need to empower parents and educators to discuss the consumption of sexy images or pornographic materials and its possible consequences for tween girls.

Fourth, engagement in intimate relationships with the opposite sex was perceived to be risky by the interviewees because of the possible bad consequences, including pre-marital pregnancy, abortion, and the leaking out of intimate images. Regarding pre-marital pregnancy, the girls were concerned about the well-being of both the mothers and the babies. They discussed the responsibility of mothers, and not fathers, in shouldering the care of babies. Through a media scandal exposed in the news, the interviewees "learned" that they should not put unreserved trust in their sex partners and should take care to protect their reputation.

Tween girls' fear of pre-marital pregnancy is understandable. A study of Chinese pregnant adolescents in Hong Kong found that their reaction to unplanned pregnancy ranged from shock and fear to avoidance and guilt. All of them described how they had tried to deny the existence of their pregnancy through various means, including faking their menstrual periods. Some of them also attempted to harm the fetus and trigger a natural abortion (Woo & Twinn, 2004). This indicates that adolescence pregnancy is not acceptable in the Chinese society.

Previous studies have found that media figures play an important role in helping adolescents develop their identities by shifting away from identification with parents, and moving towards autonomy (Giles & Maltby, 2004). How media figures act and react provides adolescents with models for how to think and feel in different situations (Larson, 1995). Media figures also provide adolescents with cultural materials for developing gender role identity, values, and for learning about sexual and romantic encounters (Arnett, 1995; Brown, Childers & Waszak, 1990). In the current study, we found that tween girls seemed to rehearse the threat of being betrayed by an intimate partner through a particular media scandal that had taken place in society. Several interviewees perceived the female media celebrities as victims of the event. The interviewees expressed fear and regret about the loss of reputation as well as professional career of the female celebrities involved in the media scandal.

In the present study, the social learning process was demonstrated by the interviewees through modeling and identification. The interviewees observed the media images in term of what was acceptable or not acceptable. The images captured by the interviewees showed that they paid considerable attention to media celebrities, and often made reference to them in defining moral standards.

Conclusion

The present study provides us with a better understanding of how some female tweens in Hong Kong consume and interpret media images dealing with sexuality. One novel idea in the research methodology was the combination of visual method and the application of qualitative methodology to the study of media effects. A second novel idea was the use of interviewees as data collectors. Based on the images collected, we were able to ask contextually relevant questions and understand the meanings of the images captured. The research process enabled us to gain insights about tweens' media consumption and interpretation of the content that they pay attention to.

Acknowledgements

This is part of a cross-cultural study on tween girls' sexuality and gender roles conducted with Dr. Birgitte Tufte of Copenhagen Business School and Ms. Gianna Cappello of University of Palermo. The Hong Kong part of the study was fully supported by the Centre for Media and Communication Research of Hong Kong Baptist University.

Images included in the article are taken by research interviewees and reproduced with permission from the interviewees.

References

American Psychological Association, Task Force on the Sexualization of Girls. (2007), Report of the APA Task Force on the Sexualization of Girls. American Psychological Association, Washington, DC. Retrieved on May 17, 2010 from www.apa.org/pi/wpo/sexualization.html

Andersen, L., Tufte, B., Rasmussen, J. & Chan, K. (2008), "The tweens market and responses to advertising in Denmark and Hong Kong", *Young Consumers*, Vol. 9 No. 3, pp. 189-200.

Arnett, J.J. (1995), "Adolescents' use of media for self-socialization", *Journal of Youth and Adolescents*, Vol. 25, pp. 519-534.

Bandura, A. (1986), *Social Foundations of Thought and Action: A Social Cognitive Theory*, Prentice Hall, Englewood Cliffs, N.J.

Brown, J.D., Childers, K.M. & Waszak, C.S. (1960), "Television and adolescents sexuality", *Journal of Adolescent Health Care*, Vol. 11, pp. 62-70.

Census and Statistics Department (2009a), Findings of the "Household Survey on IT Usage and Penetration" and the "Annual Survey on IT Usage and Penetration in the Business Sector" for 2009 released, press release on 21 December 2009. Retrieved on January 5, 2010 from http://www.censtatd.gov.hk/press_release/press_releases_on_statistics/index.jsp?sID=2463&sSUBID=15188&displayMode=D

Census and Statistics Department (2009b), "*Women and Men in Hong Kong: Key Statistics*", Hong Kong SAR Government, Hong Kong.

Chan, K. (2000), "Hong Kong children's understanding of television advertising", *Journal of Marketing Communications*, Vol. 6 No. 1, pp. 37-52.

Cheung, F.M. (1996), "Gender role development", in Lau, S. (Ed.) *Growing Up the Chinese Way: Chinese Child and Adolescent Development*, Chinese University Press, Hong Kong, pp. 45-67.

Comstock, G. (1991), *Television and the American Child*, Academic Press, San Diego, CA.

Cook, D.T. & Kaiser, S.B. (2004), "Betwixt and be tween", *Journal of Consumer Culture*, Vol. 4 No. 2, pp. 203-27.

Gauntlett, D. (2008), *Media, Gender and Identity: An Introduction 2nd edition*, Routledge, London; New York.

Giles, D. C. & Maltby, J. (2004), "The role of the media in adolescent development: Relations between autonomy, attachment, and interest in celebrities", *Personality and Individual Differences*, Vol. 36, pp. 813-822.

Goodwin, R. & Tang, C.S.K. (1996), "Chinese personal relationships", in Bond, M.H. (Ed.) *The Handbook of Chinese Psychology*, Oxford University Press, Hong Kong, pp. 294-308.

Ho, P.S.Y. & Tsang, A.K.T. (2002), "The things girls shouldn't see: relocating the penis in sex education in Hong Kong", *Sex Education*, Vol. 2 No. 1, pp. 61-73.

Hong Kong Federation of Youth Groups (2001), Youth Trends in Hong Kong 2001. Retrieved on May 11, 2010 from http://yrc.hkfyg.org.hk/english/yr-hkyt-01-e.html

Ip, W.Y., Chau, J.P.C., Chang, A.M. & Lui, M.H.L. (2001), "Knowledge of and attitudes toward sex among Chinese adolescents", *Western Journal of Nursing Research*, Vol. 23 No. 2, pp. 211-223.

Janghorbani, M., Lam, T.H. & The Youth Sexuality Study Task Force (2003), "Sexual media use by young adults in Hong Kong: Prevalence and associated factors", *Archives of Sexual Behavior*, Vol. 32 No. 6, pp. 545-553.

Kilbourne, J. (2000), Killing us Softly 3 Advertising's Image of Women, video, Media Education Foundation, Northampton, MA.

Larson, R.W. (1995), "Secrets in the bedroom: adolescents' private use of media", *Journal of Youth and Adolescents*, Vol. 24, pp. 535-550.

Lee, J.F.K. & Collins, P. (2008), "Gender voices in Hong Kong English textbooks – Some past and current practices", *Sex Roles*, Vol. 59 No. 1-2, pp. 127-137.

Lindstrom, M. (2004), "Branding is no longer child's play!", *Journal of Consumer Marketing*, Vol. 21 No. 3, pp. 175-182.

Lindstrom, M. & Seybold, P.B. (2003), *BRANDchild: Remarkable Insights into the Minds of Today's Global Kids and their Relationships with Brands*, Kogan Page, London.

Marshall, C. & Rossman, G.B. (1999), *Designing Qualitative Research 3rd ed.*, Sage, CA.

Michael, R.T., Gagnon, J.H., Laumann, E.O. & Kolata, G. (1994), *Sex in America: A Definitive Survey*, Little Brown, Boston.

Ng, M.L. (1998), "School and public sexuality education in Hong Kong", *Journal of Asian Sexology*, Vol. 1, pp. 32-35.

Rice, F.P. & Dolgin, K.G. (2005), *The Adolescent: Development, Relationships, and Culture 11th Edition*, Pearson, Boston, MA.

Siegel, D.L., Coffey, T.J. & Livingston, G. (2004), *The Great Tweens Buying Machine: Capturing Your Share of the Multi-billion-dollar Tween Market*, Dearborn Trade Publishing, Chicago, IL.

Strasburger, V.C. & Wilson, B.J. (2002), *Children, Adolescents and the Media*, Sage, Thousand Oaks, CA.

Strauss, A.L. (1987), *Qualitative Analysis for Social Scientists*, Cambridge University Press, MA.

Tang, C.S., Wong, C. & Lee, A.M. (2001), "Gender-related psychosocial and cultural factors associated with condom use among Chinese married women", *AIDS Education and Prevention*, Vol. 13 No. 4, pp. 329-342.

The Family Planning Association of Hong Kong (2000), *Youth Sexuality Study 1996: Form 3-7 Student Survey*. Family Planning Association of Hong Kong, Hong Kong.

The Family Planning Association of Hong Kong (2007), FPAHK Report of Youth Sexuality Study 2006, press release on 23 November 2007. Retrieved on May 14, 2010 from http://www.famplan.org.hk/fpahk/en-text/info/press/071123.pdf

Wong, V. (2000), "A never-ending obsession with breasts", in Wong, V., Shiu, W. & Har, H. (Eds.) *From Lives to Critique*, Hong Kong Policy Viewers, Hong Kong. (In Chinese)

Woo, H. & Twinn, S. (2004), "Health needs of Hong Kong Chinese pregnant adolescents", *Journal of Advanced Nursing*, Vol. 45 No. 6, pp. 595-602.

Appendix. List of questions

1. Based on these pictures, what do you think about what girls or women should be or should not be?
2. Based on these pictures, what behavior(s) do you think are appropriate or inappropriate for girls or women?
3. Who creates these images and why do they create them in this way?
4. Are you satisfied with the way images of girls or women are created now?
5. If you were a media owner or a media producer, what would you do in constructing images of young girls or women?

Media Sexual and Reproductive Health Taboos in the Middle East and North Africa (MENA)

Ibrahim Saleh

> It is very difficult to write about or discuss publicly the sexual and reproductive health, particularly in the Middle East and North Africa (MENA). (Farzaneh Roudi-Fahimi & Lori Ashford, 2008: 37-54)

Female adolescents in many developing societies are still facing various forms of discrimination due to their gender, race and class. Communication must become central to development thinking and practice in relation to the Middle Eastern and North African nations (MENA), otherwise any regional initiatives to improve the lives of people in this troubled region will never succeed.

One could say that this same reality is a major cause of the current widespread incidence of sexually transmitted diseases among adolescents as a result of poverty, poor health status, low literacy level, high number of young people, and inadequate knowledge about the diseases. In addition, the cultural paradigm of polygamy, violence and cultural pressures to present one's premarital relationship as moral have prevented young girls from negotiating safer sex (Lau & Muula, 2004; Smith, 2004; Owolabi et al., 2005).

Worldwide, young people have been identified as being at particular risk of HIV infection, with the majority of infections due to unprotected sexual intercourse. Several studies have established early sexual debut, multiple sexual partners, and low and inconsistent rate of condom use (Olayinka & Osho, 1997) as risk factors among youths.

On the surface, MENA is known for its strong family values and conservative and patriarchal culture, which is a cliché used to hide the realities of the situation in MENA. Some of these same norms can become barriers to informing young people, especially girls, about the health hazards of sexual activity and about reproductive health.

In the available social science literature, or in the information disseminated to the general public and policymakers, it is very common for the child or adolescent to be seen as separate from the family and the community. Moreover, in a male-dominated society, the cultural setting is typically biased towards the male with the utmost power, while the female is degraded, regardless of all the cosmetic empowerment. There is also an obvious lack of integration among the multiple service delivery systems in the MENA region. As such, when it comes to allocating funds, there is an urgent need to achieve an aggregate view on health, education, media and social services dealing with children and adolescents.

It is, thus, mandatory to think of sexual and reproductive challenges using a single service delivery system mindset, and to look across systems, in contrast to the current dilemma of lack of vision. Among the many obstacles facing media literacy in MENA are sexual and reproductive health issues, where premarital sexual relationships are generally forbidden, and the media's tackling of them is often considered taboo (Saleh, 2009). This situation reflects a society characterized by extreme hypocrisy and self-denial, where everyone thinks about it, but no one admits it. The problem of sexual taboos is also a result of the reality of a male-dominated society that allows men to have pre-marital sex while condemning women for the same thing. The media systems in MENA are still not grasping the fact that today's audience is much smarter than the media give them credit for, and those who are able to take advantage of that fact will reap the future rewards (Saleh, 2010).

Factors reinforcing sexual taboos

The present article analyses the persistence of the current sexual taboos as a result of concurrent factors: the inadequate understanding of life-span development, divergence in the public and political will, lack of professional development of media educators, and the disconnection between research, policy, and practice in the field of media development.

The inadequate understanding of the life span factor is explained as a result of focusing on preventing illness and injury by thinking about pathology instead of thinking about development. Hence, most of the media discourses prioritize prevention instead of optimizing development.

At the same time, building up the public and political will as a vehicle for improving health and media education is an overarching issue. Politics and political communication in many parts of the MENA region focus on personal gain and economic restructuring with minimal interest in encouraging a change in the current cultural mindset, which obviously hinders development. It is believed that a major impediment to development is a lack of understanding of the extent to which individual attitudes and policymakers' attitudes towards making public investments affect the youth in the societies and generations to come, as a result of this marginalization and negligence in many situations. And in oppressive societies such as MENA, the public usually reaches a state of hospitality because of the continuous hardships they encounter on a daily basis.

Many intellectuals and activists in MENA share a collective scepticism about the lack of professional development in related fields such as media and health care. It is thus common to find many of them supposedly knowing nothing about tactics and strategies to reach out to the younger generation, and they are often entrapped in their own fear of speaking out and stirring the stagnant waters. The current public health workforce is both insufficient in size and education to adequately implement health promotion strategies and collaborative practices, in addition to its lack of interest and even motivation with regard to using the available scarce resources for training and professional development.

Last but definitely not least, the disconnection between research, policy, and practice has made the situation toned with absolute oxymora (Saleh, 2009). In many cases, the suggested official policies do not address the challenges of such taboos, resulting in a real dialogue of the deaf between science, media and policies. The irony here is policymakers' persistence in focusing on the problem and adopting a diagnostic normative approach to it, instead of taking a rather bold prescriptive approach by offering solutions and at least utilizing the experiences of other show cases in the global south. Furthermore, the political culture in MENA has imposed the same syndromes and illnesses on the media and science, which is why there is no real consensus about what constitutes well being. As such, there is reluctance concerning the lack of comprehensive data, the lack of longitudinal data, and the need for more funding for data collection. Some respondents also believe that there is a lack of clearly defined outcomes. For example, "youth development" has become a catchall phrase that means everything and nothing.

In many occasions, policymakers in the region do not do enough to support more open, transparent information and communication systems. Nonetheless, it is time to wake up and harness the growing power of information and communication technologies (ICTs), such as mobile telephones and the Internet, and to do more to support the media in addressing these burning issues that threaten the whole society. Many adolescents in MENA divert to other satellite channels and navigate through the Internet for the entertainment they want, though the same communication channels could include embedded and direct public awareness campaigns, if the situation were carefully monitored and the messages carefully designed, packaged and branded.

In all cases, media experts need to move and evolve past this, and deal with the culture on a more sophisticated, adult level. Until this move is fully realized, the sexual taboos will always move the MENA region backward, jeopardizing the lives of young uninformed people.

These two problems – self-denial and male hypocrisy – must be transformed into openness and equality through dialogue and media discourse, as the risks associated with sexual relationships, both married and unmarried, are heightened by young people's lack of access to information and services related to sexual and reproductive health.

It is important to note that the situation is not homogeneous in MENA, as young people's experiences of marriage and childbearing vary greatly across the region. However, young people generally feel reluctant to seek information about sexuality and reproduction from their parents, fearing their parents will assume they are engaged in forbidden activities. Moreover, given the societal context, parents themselves also feel awkward discussing sexuality with their children, and they are not prepared to do it.

Data on sexually transmitted infections are scarce, and little of the existing data are disaggregated by age. And the media's credibility as regards giving detailed and accurate information is questionable. There is an adage that says you cannot give what you do not have. Thus, the *mal-fatigue* of the media is reflected in their failure to provide informative and appropriate discourses, though it should be very important for them to be able to deliver high quality information that will impact positively on the behaviour of schoolchildren and adolescents.

Nevertheless, great disparities in knowledge remain between the different mass media and among different countries in the MENA zone. The limited available data show that the threat of sexually transmitted illnesses (STI) is more common among young people than among other age groups. The 2005 Demographic and Health Survey in Egypt revealed that only 18 per cent of the married women aged 15 to 24 had heard of gonorrhoea, syphilis, or Chlamydia, all of which can be transmitted through sexual contact. However, 22 per cent of these women reported having had abnormal genital discharge and genital sores and ulcers, which could be symptoms of STIs (El-Zanaty & Way, 2006).

In a study conducted in Morocco, 40 per cent of STIs recorded were among young adults aged 15 to 29, putting the estimated number of new infections in this age group at 240,000 per year (Tawilah, 2002).

A recent study of married women in Oman found age to be the most important risk factor for STIs. Women under age 25 were twice as likely to have an STI as women aged 25 and older (Mabry, Al-Riyami & Morsi, 2004).

The Pan Arab Project for Family Health investigated the knowledge of young people about sexually transmitted diseases – see Table 1.

Table 1. Knowledge among young people about sexually transmitted infections, per cent

Sexually transmitted infection	Tunisia (2001) Ages 18-29	Syria (2001) Ages 15-24	Algeria (2001) Ages 15-29
HIV/AIDS	86	85	96
Genital Warts	20	2	0
Candidacies	40	10	2
Gonorrhea	37	10	2
Syphilis	28	14	7

Source: Pan Arab Project for Family Health, *Arab Family Health in Numbers,* Youth, No. 7 (2006)

The role of media and media literacy

For various religious and cultural reasons, media educators never acknowledge the role of media literacy in reducing the risk of many health problems, such as unintended pregnancies and unsafe abortions, as well as acquiring HIV/AIDS. The irony here is that the majority of people in MENA have only heard about HIV/AIDS, yet they still may not know how it is transmitted.

Sex education curricula in MENA schools are rare, and where they do exist, the sections on sexual and reproductive health are often skipped because teachers are unprepared or embarrassed to teach them.

The media in MENA have promoted a sort of adolescent sensibility in relation to sexual taboos, by following the slogan that the MENA region is a value-protected society.

The social impact of the media includes improving the quality of education, informing the public about health threats and safe practices to avoid them, serving local communities by bringing attention to their needs, and in times of disaster, providing information and sources of assistance to people displaced from their homes.

The media are not used to serving the local communities by providing information relevant to them. For example, there is a lack of consideration for community-level needs to access information (Graves, 2007). Many times even the radio, which is the most suitable medium in the region due to the illiteracy rates and poverty, is entrapped between the financial squeeze, commercialization, weak content and the patron state's control and exploitation of its ownership and management. Indeed, the situation in the more elite print media and the new media is no different.

Eliminating poverty is a cornerstone of the overarching strategy for addressing such complicated issues and realizing the millennium development goals. The MENA societies are at the crossroads of differential knowledge. Those who are well connected are doing well, but the majority of the public are forgotten by the military or business elites. Having said so, economic and educational factors must be carefully addressed before any specific health needs can be met, because there is an increasing excess risk in the current poor environment, with the exception of few oil-producing countries in the region, indicating that improvement of the environment offers protective effects.

However, the media could still play a significant role in addressing this issue in three situations:

- First, if the media were used as a powerful tool to break the culture of silence surrounding sexual and reproductive health.
- Second, if the media were to provide information to the general public, by making sexual and reproductive health a hot topic on governments' development agendas.

- Third, if the media were to become a refuge to fill the gap, by talking openly about sexual and reproductive health to limit the potential risks for young people in MENA.

Media education and media literacy could encourage democratic development by giving people a voice and providing a window for transparency in government; by informing citizens; and by educating the public about social concerns, including those of marginalized groups.

The media could certainly improve health practices related to reproductive and sexual diseases. For example, a 2001 study found that 38 per cent of teenage African respondents with high exposure to *Soul City TV* said they always use condoms, compared to 31 per cent with medium exposure and 28 per cent with low exposure. And uneducated women in Zambia who are regularly exposed to broadcast media are twice as likely to use birth control as those exposed to no media (Garenne, Tollman, Kahn, Collins & Ngwenya, 2001).

Communication and media are essential "public goods" that could urge governments and civil society to take an integrated and sustained approach to their development, which could empower the people to be unleashed to meet the millenium development goals, though as yet there is no clear commitment to them. Panos London's 2007 report *At the Heart of Change* states that political processes are communication processes and that communication lies at the heart of good governance through inclusion of the marginalized in the debates and decisions that affect their lives.

Conclusion

In conclusion, the media can certainly influence public policy. But youth sexuality is still a sensitive topic, and many societies in MENA pay insufficient attention to the rights of young people. Moreover, both media educators and policymakers must take into account the political, social, and economic context surrounding young people lives and consider how this affects young people's sexual and reproductive health.

Governments and NGOs (non-governmental organizations) should play a more proactive role in promoting comprehensive sex education in the schools, particularly by working with parents and training teachers. In the meantime, drop outs and illiteracy must be considered and included in media campaigns to ensure that the message gets to out-of-school youth who may be particularly vulnerable to sexual and reproductive health risks.

There is an urgent need in MENA to expand education and communication on sexually transmitted infections, including HIV/AIDS, using the mass media, the Internet, and telephone hotlines.

It is crucial to integrate sexual and reproductive health services for young people into existing primary health care services, ensuring that staff will be receptive to young people, guarantee their privacy and avoid judgemental behaviour.

A cornerstone in overcoming this miserable situation is to adopt and develop innovative and culturally appropriate ways to provide condoms and make them socially acceptable. Priority must be given to research conducted on the sexual behaviour of young people, including those who are unmarried, and on their perceptions about their sexual and reproductive health needs.

This issue relates to youth, and hence they must be involved in the media design of sexual and reproductive health programmes to ensure that such programmes are relevant and understood, and to motivate young people to take responsibility for their health.

There is much to be learnt from similar settings in the global south, though the iceberg of cultural beliefs and the way of life in MENA make it imperative to conduct local research on the legal, cultural, social, and other barriers that stand in the way of improved sexual and reproductive health. The region is desperate to benefit from such research, from communicating the results to decision makers, and from designing culturally appropriate, evidence-based policies and programmes.

At this historical moment, it is essential to change the mindset of the younger generation through the media and work collectively to improve the role of the media in covering sexual and reproductive diseases. Researchers, academics, professionals, and advocacy groups must invest more time and energy in linking health research to the media discourse at three different levels to make a difference in the present dim picture, by facing the current challenge of change and development through the prism of agenda setting, coalition building, and policy learning.

This approach includes presenting new information at public events, engaging policymakers, and high level of management in the media, with the intention of capturing the attention of policymakers and society at large. In addition, the approach includes educating the educators in different schools and universities, as well as the media professionals and journalists at the lower managerial levels, by building their skills premium and empowering the horizontal networking of the advocacy networks or alliances. There is also a need to break barriers between academics and professionals and to connect, bridge and link health research with the media to create media messages that can accommodate the diverse public in different parts of MENA.

Lastly, media education should play its role in getting the right groups to the "table" and in getting them excited about being a part of something bigger than any one group alone. This goal can only be attained through the establishment of links throughout public health community, which could have strong and direct impact on the future development of not only youth, but also the whole society at large. This concerns especially eliminating disease, developing health behaviours, spreading knowledge about sexually transmitted illnesses and removing the veil of blindness, allowing the region to be transformed into a more harmonious society that is true and honest in its hope for development.

References

Demographic and Health Surveys (www.measuredhs.com)

El-Zanaty, F. & Way, A. (2006) Egypt Demographic and Health Survey 2005. Ministry of Health and Population, National Population Council, El-Zanaty and Associates, and ORC Macro

Garenne, M., Tollman, S., Kahn, K., Collins, T. & Ngwenya, S. (2001) Understanding Marital and Premarital Fertility in Rural South Africa, *Journal of Southern African Studies*, Vol. 27, No. 2, Special Issue on Fertility in Southern Africa: 270-290

Graves, P. (2007) Independent Media's Vital Role in Development, Centre for International Media Assistance, National Endowment for Democracy, Washington, DC, USA, http://cima.ned.org/reports/independent-medias-vital-role-in-development.html

Lau C. & Muula S. (2004) HIV/AIDS in sub-Saharan Africa, *Croatian Medical Journal,* 45(4): 402–414

London, P. (2007) At the Heart of Change: The Role of Communication in Sustainable Development. Centre for International Media Assistance, National Endowment for Democracy, Washington, DC, USA, http://gfmd.info/images/uploads/Panos_Heart_of_Change.pdf

Mabry, R., Al-Riyami, A. & Morsi, M. (2007) The Prevalence of and Risk Factors for Reproductive Morbidities Among Women in Oman, *Studies in Family Planning*, 38 (2): 121-28

Olayinka, B.A. & Osho, A. A. (1997) Changes in attitude, sexual behaviour and the risk of HIV/AIDS transmission in southwest Nigeria, *East African Medical Journal*, 74(9): 554-60

Pan Arab Project for Family Health (PAPFAM) surveys, www.papfam.org

Roudi, F. (2000) Numbers don't lie: Demography holds Iran's destiny, *The Iranian,* May 31, 2000, http://www.iranian.com/Opinion/2000/May/Majlis/index.html

Roudi-Fahmi, F. & Asford, L. (2008) Sexual & Reproductive Health in the Middle East and North Africa: A Guide For Reporters. Ford Foundation Office, *Population Reference Bureau*: 37-54

Saleh, I. (2009) Media Literacy in MENA: Moving Beyond the Vicious Cycle of Oxymora, *Mapping World Media Education Policies, Latin American Scientific Journal of Media Education Comunicar, Comunicar,* 32 (1): 155-176

Saleh, I. (2010) Media Education in the Middle East & North Africa (MENA): Dancing Naked in a Swamp of Coercive Societies, International Association for Media & Communication Research (IAMCR), Braga, Portugal

Shepard, B.L. & DeJong, J.L, (2005) *Breaking the Silence: Young People's Sexual and Reproductive Health in the Arab States and Iran*. Boston: Harvard School of Public Health, www.hsph.harvard.edu/pihhr/files/Shepard_publication.pdf and www.prb.org/pdf08/MENAYouthReproductiveHealth_Arabic.pdf

Tawilah, O., Tawil, S., Bassiri, S. & Ziady, H. (2002) Information needs assessment for HIV/AIDS and STIs in the eastern Mediterranean region, *Eastern Mediterranean Health Journal*, 8(6): 689-698

Digital Marketing and Children's Health

A Framework for Research

Kathryn C. Montgomery, Sonya Grier, Jeff Chester & Lori Dorfman

In 2009, the Finnish online entertainment company Sulake (2009) conducted an update of its annual Global Youth Survey. The month-long poll surveyed 112,000 youth between the ages of 11 and 19 in more than 30 countries, gleaning information and insights on media usage patterns and brand preferences for fast food, beverages, mobile services, and other products. To recruit their research subjects, the company drew on the huge international user base on its popular virtual world, Habbo.com, where young people create "a fully customized online character called a Habbo", and "explore many public hang-outs, participate in a variety of activities, connect with friends, decorate their own rooms, and have fun through creativity and self expression" (Sulake, 2009). Sulake aggressively promotes the site as a marketing venue, weaving a variety of products, branded avatars, and other elements into the "storylines", and offering virtual products (including furniture – called "furni") for sale through mobile phone or online credit card purchases (HabboUS, n.d.). More than 11 million individuals visit the site every month, and 132 million Habbo characters have been created, according to the company (Sulake).

Habbo is emblematic of the new global "media and marketing ecosystem" that is transforming how corporations do business with young people in the Digital Age. Broadband networks and Web 2.0 technologies are creating an interactive media culture that is increasingly participatory, pervasive, and mobile. This rapid expansion of digital media is ushering in a new set of behaviors, especially for youth, whom marketers are closely monitoring (Montgomery, 2007). There are nearly 200 million Internet users in the U.S., and over 1.6 billion people online throughout the world (Phillips, 2008; Internet World Stats, 2009). Children between 8 and 14 are online almost two hours daily, while slightly less than half of 18-to-24 year-olds are connected more than three hours each day (Phillips).

Youth are valuable to marketers not only because of their own spending power and ease with technology, but also because of their role as trendsetters in the new media environment (Montgomery, 2007; Linn, 2004; Schor, 2004; Grier, 2009). A growing number of specialized advertising agencies, boutique digital marketing specialists, and trend analysis companies are constantly tracking their every move, coining a variety of labels to define this powerful target group of users – from "N-Geners" to "Digital Kids" to "Cyberteens" (Montgomery, 2001, 2007; Tapscott, 1999, 2008). In the U.S., Hispanic and African-American youth are the fastest growing population segments, and are considered particularly influential in their use of technologies and cultural practices (Grier, 2005). An array of specialized multicultural market research firms and advertising agencies is focused exclusively on developing new-media strategies for targeting ethnic minority youth (Grier, 2009).

The global digital marketing infrastructure is dominated by a handful of companies, with U.S.-based corporations Google and Microsoft playing a particularly influential role (IAB Europe, n.d.). Leading interactive marketers have also established R&D (research and development) labs to advance the capabilities of online advertising, including facilities in China, India, and Israel. Online marketers have formed powerful regional associations to promote transnational standards for digital marketing practices. As a consequence, many of the same technologies and business models for search, mobile, gaming, and display advertising can be found in Europe, Asia, South America, North America and elsewhere (International Conference on Online Media Measurement, 2009).

The growth of digital youth marketing is particularly important in light of renewed public policy debates over the effect of marketing on children's health. In the United States, Europe, and other parts of the world, government agencies, public health professionals, and media scholars have focused increased attention on food advertising as a key contributor to the growing childhood obesity epidemic (Schor & Ford, 2007). A major 2005 study by the U.S. Institute of Medicine documented the broad changes in food and beverage consumption among children, as well as the rise in serious diseases, pointing to marketing as a key factor, and spawning a flurry of regulatory forums and industry self-policing initiatives (McGinnis et al., 2005; Wilde, 2009). The British regulatory agency Ofcom has banned television advertising of foods high in fat, salt and sugar on programs aimed at children under 16 (BBC News, 2008). International consumer and health groups have called on the World Health Organization (2006) to develop a "global standard on the marketing of unhealthy food and drink" (Consumers International, 2009; Consumers International & International Obesity Task Force, 2007).

In contrast to the burgeoning digital market research industry, comparatively few academic studies have been conducted on interactive marketing and children (McGinnis, Gootman, & Kraak, 2005; Montgomery, 2001, 2007). Even as a robust scholarly field has emerged to study youth involvement with digital media culture, serious analysis of the commercial arena of that culture is lacking. For the most part, children and media scholars have not kept pace with the rapid changes in the digital marketplace.

Interactive marketing departs in significant ways from traditional forms of advertising, challenging the prevailing theories and methods that have guided media research in the past. In today's digital marketing system, advertising, editorial content, and measurement have been intertwined (Chester & Montgomery, 2007). Marketing is now woven into the very fabric of young people's daily experiences. Children and teens are no longer passive viewers of advertising messages; they are active participants and content creators in an interactive commercial environment that pervades their personal and social lives.

The transformation of the media environment warrants corresponding conceptual models and research methods that can accommodate new digital marketing practices. While the interactive marketplace is still in a somewhat fluid, formative stage of development, it is possible to identify several of its key features, as well as the major forces that are shaping its growth and direction. They need to be understood as a new holistic *system* of marketing *strategies*. Some are adaptations of ad practices that were part of the commercial world before the introduction of the Internet, enhanced and in many ways transformed through the use of digital technology. Taken together – and viewed against the backdrop of the major changes taking place in the worlds of media, advertising, and market research – the following features comprise a new digital marketing framework:

Ubiquitous connectivity

Today's youth are growing up in an "always-on", 24/7 media environment that is accessible to them wherever they go throughout the day, creating an internalized expectation of constant connectivity to technology. Marketers design their campaigns to take advantage of young peoples' fluid media experiences, dependency on technology, and multi-tasking behaviors. This "360-degree strategy" is one of the core principles of today's youth marketing, aimed at reaching individuals repeatedly through multiple "touchpoints" (Covino, 2007). Marketers not only tap into these patterns of behavior, but also purposely cultivate them, designing campaigns that can "drive" young consumers from one medium to the next (Chester & Montgomery, 2007). Increasingly, advertisers are taking advantage of what is known as the "three-screen" viewing environment, running their ad campaigns simultaneously on television, the Web, and mobile devices (Nielsen Company, 2009). Major media companies have restructured their marketing and sales operations to facilitate cross-platform strategies where, in a single buy, advertisers can target customers across a company's media properties, online and off (New Media Age, 2008).

Mobile marketing – combining text messaging, mobile video, and other new applications – is one of the fastest growing digital commerce platforms throughout the world, and a particularly effective way to reach and engage youth (Burns, 2009). Both U.S. African-American and Hispanic youth are in the forefront of using mobile services to access content (Nielsen Company, 2008; CTIA & Harris Interactive, 2008; Briabe Media, n.d.; Grier, 2009). Through "location targeting", ads on mobile phones can reach consumers when they are near a particular business and offer electronic pitches and discount coupons (Johannes, 2005; Center for Digital Democracy and U.S. PIRG, 2009). Among the many food and beverage companies using mobile campaigns are Coca-Cola, McDonald's, Burger King, Carl's Jr., and Dominos (Center for Digital Democracy, n.d.).

Engagement

In contrast to the passive experience of watching television, the increasingly participatory environment of interactive media facilitates active engagement (Benkler, 2006). This is particularly the case for children and youth, whose enthusiastic involvement with social networks, blogs, text messaging, and online video makes them the most engaged of demographic groups (Yahoo & OMD, 2005). Rather than simply exposing consumers to a particular marketing message, product, or service, digital marketers seek to create environments in which consumers are actually *engaging* with brands, befriending the products, and integrating them into their personal and social relationships. Engagement also has a strong emotional dimension, referring to the "subtle, subconscious process in which consumers begin to combine the ad's messages with their own associations, symbols and metaphors to make the brand more personally relevant" (Nail, 2006).

Specialized companies have developed a host of new software and tools to measure engagement. For example, Innerscope Research monitors emotional engagement using "smart garments that measure arousal, respiratory, heart, and motion responses", as well as eye tracking that measures "audience gaze location and duration". These and other techniques enable the company to develop "in-depth diagnostics of moment-to-moment changes in emotional response (Advertising Research Foundation, n.d.).

User-generated content

The growth in popularity of digital video cameras and online video sharing sites such as YouTube has made it very easy for young people to create and distribute their own videos. To take advantage of this trend, marketers are encouraging young consumers to "co-create" and promote commercials for their favorite brands. The strategy is designed to foster powerful emotional connections between consumers and products, tap into a stable of young creative talent willing to offer their services for free, and produce a new generation of "brand advocates" (DoubleClick, n.d.; Meez, n.d.; Studiocom, n.d.). These practices turn the conventional model of advertising on its head, transforming children from passive viewers of commercials into ad producers and distributors.

User-generated-media campaigns employ a variety of techniques to encourage consumers to become involved in creating marketing messages. In most cases, companies create a template and provide incentives to foster participation. For example, Pepsi's Frito-Lay division urged consumers to produce their own commercial spots for Doritos tortilla chips and submit them online in the "Doritos Smash the Super Bowl Contest" (Frito-Lay North America, n.d.; Frito-Lay North America, 2007; JumpCut, n.d.; PepsiCo, 2007; Yahoo, 2007).

Personalization

Through a variety of new techniques, marketers use the data they collect from consumers to create personalized marketing and sales appeals based on an individual's unique preferences, behaviors, and psychological profile (Hallerman, 2008; Khan, Weishaar, & Polinsky et al., 2008). Behavioral targeting has become a core strategy of contemporary marketing, a linchpin of many digital media campaigns targeting young people – not only online, but also on cell phones, video games, and other new platforms (Hallerman, 2008; Khan, Weishaar, Polinsky et al., 2008). Behavioral targeting uses a range of online methods – including cookies and invisible data files – to track the online behaviors of individuals (Center for Digital Democracy and U.S. PIRG, 2006, 2007, 2009; EPIC, Center for Digital Democracy, and U.S. PIRG, 2007, April 20 and September 17). For example, Coca-Cola has been at the forefront of companies harnessing the capabilities of digital media to collect data from users. Its MyCokeRewards site, launched in 2006, was designed to generate "mass participation" through behavioral targeting. Using advanced data-mining technologies, MyCokeRewards is able to deliver highly personalized marketing to its more than 13.5 million members in the U.S. (Fredricksen, 2009).

Social graph

Youth are especially enthusiastic participants in online social networks (also called social media), which are among the fastest-growing platforms in the digital media environment (Owyang, 2010). Facebook recently reported that it had amassed a global user base of 500 million individuals (Wortham, 2010). In the U.S., 73 percent of online youth between the ages of 12 and 17 use social networking sites (Lenhart, Purcell, Smith, & Zickuhr, 2010; Williamson, 2008). These participatory online platforms enable users to create personal profiles, where they can post photos, videos, and music (Beer, 2008; Boyd, 2007; Brake, 2008; Fono & Raynes-Goldie, 2006). Social networking platforms have added a new feature to digital marketing that is distinct and important: the ability to tap into the *social graph,* which is the complex web of relationships among individuals facilitated and tracked online (Iskold, 2007). Social networking platforms are able to give marketers access to the relationships among individuals and communities in ways that were never before possible. Using a host of new techniques and measurement tools, social media marketers can know the breadth and depth of these online social relationships, as well as how they function, understanding who influences whom, and how the process of influence works.

Food and beverage companies such as Coca-Cola, Kraft, Pepsi, and Taco Bell are among the pioneers of this new marketing strategy. Social networks offer "brand-building opportunities far beyond what's available through traditional advertising" (Interactive Advertising Bureau, 2008). Social media marketing is an increasingly important strategy for brand promotion. For example, in 2009 Pepsi decided to forego most of its Super Bowl-related advertising efforts in order to conduct a new major social media marketing campaign ("Risk or Opportunity?" 2008).

Immersive environments

State-of-the-art animation, high-definition and three-dimensional video, and other multi-media applications are spawning a new generation of immersive environments, including interactive games and virtual worlds. Using "dynamic product placement", ads can be incorporated into a game's storyline, and programmed to respond to a player's actions in real time, changing, adding, or updating messages to tailor their appeal to that particular individual (Gaudiosi, 2007; Shields, 2006). In-game ad spending is projected to reach $1 billion by 2014, according to recent industry projections (Alexander, 2009). Virtual worlds are increasingly popular among youth, with six million 3-11 year-olds and 3.7 million teens 12-17 visiting some form of online virtual world each month ("$594 million Invested", 2009; Shields, 2009). Food and beverage companies are finding both online gaming and virtual worlds to be especially effective venues for brand promotion. For example, Frito-Lay worked with Microsoft's popular Xbox to "create an engaging interactive online experience" involving Doritos, targeted at 16-24 year-olds. The campaign began with a contest on the snack food company's website, Snack Strong Productions, where visitors were invited to design their own "user-generated" ideas for a "Doritos-inspired video game" built around the product's "iconic shape, color, bold flavors, and/or the intensity of the chip experience". One million users were attracted to the Doritos site as a result of the Xbox campaign (72 percent were new visitors), where they spent significant amounts of time viewing all the submissions. More than 160,000 "Doritos theme packs" were downloaded on Xbox Live (Microsoft Advertising, 2008).

New metrics

The impact of marketing is further enhanced and intensified by new forms of monitoring and measurement that were not possible before the advent of digital media. Measurement has been woven into content, delivery systems, and user interactions. Through web analytics, conversation targeting, and other forms of surveillance, marketers can now track individuals online, across media, and in the real world, monitoring their interactions, social relationships, and locations. Increasingly, these various forms of analysis can take place in real time, following users' movements and behaviors from one moment to the next, and assessing their reactions to various marketing techniques. As a result, these techniques can be tested, refined, and tailored for maximum effect.

The tools of neuroscience have also been adapted for advertising, creating a variety of *neuromarketing* techniques for measuring such responses as "degrees of attention, emotional engagement, and memory retention that consumers experience at the deep subconscious level of the brain", and to assess how "specific patterns of brain activation predict purchasing", the potential "shopping centers in the brain", and the neurological basis of purchasing (Sensory Logic, n.d.; Knutson et al., 2007; Dagher, 2007; Dooley, 2007). Through functional magnetic resonance imaging (fMRI), eye-tracking studies, galvanic skin response, and electroencephalography (EEG), marketers can hone their engagement strategies for maximum impact. Neurofocus, the leading neuromarketing company, boasts that its metrics are drawn from clinical methods for diagnosing mental illness and learning disabilities. For example, measurement of "attention level" is "based on the science behind ADD/ADHD clinical diagnosis"; "emotion" is "based on the science behind mania & phobia clinical diagnosis"; and "memory retention" measures are "based on the science behind Alzheimer's clinical diagnosis" (Bush & Padreep, 2009).

A new agenda for the digital age

The growth of digital media and marketing requires fresh thinking and new agendas for research. The traditional emphasis on the *content* of television commercials and their *effects* on behavior and attitudes of young children is rooted in an earlier set of relationships in the mass media that are not applicable to contemporary practices. We can no longer speak of marketing *messages* as isolated, measurable, units. Rather, we need to consider the synergistic nature of marketing *interactions* across a variety of platforms. Nor is marketing confined to a particular time and place; for example, it can be seeded through the *social graph* and then distributed widely, reinforced, and multiplied through a viral process that has no bounds. *Exposure* to marketing may be less important than the nature and degree of *engagement* with marketing and brands. In some cases, young people are actively *participating* in the development of the product, the design of the package, and the creation and distribution of the marketing. *Personalization* means that each individual has his or her own unique interactions and relationships with brands and the companies that produce and promote them. The increasingly *immersive* nature of all digital media means that young people are not just *viewing content,* but *inhabiting media environments* where entertainment, communication, and marketing are combined in a seamless stream of compelling sounds and images.

Flexible and innovative approaches are needed to understand the complex ways that youth are interacting with this new commercial media culture. Collaborative, interdisciplinary studies should combine expertise from various fields, including communications, cultural studies, new media, psychology, and marketing. Some of the new research on how young people are engaging with digital media culture, for example, including qualitative, ethnographic investigations of youth subcultures, could provide useful insights and possible models for exploring digital marketing (MacArthur Foundation, n.d.; Livingstone, 2007).

The needs of adolescents should not be overlooked (Chester & Montgomery, 2009). Even though teenagers are at serious risk for obesity, food marketing to this age group has not received the same level of scholarly attention that has been focused on younger children (McGinnis, Gootman, & Kraak, 2005). Today's teens are being socialized into this new commercial digital culture, which resonates so strongly with many of their fundamental developmental tasks, such as identity exploration, social interaction, and autonomy (Harter, 1990; Uhlendorff, 2004; Hill, 1983; Subrahmanyam & Greenfield, 2008). Thus, they may be internalizing and normalizing the marketing practices that have been so integrally woven into their everyday actions and experiences. Recent research within the fields of neuroscience, psychology, and marketing has identified key biological and psychosocial attributes of the adolescent experience that may make members of this age group more susceptible to certain kinds of marketing (Pechmann et al., 2005). Scholars have challenged the notion that cognitive defenses enable adolescents to resist advertising (particularly in new media) more effectively than younger children (Livingstone & Helsper, 2006). Rather than communicating rational or factual appeals, many digital marketing techniques are forms of "implicit persuasion", promoting "subtle affective associations" that often circumvent a consumer's explicit persuasion knowledge (Nairn & Fine, 2005).

Any studies undertaken on youth and digital marketing must be grounded in the "real-world" practices of the contemporary marketplace, which is not static but constantly evolving. This will require close, ongoing monitoring of market research, theories, platforms, and techniques. The toolbox of techniques that digital market researchers use to assess youth consumer behavior could also be adapted for academic researchers, as long as these techniques are employed in accordance with academic standards for ethical research.

Finally, as governments across the globe consider appropriate safeguards for youth, it will be important to position young people in ways that acknowledge their unique vulnerabilities to marketing (including those described above), while honoring and respecting their rights as active participants (and important influencers) in both the media culture and the larger society.

Acknowledgement

The authors wish to thank the Robert Wood Johnson Foundation's Healthy Eating Research project for supporting the research and writing of this article.

References

"$594 million Invested in 63 Virtual Worlds-Related Companies in 2008." (2009, January 20) Virtual Worlds News. Retrieved June 7, 2009, from http://www.virtualworldsnews.com/2009/01/594-million-invested-in-63-virtual-worldsrelated-companies-in-2008.html.

Advertising Research Foundation. (n.d.) "Building Engagement on Two Levels," PowerPoint presentation.

Alexander, L. (2009, May 26) "Analyst: In-Game Ad 'Spending to Reach $1 Billion By 2014,'" Gamasutra. Retrieved June 7, 2009, from http://www.gamasutra.com/php-bin/news_index.php?story=23751.

BBC News. (2008, January 1) "Ban on Junk Food Ads Introduced," *BBC News*. Retrieved August 3, 2009, from http://news.bbc.co.uk/2/hi/health/7166510.stm.

Beer, D. (2008) "Social Network(ing) Sites... Revisiting the Story So Far: A Response to danah boyd & Nicole Ellison," *Journal of Computer-Mediated Communication*, Vol. 13, No. 2, pp. 516-529.

Benkler, Y. (2006) *The Wealth of Networks: How Social Production Transforms Markets and Freedom*. New Haven, CT: Yale University Press, p. 272.

boyd, D. (2007) "Why Youth (Heart) Social Networks," in Buckingham, D. (Ed.), *Youth, Identity, and Digital Media* (pp. 119-142). Cambridge, MA, MIT Press.

Brake, D. (2008) "Shaping the 'Me' in MySpace: The Framing of Profiles on a Social Network Site," in K. Lundby, ed., *Digital Storytelling, Mediatized Stories: Self-Representations in New Media*. New York: Peter Lang.

Briabe Media. (n.d.) *Mobile Marketing to Multicultural Audiences*. Retrieved August 4, 2009, from http://briabemedia.com/documents/articles/Mobile_Marketing_to_Multicultural_Audiences.php.

Burns, E. (2009, February 25) "U.S. Mobile Ad Revenue to Grow Significantly through 2013," *ClickZ*. Retrieved August 4, 2009, from http://www.clickz.com/3632919.

Bush, J., & Padreep, A.K. (2009, March 8) "Maximizing Message Impact for Alcon Laboratories," presentation to the 2009 Annual National Conference of the PMRG.

Center for Digital Democracy and U.S. PIRG. (2006, November 1) "Complaint and Request for Inquiry and Injunctive Relief Concerning Unfair and Deceptive Online Marketing Practices," Federal Trade Commission Filing. Retrieved October 12, 2009, from http://www.democraticmedia.org/files/pdf/FTCadprivacy.pdf.

Center for Digital Democracy and U.S. PIRG. (2007, November 1) "Supplemental Statement In Support of Complaint and Request for Inquiry and Injunctive Relief Concerning Unfair and Deceptive Online Marketing Practices," Federal Trade Commission Filing. Retrieved October 12, 2009, from http://www.democraticmedia.org/files/FTCsupplemental_statement1107.pdf.

Center for Digital Democracy and U.S. PIRG. (2009, January 13) "Complaint and Request for Inquiry and Injunctive Relief Concerning Unfair and Deceptive Mobile Marketing Practices." Federal Trade Commission Filing. Retrieved June 7, 2009, from http://www.democraticmedia.org/current_projects/privacy/analysis/mobile_marketing.

Center for Digital Democracy (n.d.) "Digital Marketing Update: News on Digital Food Marketing Since Our Report was Released." Retrieved June 7, 2009, from http://www.digitalads.org/updates.php.

Chester, J., & Montgomery, K. C. (2007) *Interactive Food & Beverage Marketing: Targeting Children and Youth in the Digital Age*. Berkeley, CA: Berkeley Media Studies Group.

Consumers International. (2009). *World Consumer Rights Day 2009*. Retrieved August 29, 2009 from http://junkfoodgeneration.org/index.php?option=com_content&task=view&id=80.

Consumers International & International Obesity Task Force. (2007) *Recommendations for an International Code on the Marketing of Food and Non-alcoholic Beverages to Children*. Retrieved August 29, 2009 from http://www.junkfoodgeneration.org/documents/marketing_code.pdf.

Covino, R. M. (2006, March) "Tapping into Kids' Touchpoints," *Confectioner*. Retrieved April 25, 2007, from http://www.confectioner.com/content.php?s=CO/2006/03&p=9.

CTIA & Harris Interactive. (2008) *Teenagers: A Generation Unplugged*. Retrieved August 4, 2009, from http://www.ctia.org/content/index.cfm/AID/11483.

Dagher, A. (2007) "Shopping Centers in the Brain," *Neuron* 53(1), 7-8. doi:10.1016/j.neuron.2006.12.014.

Dooley. R. (2007, January 5) "Brain Scans Predict Buying Behavior," *Futurelab*. Retrieved August 4, 2009, from http://blog.futurelab.net/2007/01/brain_scans_predict_buying_beh.htm.

DoubleClick. (n.d.) *DoubleClick Rich Media and Video*. Retrieved August 5, 2009, from http://www.doubleclick.com/products/richmedia/index.aspx.

EPIC, Center for Digital Democracy, and U.S. PIRG. (2007, April 20) "In the matter of Google, Inc. and DoubleClick, Inc., Complaint and Request for Injunction, Request for Investigation and for Other Relief, before the Federal Trade Commission." Retrieved October 12, 2009, from http://www.epic.org/privacy/ftc/google/epic_complaint.pdf.

EPIC, Center for Digital Democracy, and U.S. PIRG. (2007, September) "In the matter of Google, Inc. and DoubleClick, Inc., Second Filing of Supplemental Materials in Support of Pending Complaint and Request for Injunction, Request for Investigation and for Other Relief." Retrieved October 12, 2009, from http://epic.org/privacy/ftc/google/supp2_091707.pdf.

Fono D., & Raynes-Goldie, K. (2006) "Hyperfriends and Beyond: Friendship and Social Norms on LiveJournal," *Internet Research Annual*, Vol. 4, pp. 91-103. Retrieved March 23, 2009, http://k4t3.org/publications/hyperfriendship.pdf.

Fredricksen, C. (2009, November 25) "My Coke Rewards: Combining Mobile and Social Media to Drive Brand Loyalty," The eMarketer Blog. Retrieved September 12, 2010, from http://www.emarketer.com/blog/index.php/my-coke-rewards-combining-mobile-social-media-brand-loyalty/.

Frito-Lay North America. (n.d.) "Doritos Presents Crash the Super Bowl." Retrieved October 2, 2010, from http://crashthesuperbowl.com/.

Frito-Lay North America. (2007) "Doritos Surprises Super Bowl Television Audience Airing Two Consumer-created Commercials: 'Live the Flavor' and 'Check Out Girl.'" Retrieved October 2, 2008, from http://www.fritolay.com/fl/flstore/cgi-bin/ProdDetEv_Cat_304_NavRoot_303_ProdID_544013.htm

Gaudiosi, J. (2007, March 7) "Google gets In-game with Adscape," *The Hollywood Reporter*. Retrieved August 5, 2009, from http://www.hollywoodreporter.com/hr/content_display/business/news/e3i898ca0de1754206ae43bdbc6ee2d9ffd (subscription required).

Grier, S. (2005) "What is Different about Targeted Marketing to Ethnic Minority Children?" In The Past, Present and Future of Marketing Foods to Children Panel. The Federal Trade Commission and the Department of Health and Human Services workshop: Perspectives on Marketing, Self-Regulation & Childhood Obesity, July 14-15, Washington, DC.

Grier, S. (2009) "African American & Hispanic Youth Vulnerability to Target Marketing: Implications for Understanding the Effects of Digital Marketing." Memo prepared for the Second NPLAN/BMSG Meeting on Digital Media and Marketing to Children for the NPLAN Marketing to Children Learning Community, Berkeley, CA, June 29-30, 2009.

HabboUS. (n.d.) *FAQ*. Retrieved August 3, 2009, from http://www.habbo.com/help/42#011.

Hallerman, D. (2008) "Behavioral Targeting: Marketing Trends." Retrieved August 4, 2009, from http://www.emarketer.com/Reports/All/Emarketer_2000487.aspx.

Harter, S. (1990) "Processes Underlying the Construction, Maintenance and Enhancement of the Self-concept in Children," *Psychological Perspective on the Self*, Vol. 3, pp. 45-78.

Hill, J. (1983) "Early Adolescence: A Framework," *Journal of Early Adolescence*, Vol. 3, No. 1, pp. 1-21.

IAB Europe. (n.d.) *Welcome to the IAB Europe website*. Retrieved August 3, 2009, from http://www.iabeurope.eu/.

Interactive Advertising Bureau. (2008, April) "IAB Platform Status Report: User Generated Content, Social Media, and Advertising—An Overview." Retrieved September 12, 2010, from http://www.iab.net/media/file/2008_ugc_platform.pdf.

International Conference on Online Media Measurement. (2009) *Patronage Organizations: Global Summit*. Retrieved August 29, 2009, from http://i-com.org/patronage-organisations-global/.

Internet World Stats. (2009) *Internet Usage Statistics*. Retrieved August 3, 2009, from http://www.internetworldstats.com/stats.htm.

Iskold, A. (2007, September 12) "Social Graph: Concepts and Issues," ReadWriteWeb. Retrieved October 2, 2008, from http://www.readwriteweb.com/archives/social_graph_concepts_and_issues.php.

Johannes, A. (2005, October 26) "McDonald's Serves Up Mobile Coupons in California," *PROMO Magazine*. Retrieved August 4, 2009, from http://promomagazine.com/incentives/mcds_coupons_102605/.

JumpCut. (n.d.) *Contest Page*. Retrieved October 2, 2008, from http://www.jumpcut.com/groups/detail?g_id=11752B7457BE11DB90D6961586523BC9.

Khan, I., Weishaar, B., & Polinsky, L. et al. (2008) "Nothing but Net: 2008 Internet Investment Guide." Retrieved March 23, 2009, from https://mm.jpmorgan.com/stp/t/c.do?i=2082C-248&u=a_p*d_170762.pdf*h_-3ohpnmv.

Knutson, B., Rick, S., & Wimmer, G. E. et al. (2007) "Neural Predictors of Purchases," *Neuron*, Vol. 53, No. 1, pp. 147-156.

Lenhart, A., Purcell, K., Smith, A., & Zickuhr, K. (2010) "Social Media and Young Adults," Pew Internet & American Life Project. Retrieved March 23, 2010, http://www.pewinternet.org/Reports/2010/Social-Media-and-Young-Adults.aspx.

Linn, S. (2004) *Consuming Kids: The Hostile Takeover of Childhood.* New York: The New Press.

Livingstone, S., & Helsper, E. J. (2006) "Does Advertising Literacy Mediate the Effects of Advertising on Children? A Critical Examination of Two Linked Research Literatures in Relation to Obesity and Food Choice," *Journal of Communication*, Vol. 56, No. 3, pp. 560-584.

MacArthur Foundation. (n.d.) *Building the Field of Digital Media and Learning*. Retrieved August 7, 2009, from http://www.digitallearning.macfound.org/site/c.enJLKQNlFiG/b.2029199/k.BFC9/Home.htm.

McGinnis, J. M., Gootman J. A., & Kraak, V. I., (Eds.) (2005) *Food Marketing to Children and Youth: Threat or Opportunity?* Washington, DC: National Academies Press.

Meez. (n.d.) *Advertise with Us*. Retrieved August 5, 2009, from http://www.meez.com/help.dm?sect=8

Microsoft Advertising. (2008, December 23) "Doritos and Xbox Put Fans in Control." Retrieved June 7, 2009, from http://advertising.microsoft.com/research/Doritos-Xbox

Montgomery, K. C. (2007) *Generation Digital: Politics, Commerce, and Childhood in the Age of the Internet*. Cambridge, MA: MIT Press.

Montgomery, K. C. (2001) "Digital Kids: The New Online Children's Consumer Culture," in Singer D., & Singer, J. (Eds.) *Handbook of Children and the Media*. Thousand Oaks, CA: Sage Publications, pp. 635-650.

Montgomery, K. C., & Chester, J. (2009) "Interactive Food & Beverage Marketing: Targeting Adolescents in the Digital Age," *Journal of Adolescent Health*, Vol. 45, pp. S18–S29.

Nail, J. (2006, October 13) "The 4 Types of Engagement," *iMedia Connection*. Retrieved August 4, 2009, from http://www.imediaconnection.com/content/11633.asp.

Nairn, A., & Fine, C. (2005) "Who's Messing with My Mind? The Implications of Dual-Process Models for the Ethics of Advertising to Children," *International Journal of Advertising*, Vol. 27, No. 3, pp. 447-470.

New Media Age. (2008) *NMA Marketing Services Guide 2008*. Retrieved August 4, 2009, from http://www.nma.co.uk (subscription required).

Nielsen Company. (2008) "46% of U.S. Tweens use a Cell Phone, Nielsen Reports." Retrieved June 7, 2009, from http://www.nielsenmobile.com/html/press%20releases/MobileKids.html.

Nielsen Company. (2009) "Americans Watching More TV than Ever; Web and Mobile Video Up Too." Retrieved August 4, 2009, from http://blog.nielsen.com/nielsenwire/online_mobile/americans-watching-more-tv-than-ever/.

Owyang, J. (2010, January 19) "A Collection of Social Network Stats for 2010," Web Strategy. Retrieved March 13, 2010, from http://www.web-strategist.com/blog/2010/01/19/a-collection-of-social-network-stats-for-2010/.

Pechmann, C., Levine, L., & Loughlin, S. et al. (2005) "Impulsive and Self-conscious: Adolescents' Vulnerability to Advertising and Promotion," *Journal of Public Policy & Marketing*, Vol. 24, No. 2, pp. 202-221.

PepsiCo. (2007) "Doritos Reveals Final Five Consumer-created Commercials Competing to Air during Super Bowl XLI." Retrieved October 2, 2008, from http://phx.corporate-ir.net/phoenix.zhtml?c=78265&p=irol-newsArticle&ID=947181&highlight=.

Phillips, L. E. (2008, February) "U.S. Online Population." Retrieved August 3, 2009, from http://www.emarketer.com/Report.aspx?code=emarketer_2000486.

"Risk or Opportunity? PepsiCo Pulls Beverage Ads From Super Bowl." (2008, December 18) Loyalty360.org. Retrieved September 12, 2010, from http://www.loyalty360.org/industry_news/risk_or_opportunity_pepsico_pulls_beverage_ads_from_super_bowl/.

Schor, J. B. (2004) *Born to Buy: The Commercialized Child and the New Consumer Culture*. New York: Scribner.

Schor, J. B., & Ford, M. (2007) "From Tastes Great to Cool: Children's Food Marketing and the Rise of the Symbolic," *Journal of Law, Medicine & Ethics*, Vol. 35, No. 1, pp. 10-21.

Sensory Logic. (n.d.) *Research*. Retrieved August 4, 2009, from http://www.sensorylogic.com/home/research.html.

Shields, M. (2006, April 12) "In-game Ads Could Reach $2 Bil," *Adweek*. Retrieved August 5, 2009, from http://www.adweek.com/aw/national/article_display.jsp?vnu_content_id=1002343563.

Shields, M. (2009, May 22) "Kids' Virtual Worlds Gain Traction," *AdWeek*. Retrieved June 7, 2009, from http://www.adweek.com/aw/content_display/news/digital/e3i9659c5aa3ebf280624968f-ca48925660.

Studiocom. (n.d.) *Immersive Online Experiences*. Retrieved August 5, 2009, from http://www.studiocom.com/godeep/.

Subrahmanyam, K., & Greenfield, P. (2008) "Online Communication and Adolescent Relationships," *The Future of Children*, Vol. 18, No. 1, pp. 119-146.

Sulake. (2009) "Global Habbo Youth Survey 2009 Uncovers American Teens' Unique Attitudes Towards Brands." Retrieved August 3, 2009, from http://www.newsguide.us/technology/multimedia/Global-Habbo-Youth-Survey-2009-Uncovers-American-Teens-Unique-Attitudes-Towards-Brands/.

Tapscott, D. (1999) *Growing Up Digital: The Rise of the Net Generation*. New York: McGraw-Hill.

Tapscott, D. (2008) *Grown Up Digital: How the Net Generation is Changing Your World*. New York: McGraw-Hill.

Uhlendorff, U. (2004) "The Concept of Developmental Tasks," *Social Work & Society*, Vol. 2, No. 1, pp. 54-63.

Wilde, P. (2009) "Self-regulation and the Response to Concerns about Food and Beverage Marketing to Children in the United States," *Nutrition Reviews*, Vol. 67, No. 3, pp. 155-166.

Williamson, D. A. (2008) "Kids and Teens: Communications Revolutionaries," eMarketer. Retrieved March 23, 2009, from http://www.emarketer.com/Report.aspx?code=emarketer_2000539.

World Health Organization. (2006) *Marketing of Food and Non-alcoholic Beverages to Children*. Report of a WHO forum and technical meeting, Oslo, Norway, May 2-5. 2006. Retrieved August 29, 2009, from http://www.who.int/dietphysicalactivity/publications/Oslo%20meeting%20layout%2027%20NOVEMBER.pdf.

Wortham, J. (2010, July 21) "Facebook Tops 500 Million Users," *New York Times*. Retrieved August 26, 2010, from http://www.nytimes.com/2010/07/22/technology/22facebook.html?_r=2.

Yahoo. (2007) "Doritos Asked Ordinary People to Help Them Make a Commercial for the Big Game. What Happened was Extraordinary." Retrieved October 2, 2008, from http://promotions.yahoo.com/doritos/jumpcut/.

Yahoo & OMD. (2005) "Truly, Madly, Deeply Engaged: Global Youth, Media and Technology." Retrieved March 27, 2007, from http://www.iabaustralia.com.au/Truly_Madly_Final_booklet.pdf.

Juanita Publicly Asks "What Will You Do for Me, Mayoral Candidate?"

Children, Media, and Health Advocacy in Colombia[1]

Arvind Singhal

The legendary Jim Grant, Executive Director of UNICEF (from 1980 to 1995), was fond of telling the story of a young woman who was walking along the beach, picking up the beached starfish and throwing them back into the sea. When an old man asked her why she was doing this, she said: "If left on the sand, the starfish would die." "But there are thousands of beached starfish", countered the old man. "How can your effort make any difference?" The young woman threw the starfish she had in her hands into the water and replied: "It makes a difference to this one."

Under Grant's leadership, UNICEF launched the Child Survival and Development Revolution (CSDR) – an ongoing, multi-year initiative which included several highly creative and innovative advocacy, mobilization, and strategic communication interventions to defend, uphold, and nurture childhood causes globally. As a result of UNICEF's CSDR, tens of millions of children's lives have been saved, and the quality of life of many more has been enhanced.

The present article describes and analyses a national-level communication intervention in Colombia in the late 1980s, in which children served as their own health advocates, harnessing the power of the mass media to mobilize political will and actions for their cause. While implemented over two decades ago, relatively little is known about this Colombian campaign in the mainstream literature on media, children, and health advocacy. Through the historical backdrop of UNICEF's Child Survival and Development Revolution of the 1980s, which sparked countless global, national, and local initiatives to safeguard and enhance the health of the world's children, we specifically focus on the Juanita Communication Initiative in Colombia which translated national-level goals for children's causes into local plans for action. In a world where children's voices are largely muted and goes undefended, the Juanita Communication Initiative provides important lessons on the role of communication strategies in defending and nurturing childhood.

The Child Survival and Development Revolution

In the early-1980s, UNICEF, under Grant's leadership, launched the Child Survival and Development Revolution (CSDR), riding on four available, simple, and low-cost technologies (acronym GOBI): G for growth monitoring to detect under-nutrition in children; O for oral rehydration therapy to treat childhood diarrhoea; B for breast feeding;[2] and I for immunization against the six childhood diseases (tuberculosis, polio, diphtheria, tetanus, whooping cough, and measles).

Grant was a master of high-level global advocacy, meeting personally with more than 100 Heads of State during the decade of the 1980s to enlist their personal and political support for the achievement of CSDR goals. He kept his messages simple and pockets full. Sitting with a prime minister, a president, or a king, he would pull out a packet of oral rehydration salts and say: "Do you know that this costs less than a cup of tea and can save hundreds of thousands of children's lives in your country."[3]

Grant provided incentives for UNICEF country offices to work with national government agencies to mobilize around GOBI (and later GOBI-FFF[4]). He utilized the annual State of the World Children's Report (SOWCR), which he launched in 1980 upon assuming office, as a forum to both report and rank child survival achievements by country. SOWCR became a leading tool of advocacy on behalf of the world's children, achieving worldwide outreach. Released annually with fanfare, it often received front page media coverage. Now a country's performance in meeting the goals of the Child Survival and Development Revolution were more visible.[5] No nation could hide. Not only one knew what were the rates within a country but, more importantly, how they compared with others.[6]

Grant orchestrated a global movement – a "Grand Alliance for Children" – in which governments, civil society, international agencies, and non-governmental organizations formed creative and dynamic partnerships for children and sustainable human development. UNICEF forged partnerships with hundreds of groups – the Red Cross and Red Crescent Societies, the Catholic Church, the International Council of Nurses, Associations of Pediatricians, Mayors Associations and others. UNICEF was also instrumental in mobilizing Rotary International to underwrite the costs of all the vaccines needed to eradicate polio. Rotary pledged to raise $100 million within a few years. By 2000, they had raised over $400 million.

In 1984, Grant persuaded Belisario Betancur, President of Colombia, to back a national vaccination campaign. Betancur grew up in a large family in which a number of his siblings died young. Three national vaccination days were declared. Media promoted the campaign and 100,000 volunteers from the Church, police, military, trade unions, public school teachers, Boy Scouts and Red Cross vaccinated 800,000 children. It was the first large-scale nationwide effort at mobilizing all sectors of society, and proved to be a trend-setter for dozens of other countries that followed suit.

In 1985, Grant worked closely with Turkish Prime Minister Turgut Ozal to launch a massive immunization campaign. At this time, Turkey's immunization rate was dismal, covering only 20 percent of young children. Grant and Ozal conceived and implemented a social mobilization campaign to vaccinate five million children. On the launch day, Prime Minister Ozal, President Evren, the Turkish Minister of Health, the Chief Imam, and Jim Grant vaccinated a baby against polio. It was covered by the national electronic and print media, and hailed as a momentous national event. For the Turkish launch, Grant and Ozal personally invited the ministers of health from Egypt, Pakistan, Sudan and Syria to attend the launch ceremony. In the next several years, these guests would become champions of such immunization drives in their respective countries.

In Turkey, along with extensive mass media coverage, 200,000 school teachers, 54,000 *imams*, and 40,000 *muhtars* (village leaders) were mobilized to help out with the immunization campaign. The country's meat and fishing industries put their cold storage facilities at the disposal of the campaign to preserve the efficacy of the vaccines. Vaccines were moved on cars, trucks, horseback, mules, and foot. Constant radio and television announcements had reached 30 million Turkish homes, ensuring everyone knew what was at stake, what to do and where to go. Within two months of the campaign's launch, 84 percent of the target group was immunized.[7]

With Colombia and Turkey as spectacular showcases, dozens of countries in Asia, Africa, and Latin America followed suit soon thereafter. Amazingly, the 1990 CSDR goal of immunizing 80 percent of the world's under one-year olds with vaccines against the six major child-killing and crippling diseases was realized, up from a meager 20 percent a decade before. While some countries did better than others, an estimated four-to-five million child deaths were now being prevented each year from immunizations and diarrhea control. Millions who would have been crippled by polio could walk and run; millions who would have been blinded from lack of Vitamin A could see. An estimated 50 million children's lives were saved during the decade of the 1990s; and an estimated 20 to 25 million during the decade of the 1980s, when the CSDR was launched and implemented globally.[8]

Although working with various partners, UNICEF could claim to be the moving force behind these spectacular achievements and strategic communication – in the form of global, national, and local advocacy; cross-sectoral mobilization of civil society groups, and behavior change communication for demand creation. Here we profile one of UNICEF's exemplary strategic communication initiatives in Colombia – The Juanita Initiative, which holds important scholarly and practice implications for child-driven, mass-mediated health advocacy.

The Juanita Communication Initiative in Colombia[9]

In 1988, children's voices helped set the national and local agendas for child-related causes in Colombia. That year, Mayoral elections were being held in Colombia for the first time; prior to 1988, they were appointed by the provincial governors. As part of a UNICEF-led campaign, each Mayoral candidate received a letter from a young fictional schoolgirl, Juanita. On a page torn from her school note book, and in her own handwriting (with punctuation glitches), Juanita tells the future mayor about the problems facing Colombian children and asks for help.

> I am Juanita, you do not know me, but I know you. I know you are a very important person. Who is going to be in charge here. Who is liked and respected by people. My mother says that you are going to do a lot for us, because now there is money to do things in this community, and that you will do them. For this, you must think about me and the other children like me. I would like you to know that we are lacking schools, clean water, food, and health. Our problems are many but there are easy solutions that don't need much money, only that you want to do them. I cannot vote because I am a child.
>
> I cannot give you my support yet, but you, yes, you can give me yours. Excuse me and thank you!!!
>
> Juanita

Juanita's letter arrived on each mayoral candidate's desk in the form of a leaflet which had a photograph of the face of Juanita (Image 1), with a thoughtful face, and with the campaign slogan: "Mr. Mayor, I cannot give you my support yet, but you, yes, you can give me yours. Juanita."

The leaflet, on the back side, contained information about the problems of children in Colombia, including high rates of infant mortality, malnutrition, lack of access to pre-school child care and primary education, and vulnerability of certain children and youth. Each problem was defined, elaborated, and solutions suggested: for instance, 34,000 of the 700,000 children born in Colombia each year died before their first birthday; these deaths occurred as not enough doses of vaccines were available against diseases such as measles, polio, tetanus, diphtheria, and whooping cough. Mayors could take corrective actions by procuring vaccines and launching immunization drives, for instance.

Image 1. Juanita, the fictional symbol representing Colombian children
Source: Colin Fraser and Sonia Restrepo-Estrada, used with permission.

Through their representative, Juanita, the Colombian children had laid out a challenge to the hundreds of mayoral candidates all over the country, asking *what they would do for them locally, and how their plan was better than their local competitors'?*

Linking local mayoral elections with children's causes, and placing the burden of articulating a plan on the mayoral candidates, who once elected could be held accountable was brilliant in its creativity, simplicity and audacity. Its timing was uncanny – for it was only two years previously (in 1986) that Colombia had begun its political and administrative decentralization. Local municipalities run by Mayors had assumed responsibility for providing services such as primary health care, water and sanitation and primary and secondary education. Thus, in 1988, when the Mayoral elections were announced, UNICEF considered this new political situation in the country as an unusual opportunity for advocating for children's causes, and anchoring it with electoral platforms and election campaigning.

The final sentence of Juanita's letter to the mayor, "I cannot give you my support yet, but you, yes, you can give me yours" became the slogan for this campaign and was reproduced and repeated in all the communication media – the main newspapers, all radio networks, private television stations and Inravisión, the National Radio and Television Institute in Colombia. This slogan was accompanied by the motto of the campaign: "The children of Colombia: a great responsibility for mayors and communities."

Radio and television spots, featuring Juanita, were crafted and broadcast widely. The main purpose of these spots was to orchestrate public consciousness so that voters would choose the mayoral candidate who offered the best programs for the children in their municipality. Further, to publicize the tie-in, Juanita's face, her letter, and the campaign slogan appeared on large posters in streets all over Colombia, next to the candidate's campaign posters (Image 2).

The Juanita materials were also sent to the various mass media outlets (radio, television, and print) with a personalized cover letter explaining the strategy and asking for their support. Dozens of journalists thus quizzed the mayoral candidates about their electoral platform with regard to children's interests. Children became, for the first time, a theme of Colombian political campaigns.

The Juanita campaign was the brainchild of Programme Communication officer Sonia Restrepo-Estrada, in UNICEF's Bogota office who, along with her team, worked with various in-country partners to make it a reality. In a personal interview in Fall, 2007, when I asked Sonia to elaborate on the conceptual genesis of the Juanita campaign, she told me that her undergraduate training was in social communication and her post-graduate work in political science. The Juanita campaign was a creative and strategic layering of political processes with localized communication advocacy. The premise guiding the Juanita campaign was that democracy is fundamentally local. That is, only when the issues and actors are rooted and/or relevant locally, can effective action and accountability be assured. Not surprisingly, in the World Summit for Children in 1990, heads of state insisted on the importance of translating national action plans into provincial and local plans. UNICEF Colombia was ahead of the game.

The reasons for the effectiveness of the Juanita campaign, especially with respect to advocacy for children's causes at the local level, was the linkage between the campaign activities, children's causes, and current political events within Colombia. While the news services covered the first ever mayoral elec-

Image 2. Juanita's poster side-by-side with candidate's posters
Source: Colin Fraser and Sonia Restrepo-Estrada, used with permission.

tions in Colombia, UNICEF and its partners strategically dovetailed the various components of the Juanita campaign with the current political events, eliciting widespread media coverage. Another key reason for the campaign's effectiveness was the high quality of the printed and audiovisual materials.

In 1989, a year after the original Juanita campaign was carried out, another opportunity arose for UNICEF to capitalize on the experience gained. Colombia was working feverishly, along with other Latin American countries, to eradicate polio from the continent by 1990. UNICEF's Colombia country office worked with the Ministry of Health to implement a "Juanita 2" communication strategy at the local level to achieve Universal Child Immunization and eradicate polio. The strategy consisted of converting the national immunization objectives, for which the responsibility was often diffused and diluted between partnering institutions, into limited but concrete and municipal objectives for local authorities to achieve.

For each of the 1,018 municipalities in Colombia, customized printed materials – posters and leaflets – with immunization data on the five preventable childhood diseases were compiled and delivered to each Mayoral office. Specific proposals, tailored to the local conditions, were provided to the mayors for actions they might take to benefit children within their localities. A parallel purpose was to sensitize and mobilize local communities to immunize their children.

There was a need to avoid any possibility that mayors receiving posters that showed poor vaccination coverage might hide them in their bottom drawer.

Strategically, they were also sent to the local health service outlets, and a whole raft of other local entities who were asked to display them in the municipality. This meant, as Sonia Restrepo-Estrada explained:[10] "That any mayor who hid his posters would find the things plastered all over the town!" An average of seven separate packages of posters was mailed to local entities in each municipality.

The idea of the customized immunization posters drew upon the previous Juanita campaign experience in the 1988 mayoral elections. Municipalities were categorized into three groups: (1) good – for those that had already reached 80 percent immunization coverage; (2) fair – for those that were between 60 to 79 percent coverage; and (3) poor – for those that had below 60 percent coverage, and had reported cases of polio in the previous three years. For each municipality, data on the numbers of children who were not covered for each of the five antigens were obtained and listed. The idea was not to say that so much success has been achieved, but rather, how much more distance needed to be covered. For each municipality, the immunization rates for each antigen (polio, DPT and measles) were converted into three simple ratings: good, fair and low. In this way, 1,018 different posters, one for each municipality were designed, with print-runs that varied from 50 to 3,000 copies, depending on the municipal population.

Cleverly, the poster reproduced the final part of Juanita's letter (on her handwritten notebook paper) to the mayor with its punch line – "I cannot give you my support yet, but you, yes, you can give me yours". The purpose was for mayors, as well as the public, to make the link with the commitments made in the previous year's campaign. In the lower part of the poster was the campaign slogan, a call to action: "Mr. Mayor, let no child remain without immunization at the end of your term of office."

Leaders of all partner agencies – the Colombian Ministry of Health, the Corporation Agency for the Promotion of Municipal Communities (PROCOMÚN), UNICEF, the Pan American Health Organization (PAHO)/WHO, and Rotary International signed a letter addressed personally to each mayor, and this letter was sent to them with their respective customized posters and leaflets. The letter explained Colombia's commitment to Universal Child Immunization and the national eradication of polio.

The printed materials were complemented by 30-second television and radio spots, designed to sensitize the mayors and municipal officials about their role, and to generate public awareness about participating in the immunization campaign. Inravisión (the National Radio and Television Institute), private television stations and radio networks provided free airtime to broadcast the spots. An immunization tsunami was being triggered as a result.

The immunization campaign was launched with fanfare in Bogota with representatives of partner organizations, journalists, and prominent Bogota citizens in attendance. A special invitation card was designed for guests that on the outside said: "Do you know what immunization rating your municipality was given?" Upon opening, it read: "Please make yourself aware of it and commit to ensuring that, in the municipality where you were born, no child remains unvaccinated." Upon arrival, each guest was given a copy of a poster with vaccination figures for their local municipality. The intention was to obtain their commitment, whatever his or her field of activity, to support the immunization targets set for their municipalities.

The strength of the second Juanita campaign was that national level data was compiled and broken down into localized figures that were meaningful to the community. These figures revealed the local reality, which national figures often hide. In so doing, an alliance for children's health was created at the national level, yet firmly rooted in local municipalities. Further, as the rates of vaccination coverage were presented in terms of how many children were still not covered, precise targets for every municipality were established. This generated momentum in many communities to find the non-immunized children.

The final outcome: Colombia not only met its immunization target of 80 percent coverage for children under five years of age against preventable diseases, it exceeded it. However, in spite of its widespread appeal and accompanying national and local buzz, regrettably, no formal monitoring and evaluation was done of the two Juanita campaigns. Informal monitoring conducted by the publicity agency that was executing the campaign on behalf of UNICEF, showed that "the majority of the Colombian population had received the Juanita message and were favorably disposed to it."[11]

A qualitative study, comprising some 60 in-depth interviews in 12 municipalities with a range of respondents who were directly involved with the initiative or were targets of the campaigns, showed that Juanita's "direct appeal to Mayoral candidates was perceived as ingenious", and the call for actions on behalf of children was perceived to be "non-political" and non-partisan in spite of its overt tie-in with the current political events in Colombia. One Mayoral candidate wrote a public letter addressed to Juanita saying "that he too had been a poor child, and that through hard work and study had qualified as a lawyer, and pledged that children would be his main priority if he was elected".

Was the Juanita campaign a "one-off" burst of brilliance, or has its experience influenced other UNICEF initiatives? While the lessons from Juanita were not immediately and fully capitalized on (as lamented by Sonia Restrepo-Estrada in a personal conversation), UNICEF's current high profile *Hechos y Derechos* (Facts and Rights) initiative in Colombia, in which local authorities are held accountable for creating an enabling environment for the realization of children's rights, builds on the experiences gained in the municipality-focused advocacy and social mobilization strategies employed in the Juanita campaigns of the late 1980s.[12]

Lessons learned

What lessons can be learned from the Juanita Initiative in Colombia about harnessing the power of the mass media to mobilize political will, resources, and actions for children's causes? What implications does the Colombian case hold for scholars and practitioners interested in child-driven, mass-mediated health advocacy?

1. The power of Juanita-type campaigns lies in that they are essentially political: they aim at making democracy deliver on its promises by holding elected officials accountable for children's rights and well-being.
2. Strategic communication initiatives at the national level are more likely to succeed if the issues become meaningful at the local level.
3. Harnessing disaggregated data with messages tailored to local communities are key factors for successful communication and advocacy interventions.
4. Children need not be construed as only "objects" of a campaign, but as activist subjects, as was the case with Juanita.
5. When children pose questions, adults tend to listen. When children throw out public challenges, adults tend to respond with a sense of public accountability and responsibility. In this sense, children represent an invaluable resource as health advocates.
6. Mass mediated strategies and tools like Juanita can be used by a wide variety of implementing partners for a wide variety of social topics, galvanizing a process of advocacy, social mobilization, and individual-level behavioural changes.

Notes

1. This chapter builds on the author's previous writings on the role of communication strategies for overcoming childhood vulnerability (Singhal, 2008; Singhal & Howard, 2003; Singhal and Rogers, 1999; 2003), including a presentation the author made in a conference on *Undefended Childhood in Global Contexts* held at Michigan State University in 2008. The author thanks UNICEF's Communication for Development (C4D) Unit in New York for supporting the documentation of this project, and especially acknowledges Colin Fraser and Sonia Restrepo-Estrada for serving as key informants for the Juanita Communication Initiative in Colombia, generously sharing archival material on the campaign. Robert Cohen, Ketan Chitnis, and Rina Gill of UNICEF's C4D also provided helpful comments on a draft version of this manuscript.
2. By the early 1980s breast feading had declined precipitously due to working mothers and aggressive marketing of infant formula by multinationals such as Nestle.
3. Cited in Borstein (2004, p. 248).
4. Later GOBI became GOBI – FFF as food supplements, family planning, and female education were added. See McKee (1992); McKee et al. (2000); and Servaes (1999).
5. Grant realized that under-5 mortality rate was the best science-based proxy for gauging a country's treatment of its youngest citizens.
6. Later, another annual report, *Progress of Nations*, was launched, which judged nations by the protection that they afforded to the growing minds and bodies of their children.
7. See Bornstein (2004).
8. Black (1986; 1996) and Jolly (2001).
9. This draws upon a personal conversation with Colin Fraser and Sonia Restrepo-Estrada in October, 2007; several rounds of follow-up email correspondence; Fraser and Restrepo-Estrada (1994); and Juanita and Related Immunization Campaign in Colombia: Programme Experiences.

Source: http://www.comminit.com/experiences/pds2005/experiences-3185.html. Immunisation Poster Campaign – Colombia Source: http://www.comminit.com/experiences/pds2005/experiences-3300.html .

10. In an email memo to the present author on March 10, 2008.
11. See Fraser and Restrepo-Estrada (1994; 1998)
12. See http://www.unicef.org/colombia/pdf/FactsRigths1a.pdf

References

Black, M. (1996). *Children First: The Story of UNICEF, Past and Present.* New York: Oxford University Press.

Black, M. (1986). *The Children and the Nations.* New York: UNICEF.

Borstein, D. (2004). *How to Change the World: Social Entrepreneurs and the Power of New Ideas.* New York: Oxford University Press.

Fraser, C. and Restrepo-Estrada, S. (1998). *Communicating for Development: Human Change for Survival.* London/New York: I.B. Tauris

Fraser, C. & Restrepo-Estrada, S. (1994). *Juanita: Putting Children in the Electoral Arena. A case-study of advocacy and social mobilisation for children linked to decentralisation and elections in Colombia.* Bogota, Colombia: UNICEF.

Jolly, R. (Ed.) (2001). *Jim Grant: UNICEF visionary.* New York: United Nations Publications.

McKee, N. (1992). *Social Mobilization and Social Marketing in Developing Countries: Lessons for Communicators.* Penang, Malaysia: Southbound.

McKee, N., Manoncourt, E., Chin, S.Y. & Carnegie, R. (Eds.) (2000). *Involving People, Evolving Behaviour.* New York: UNICEF; Penang, Malaysia: Southbound.

Servaes, J. (1999). *Communication for Development: One World, Multiple Cultures.* New Jersey: Hampton Press.

Singhal, A. and Howar, W.S. (Eds.) (2003). *The Children of Africa Confront AIDS: From Vulnerability to Possibility.* Athens, OH: Ohio University Press.

Singhal, A. and Rogers, E.M. (2003). *Combating AIDS: Communication Strategies in Action.* Thousand Oaks, CA: Sage Publications.

Singhal, A. and Rogers, E.M. (1999). *Entertainment-Education: A Communication Strategy for Social Change.* Mahwah, NJ: Lawrence Erlbaum Associates.

Panel Session on
Media Ethics and Social Responsibility

Introduction

Sirkku Kotilainen

For the most part, ethics and social responsibilities have been discussed from the viewpoint of accountabilities in public and global institutions, for example, in global governance, non-governmental organizations and private enterprises (e.g., Ebrahim & Weisband, 2007). Accountability has been widely debated and theorized in the social sciences, but one can say that it is about an organization's position and ethical actions within wide fields of power and social networks, including citizen participation (Lewis, 2007: 133). As an organization, the media are public or private institutions that interact with their audiences, i.e., different groups of people. How, then, do the globalized media take into account their marginalized audiences, especially children and the young? What about national and international media policies?

One can presume that ethically and socially responsible activities belong to the accountabilities of the media – and media policies – if the media are interested in having well-informed, participatory audiences in the future. As such, recognition of children's rights to communication and self-expression, and of enhancement of participatory practices for youngsters and children, is important, for example, possibilities to participate in the production of their own media content. A "strong social responsibility ethos" – as Firdoze Bulbulia (2010) puts it in the newsletter of The International Clearinghouse on Children, Youth and Media – also includes recognition of the importance of developing youth media literacies, i.e., ensuring that young people can critically evaluate and create media.

The presentations of the Research Forum session "Media Ethics and Social Responsibility" highlight the issues of social responsibilities and accountabilities from different angles and different geographical viewpoints, as they focus on several continents around the globe:

Sonia Livingstone takes a look at the European situation: how best to facilitate online opportunities while also reducing or managing the associated risks. She draws on findings from the EU Kids Online research network of 25 European countries to pinpoint four complicating factors that must guide future research and policy priorities, namely the interconnections between (i) online opportunities and online risks, (ii) online and offline risks, (iii) risk and harm, and (iv) sources of vulnerability and resilience.

Divina Frau-Meigs continues the European perspective and states that turning civic apathy into civic agency implies focusing on youth as media consumers, but also as producers and creators of the network cultures online. Civic engagement is positively correlated with media literacy, and the reality of this hyper-connected generation needs to be fully integrated when dealing with media education. She asks, for example, what action plan could be elaborated so that all actors, from inter-governmental organizations to teachers and media activists, could be implicated and could imagine creative partnerships?

Manisha Shelat gives an overview of policy-level efforts to focus on young people in India. She concentrates on some key issues that youth media policy in India needs to address. Some of these issues have a developmental rather than regulatory role in youth media policy, for example, the need to support media education and research. The liberalization of the Indian economy and rapid spread of digital technology have brought about many changes in India, and yet so many deep-rooted structural and cultural aspects have changed very little.

Tatiana Merlo Flores from Argentina presents a study that aims to explain and measure the need to take into account the new demands from the point of view of children and youngsters, based on what they feel, express and perform. One result of the study is an Index of Social Responsibility that measures, for example, the contextualization and problematization of the most important problems that kids and adolescents perceive to be their own. Moreover, the final product is an Index of the processes and levels of audience involvement. She looks forward to fostering – through the media – social and human development as well as respect for children's rights, mainly the right to be included and to participate, and to exert their right as citizens.

Sirkku Kotilainen, Annikka Suoninen, Irma Hirsjärvi and Sara Kolomainen present preliminary results of an ongoing international study on youth media participation. They look at social responsibilities from the viewpoints of young people interacting through media: youngsters' expressions of responsible citizenship through media diaries written and collected in Argentina, Egypt, Finland, India and Kenya in the first half of 2010. The results show, for example, that youngsters' involvement in societal issues is occurring through media worldwide, and that media literacies are being practised in several ways.

References

Bulbulia, Firdoze (2010) Africa's Best Channel for Children, *News on Children, Youth and Media in the World*, No. 1, 2010, The International Clearinghouse on Children, Youth and Media at Nordicom, Göteborg University. Available online: http://www.nordicom.gu.se/cl/publ/letter.php (retrieved 27 September, 2010)

Ebrahim, Alnoor & Weisband, Edward (Eds.) (2007) *Global Accountabilities: Participation, Pluralism, and Public Ethics*. New York: Cambridge University Press

Lewis, David (2007) Bringing in Society, Culture, and Politics: Values and accountability in a Bangladeshi NGO, in Ebrahim, Alnoor & Weisband, Edward (Eds.) *Global Accountabilities: Participation, Pluralism, and Public Ethics*. New York: Cambridge University Press, pp. 131-148

Positioning Children's Interests within Debates over Internet Governance[1]

Sonia Livingstone

As many have observed, the internet promises wonderful opportunities for learning, communicating, participating and having fun; yet the same medium is also a means of bringing into the privacy of the home the very worst of society; most online content and activities fall somewhere – often ambiguously – in between (Livingstone, 2009). Governments worldwide are not only promoting broadband infrastructure and internet use throughout society but they are also making parallel efforts to recognise and address the associated risks. The opportunities and risks afforded by the internet to children and young people have attracted particular attention, itself not always in children's best interests. Indeed, the early regulatory debates, typically led by moral panics about the internet's undermining of childhood innocence, often served to polarise rather than advance policy developments regarding online risks and opportunities.

Since those early days, regulatory debates have matured, seeking neither to establish a wholly new enterprise of online regulation but nor assuming that what holds offline straightforwardly applies online, although as a general principle this latter is accepted (van Dijk, 2006). The evidence base has also developed (as reviewed in Hasebrink, Livingstone, & Haddon, 2009; Internet Safety Technical Task Force, 2008; ITU, 2009), thereby supporting more informed multi-stakeholder deliberations. Developing the evidence base further, so as to understand which risks are encountered by which children and, crucially, when and why harm does or does not result, remains a major research task, along with the related task of identifying which policy solutions are effective – particularly, which can bring about harm reduction without also curtailing children's online opportunities. Linking these tasks is the effort to ensure that research findings are appropriately used by policy makers and other stakeholders in framing internet regulation and governance in the best interests of children.

This article reflects on emerging governance practices in the United Kingdom (UK), European Union (EU) and United States (US), to explore how competing interests are being managed in practice. Specifically, I draw on my experiences in representing the EU Kids Online network in a range of policy settings, including working with the EC's Safer Internet Programme, the UK Council for Child Internet Safety and, before that, the Byron Review (Byron, 2008) and the Internet Watch Foundation in the UK. My aim is thus to combine what Bohman (1991) calls contextualised interpretation, in which the researcher draws on insider (or engaged) knowledge, and rational interpretation, in which the researcher draws on outsider (or independent, critical) knowledge. For a more developed version of these arguments, see Livingstone (2011).

Three starting points should be clarified at the outset. The first is to define children's interests, which I take from the UN Convention on the Rights of the Child (1989), also echoed in the Children's Television Charter (World Summit on Media for Children Foundation, n.d.), and set out in Livingstone (2009a: 211) as a Children's Internet Charter:

1. 'Children should have online contents and services of high quality which are made specifically for them, and which do not exploit them. In addition to entertaining, these should allow children to develop physically, mentally and socially to their fullest potential';
2. 'Children should hear, see and express themselves, their culture, their languages and their life experiences, through online contents and services which affirm their sense of self, community and place';
3. 'Children's online contents and services should promote an awareness and appreciation of other cultures in parallel with the child's own cultural background';
4. 'Children's online contents and services should be wide-ranging in genre and content, but should not include gratuitous scenes of violence and sex';
5. 'Children's online contents and services should be accessible when and where children are available to engage, and/or distributed via other widely accessible media or technologies';
6. 'Sufficient funds must be made available to make these online contents and services to the highest possible standards';
7. 'Governments, production, distribution and funding organizations should recognize both the importance and vulnerability of indigenous online contents and services, and take steps to support and protect it'.

Given this deliberately ambitious conception of children's online interests, a second and complementary starting point is to identify the risks posed to children's interests by the advent of the internet. These have been classified by the EU Kids Online network first in terms of areas of the lifeworld (aggressive, sexual, values, commercial) and, secondly, in terms of the child's role. This is to distinguish content risks (which position the child as recipient), contact risks (in which the child in some way participates, if unwillingly) and conduct risks (where the child is an actor) – see Table 1 (where the cells contain exemplars only) (Livingstone & Haddon, 2009):

Table 1. Risks posed to children's interest in the internet

	Content *Receiving (typically) mass-produced content*	*Contact* *Participating, not necessarily willingly, in a (typically) adult-initiated activity*	*Conduct* *Perpetrator or victim in peer-to-peer exchange*
Aggressive	Violent / gory content	Harassment, stalking	Bullying, hostile peer activity
Sexual	Pornographic content	'Grooming', sexual abuse or exploitation	Sexual harassment, 'sexting'
Values	Racist / hateful content	Ideological persuasion	Negative user-generated content
Commercial	Embedded marketing	Personal data abuse	Gambling, copyright infringement

Balancing opportunities and risks as identified above will not happen by itself. Thus, the third crucial starting point for the present article is to clarify what may be expected of 'governance' and 'regulation'. In this article, I use the term regulation in the broadest sense to refer to the relation between power and the ordering of social behaviour at all levels of society from the transnational organization, the nation-state, the subnational organization or community down to the level of the individual. Without developing the point here (see Livingstone, 2011), I thus position the present arguments in the context of the significant shift underway in developed market economies away from top-down, state-led models of regulation towards a conception of governance that emphasises 'the dynamic structure of rules between actors that are linked in different networks and permanently forced to negotiate, without a center that has the power to command and control' (Donges, 2007). In other words, not only has the internet brought social changes but so too is the nature of regulation and the role of the state changing; the network metaphor, intriguingly, characterises both changes (Castells, 2002).

'We will not regulate the internet'

Yet surprising to some, it is commonly claimed that – as asserted by the UK's then Secretary for State, Media, Culture and Sport, Tessa Jowell, in 2002 and echoed before and since by many others – 'we [society, the UK government] do not intend to regulate the internet' (Commons Hansard, 2002, np). If this statement was intended to forestall debate or quell contestation over internet regulation, it failed, for rapid advances in technological innovation have meant that the rationale, prospects and practicalities of internet regulation have been hotly debated throughout the past decade. So why did Jowell say this, other than for the particular, if still puzzling, reason that she was seeking to justify why the then newly-proposed regulator, the UK's Office of Communications (Ofcom), would not encompass internet regulation along with broadcasting and telecommunications regulation, despite being a converged regulator for a converged communications landscape (Livingstone & Lunt, 2007)?

Civil libertarians, clearly, hoped she – and all others who make similar claims – meant that governments *should not* regulate the internet, to protect freedom of speech and to prevent any growth in censorship. This position holds that arguments in favour of regulation for child protection should be rejected since these threaten to restrict (adult) freedom of expression online. Thus children's needs are placed in tension with adults' needs, and in any such a balancing act of the weak versus the powerful, children will surely lose out. More subtle variants of this position fear that advocacy for child protection opens the door to censorship of speech well beyond that which may harm children and, further, to the state surveillance of citizens.

But, a simple opposition of adult freedoms and children's protection surely undermines recognition of children's positive rights, including their freedom of expression, along with adults' rights to privacy and protection from harm. Indeed, it is possible to distinguish four regulatory goals at stake – support for children's rights to freedom and to protection and support for adult's rights to freedom and to protection. Can policy makers and society agree a strategy that avoids pitting a weaker constituency against a stronger? For those following the UN Convention on the Rights of the Child (UN, 1989), the issue is that of maximizing children's online freedom while minimizing their exposure to online harm, as already noted above. Adult freedoms and rights to protection are also instantiated in national and international frameworks. The challenge is to recognise all four of these regulatory goals, not just those of child protection and adult freedom.

A second reading of Jowell's claim is that we *cannot* regulate the internet, because it is a vast and global technology, more horizontal than vertical in its structure and highly impractical to monitor. As Negroponte famously stated in 1996, '[t]he Internet cannot be regulated. It's not that laws aren't relevant, it's that the nation-state is not relevant' (cited in Drezner, 2004, p. 481). To be sure, international bodies find it difficult to attain and sustain consensus, and they typically lack the power of nation-states to enforce compliance or punish transgression. Yet this version of the claim that internet cannot be regulated tends to assume a model of top-down, command and control regulation, notwithstanding the analysis of Donges' (quoted earlier) and others regarding the growth of softer but more pervasive governance, this in turn developing partly in response to the shifting balance between national and international bodies and processes (see also Jessop, 2002). However, at least in developed countries, there are signs that international models of regulation increasingly influence rather than merely recognize or respond to the regulatory regimes of nation-states; the shifting role of regional governments such as the European Commission or the power of international organisations such as ICANN (the Internet Corporation of Assigned Names and Numbers), International Telecommunications Union or Internet Governance Forum is worth watching closely in this regard.

A third interpretation of Jowell's claim is that 'we do not intend to regulate the internet' because there is *no need* to regulate it – in short, because there is no problem. It is this argument that a wide range of child welfare professionals, children's charities, teachers and educationalists, clinicians, parenting organizations, social workers and law enforcement are marshalling their evidence to undermine, with the focus on producing empirical evidence to document the nature, incidence and severity of online harm. Nonetheless, and despite a rapidly growing evidence base regarding online risks encountered by children, the evidence remains and will remain contested, not least because the methodologies available to research children's online experiences are imperfect and because judgements of scale, reach and severity of harm are particularly hard to ground in rigorous findings, even though these judgements are vital if policy interventions are to be proportionate. More positively, considerable efforts are now being made to generate and evaluate evidence,[2] and that which is available is no less robust than for other areas of risk for children, where regulatory protections are taken for granted (Madge & Barker, 2007).

To many critics, a fourth and final reading of Jowell's claim is the most plausible, namely that it is not that we shouldn't or can't or see no need to regulate the internet but that we *will not* regulate it, because the commercial interests at stake are substantial and, while international in scale, profits largely accrue to certain dominant nation-states. Indeed, one may even suggest that, lying behind the strongly asserted arguments that one should not regulate the internet, for reasons of free speech, or that nation states cannot hope to regulate the internet in practical terms or that the evidence base for online harm to children is flawed or inadequate, it is this argument that really drives the debate. This argument, then, treats the internet as any other business, a source of both innovation and revenue, and thus one that requires a liberalized market not hampered by 'red tape' and 'unnecessary' interference from the state. Undoubtedly, as an argument in its own right, this last is supported by many market liberals and most of the internet industry.

What is most difficult in debating internet regulation, I suggest, is not the nature of any of these four arguments but rather the persistent confusion among them, with advocates of any one position tending to shift ground and take up another position when the criticism becomes fierce, and with many arguing against internet regulation without clarifying which position they endorse or, even, the conception of regulation they are relying upon. The result can be some unholy alliances – between radical freedom of speech advocates and the industry, for example, and some unfair accusations – that to advocate child protection is to favour censorship, for example. As Szoka and Thierer (2009, p. 1) point out, in multi-stakeholder deliberations, it can too often seem that 'online privacy, child safety, free speech and anonymity are on a collision course.'

'The internet has always been regulated'

Yet, as Tambini observed, citing Lessig's (1999) ground-breaking work on *Code and other laws of cyberspace* published well before Jowell's claim, 'of course, the internet has always been regulated' (Tambini et al. 2008, p. 5). To address the four arguments in turn, it should be noted first that, despite routine reference to the American constitution in defence of an anti-regulatory position, there have always been legitimate restrictions on freedom of speech, even in the U.S. – for example, restricting the dissemination of child sexual abuse images; and such restrictions are being debated anew with the expansion of hostile, bullying and harmful speech in peer-to-peer networks among both children and adults (Collier, 2009). However, as Etzioni (2010, p. 162) observes,

> both individual rights and public safety must be protected. Given that on many occasions advancing one requires some curtailment of the other, the key question is what the proper balance between these two cardinal values should be. The concept of balance is found in the [USA's] Fourth Amendment...

Second, there is growing optimism that international organizations can cooperate to good effect in shaping the internet's global infrastructure – witness the increasing interest in and support for the Internet Governance Forum, notwithstanding that it has no decision-making powers, or the 2009 shift of ICANN from American to international management (ICANN, 2009). Perhaps most telling in this instance is the work of the European Commission in implementing self-regulation of mobile and social networking operators. This work and related work on privacy, personal data abuse and information rights led the European Union to endorse the ministerial Prague Declaration in April 2009, which advocates a 'holistic' cooperation across countries, including the promotion of 'a safer online environment by fostering and assessing private sector self-regulatory initiatives, and by supporting initiatives providing parental control tools as well as positive content for children' (Czech Presidency of the Council of the EU, 2009, p. 7).

Third, as evidence grows that online experiences may harm the vulnerable, including but not only children, more and more organisations (ranging from law enforcement to children's charities, schools and clinicians, businesses and governmental bodies) are extending their traditional regulatory activities from offline to online domains in order to exercise their duty of care to their clients, customers or public. In other words, it is evident to more and more bodies going about their ordinary (offline) business that the internet, far from posing no problem at all, is making a substantial difference to their operation and not always for the better.

Fourth and relatedly, there are growing calls for regulation from business as well as third sector and state actors to impose greater obligations on online service providers so as to ensure online transactions are secure, copyright infringements are enforced, personal data are well-managed and brands have their reputations protected. The ethical discourses of corporate social responsibility departments may carry little force, but the commercial interests at stake in protecting the brand carry significantly more. Consider the struggle between Facebook and its users over privacy controls (boyd & Hargittai, 2010), the effort put in by internet service providers to implement terms and conditions for customer care that meet the satisfaction of consumers, the concerted action of the industry to eradicate illegal content or to ensure that financial frauds and scams are minimised, the development of parental tools and guidance by providers keen to be perceived as 'family friendly'. All these and many other actions may be read cynically as attempts to ward off state regulation or to compete in the domestic market rather than as positive actions to advance the interest of children; nonetheless, this latter may still be the outcome.

What regulation exists?

Recalling that EU Kids Online classified online risks to children in terms of content, contact and conduct risks, the regulatory approach emerging in each domain can be summarised as follows, recalling the complex mix of governance arrangements that fall under the heading of 'regulation', extending well beyond top-down state interventions. First, since contact risks, especially online grooming and paedophile activity, are phenomena for which society has least tolerance, these are widely though far from universally addressed by criminal law. Such legislative solutions are, however, generally reserved for high risk circumstances, since they also have the effect of constraining freedoms. The difficulty, therefore, is that they tend to presume that risk behaviours inevitably lead to harm, though in reality, children make many contacts online and only a few result in harmful encounters, albeit that these may be disastrous for their victims. Complicating matters, then, most online contacts, including most of those which lead to offline meetings, afford positive experiences for children, valuable therefore as part of their right to 'freedom of assembly'. It is this, over and above the challenges of international law enforcement, which complicates the regulatory task of using legislative solutions to minimise contact risks to children, for it cannot easily be ascertained in advance which contacts are benign and which are harmful. Nor does research as yet pinpoint the particularly vulnerable children from among the many sufficiently resilient to avoid and/or cope with potential contact risks.

'Content is by far the most contentious area of media policy' (Freedman, 2008, p. 122), far more than has been the case for dealing with contact risks. Difficult questions of community standards and cultural values, the basis of any filtering of content, are exacerbated in a transnational context. Yet there remains widespread public concern that, for example, explicit images of heterosexual, homosexual, teenage, violent or bestial sexual acts are readily accessible via a simple Google search. Although traditionally tolerated in print or film, children's access to such content has traditionally been restricted, whether through regulatory or social means (Millwood Hargrave & Livingstone, 2009). Already in the short history of the internet, regulators and industry have experimented with diverse initiatives for managing the conditions of access to inappropriate content, searching for the online equivalent of these familiar (and largely uncontroversial) means of managing content offline. Yet whether implemented through white lists, black lists, walled gardens, international content rating systems, more or less subtle filters applied at different points in the distribution chain or even outright censorship, many of these initiatives have failed. Nonetheless, filters, portals or walled gardens of one kind or another remain the preferred solution on all sides, especially if installed by parents within the household, and so efforts continue to improve these (Deloitte & European Commission, 2008; Thierer, 2009). Whether or not such filters should be, by default, turned on when the computer or internet service is first purchased, by analogy with virus protection or spam filters, remains contentious, even though any adult purchaser could easily turn them off.

More recently, the risk agenda has been broadened to encompass not only how adult society may harm children but also how children's own conduct may hurt or harm each other (and even themselves). For example, bullying has long been understood as including not only physical but also verbal and visual harassment among peers (e.g., by manipulation and circulation of images). Going beyond the important point that online bullying is often continuous with offline bullying (i.e., the bully pursues his or her victim across contexts on and offline, even into their bedroom), it is increasingly acknowledged that cyberbullying differs from offline bullying insofar as it simultaneously affords anonymity to the bully and publicity to the humiliation of the victim (Smith, Mahdavi, & Carvalho, 2008; Vandebosch & Cleemput, 2009). For regulators and, indeed, the industry, conduct risks are the least amenable, for they occur peer-to-peer and are not easily (or cheaply) observed. Thus, most regulatory efforts focus on raising awareness (among parents), encouraging considerate codes of conduct (among children), facilitating peer support (via mentoring) and providing sources of support (helplines). Much effort also is directed at making young people themselves, rather than industry, self-regulating. Yet as with any effort to increase knowledge and awareness, the reach of such initiatives is often uneven and unequal, while the translation into behaviour change is uncertain (Livingstone, 2009).

Conclusion

A recent survey of policies in place suggests considerable diversity in governance regimes worldwide, although too little is known about which forms of regulation are effective in meeting public policy goals (International Telecommunication Union, 2009). It is clear, however, that in many developed countries, regulatory regimes are generally moving towards a 'softer', more flexible, more indirect approach that disperses the role of the state, that establishes more accountable national and transnational regulatory bodies and that engages civil society (including children's welfare bodies, parenting groups and youth organisations) in processes of governance. In parallel, considerable efforts are being made to devolve regulation down to the level of the individual, encouraging in individuals (parents, teachers, children) the responsibility to conduct their own personal risk assessment. As Beck (1986/2005) put it, in the 'risk society', risk has been individualised. Consequently, everyone 'need[s] to adopt a calculative prudent personal relation to fate now conceived in terms of calculable dangers and avertable risks' (Rose, 1996, p. 58).

But Beck and Rose are critical of a situation popularly described as 'empowering' for the individual. First, it tasks individuals with sometimes burdensome responsibilities for which they may lack resources or for which resources are unequally distributed. Second, the dispersal of regulation from state to self-regulation means that governance approaches 'commonly lack[s] the procedural fairness and protection for fundamental rights that are encouraged by independent judicial and parliamentary scrutiny' (Brown, 2010; see also Schultz & Held, 2006). To equip individuals, governance regimes place increasing reliance on media or digital literacy policies, as in, for instance, the EU's Digital Agenda (European Commission, 2010; for the rising importance of media literacy as a tool of regulation, see Livingstone, 2009). To introduce principles of fairness, transparency and accountability into self-regulation, governance regimes often include some degree of oversight – where 'oversight' refers to 'second-order processes' which 'examine, review, and correct first-order processes'; this, Etzioni (2010, p. 175) argues is the second crucial balance to be achieved in regulation – 'not between the public interest and rights, but between the supervised and the supervisors' (p. 174).

Recent examples include the EC Safer Internet Programme's independent evaluation of filtering technology (Deloitte & European Commission, 2008), of the Mobile Operators' Code (PricewaterhouseCoopers, 2009) and, most recently, of the Social Networking Guidance (European Commission, 2009). In relation to both sets of policies – those addressing individuals' competence and those addressing firms' responsibilities – consideration for children's risks and opportunities online has led the way; nonetheless, the resulting governance approaches are couched in more general terms, benefiting (or otherwise) the wider public. Intriguingly, there is a degree of complementarity between media literacy policy (which is necessarily limited by the bounds of individuals' competence) and industry self-regulation (which is expected to step in as required to support the needs of individuals). For example, if children and parents understand and respect the rule that those under 13 years old are not permitted on Facebook or MySpace, then the social networking site need take no action; but insofar as individuals do not understand or respect this rule, the site is expected to take action as part of its self-regulatory guidance. Similarly, to the extent that parents lack the skill to install filtering technology, then technology providers are expected to redesign their products and provide a help desk. And so forth. In other words, the affordances of the online interface can be designed to fit more or less well with the literacies of users, and the result is more or less enabling or undermining of use.

In cases where the risk at stake is unambiguous or uncontroversial, most would agree that the online environment should be designed so that little or no reliance is placed on the individual's competence: examples might include preventing paedophiles from using social networking sites popular with children or ensuring that financial fraud is eliminated by securing payment systems; to rely on the competence of children in such cases seems unnecessarily hazardous. In such cases, a strategy of 'safety by design' (as already occurs in offline in the domains of engineering, urban planning, health and safety at work) can reduce risk without affecting opportunities. But in cases where the risk at stake is ambiguous (for example, making new online contacts may be beneficial but may be dangerous) or controversial (for example, is seeing online pornography harmless or harmful?) or dependent on circumstances (for example, most children are not tempted to take the advice of pro-harm sites but a few are vulnerable to such advice), the online environment cannot simply be designed to be risk free, for this is to undermine individual opportunities. Even then, 'safety by design' can reasonably be employed to reduce risks provided that individuals' choices are not prevented entirely: examples might include the use of default filters that can, if desired, be overridden, or programmed-in reminders on sending images or posting personal information to think carefully before acting. Though the effect of such features is likely to increase media literacy, this remains to be established by empirical research.

As should be apparent, in this article I have sought to move beyond a framework for children's interests that simply polarises consideration of online risks and opportunities, also rejecting a framework for regulation that simply polarises top-down restrictive regulation and laissez-faire avoidance of regulation in the interests of (adult) freedoms. The task for researchers, therefore, is no longer primarily to chart the possible harms experienced by children online, in order to provoke regulatory intervention. Rather, a more complex research agenda is opened up, matching the complexity of the emerging governance regime as well as the complexity of children's interests online. In short, researchers should investigate (and many now are investigating) the conditions of childhood that mean some children explore online opportunities and become resilient to the risks while (a few) others get hurt. However, they should also investigate (and here much more research is needed) the conditions of the online environment that render some sites more or less beneficial or hazardous, as a function of their design and institutional infrastructure as well as their practices of use, and some regulatory tools and strategies more or less effective, depending in part on their implications for media literacy.

Notes

1. The article is based with permission on an abbreviated form of Livingstone (2011), 'Regulating the internet in the interests of children: Emerging European and international approaches', in Mansell & Raboy (Eds.) *The handbook on global media and communication policy* (Oxford: Wiley-Blackwell). It also draws material published in Livingstone, S. (2009) *Children and the Internet: Great expectations, challenging realities* (Cambridge: Polity).
2. See in particular the ongoing work of the EU Kids Online network at www.eukidsonline.net.

References

Beck, U. (1986/2005). *Risk society: Towards a new modernity*. London: Sage Publications.

Bohman, J. (1991). *New philosophy of social science: Problems of indeterminacy*. Cambridge: Polity Press.

boyd, d., & Hargittai, E. (2010). Facebook privacy settings: Who cares? *First Monday, 15*(8).

Brown, I. (2010). Internet self-regulation and fundamental rights. *Index on Censorship, 1*, 98-106.

Byron, T. (2008). *Safer children in a digital world: The report of the Byron Review*. London: Department for Children, Schools and Families, and the Department for Culture, Media and Sport.

Castells, M. (2002). *The Internet galaxy*. Oxford: Oxford University Press.

Collier, A. (2009). School cyberbully wins free-speech case. *Journal*. Retrieved from http://www.netfamilynews.org/2009/12/school-cyberbully-wins-free-speech-case.html

Commons Hansard (2002). "House of Commons Hansard Debates for 3 Dec 2002 (pt 14)", accessed 01/01/2010, http://www.parliament.the-stationery-office.co.uk/pa/cm200203/cmhansrd/vo021203/debtext/21203-14.htm

Czech Presidency of the Council of the EU (2009). "Prague declaration: A new European approach for safer Internet for children" (20 April), Prague: Ministerial Conference 'Safer Internet for Children – fighting together against illegal content and conduct on-line', accessed 03/01/2010, http://ec.europa.eu/information_society/activities/sip/docs/events/prague_decl.pdf.

Deloitte & European Commission (2008). *Safer Internet: Protecting our children on the net using content filtering and parental control techniques: A report prepared for the Safer Internet Plus Programme*. Belgium: Deloitte Enterprise Risk Services, accessed 03/01/2010, http://www.sip-bench.eu/index.html .

Donges, P. (2007). The new institutionalism as a theoretical foundation of media governance. *Communications: The European Journal of Communication Research*, 32(3), 325-329.

Drezner, D. W. (2004). The global governance of the Internet: Bringing the State back in. *Political Science Quarterly*, 119(3), 477-498.

Etzioni, A. (2010). Privacy and security policy in the digital age. In W. R. Newman (Eds.), *Media, technology, and society*. Ann Arbour: University of Michigan Press (163-178).

European Commission (2009). "Safer social networking principles for the EU", Brussels: European Commission, accessed 03/01/2010, http://ec.europa.eu/information_society/activities/social_networking/docs/sn_principles.pdf.

European Commission. (2010). *A digital agenda for Europe*. Brussels: European Commission.

Freedman, D. (2008). *The politics of media policy*. Cambridge: Polity Press.

Hasebrink, U., Livingstone, S., & Haddon, L. (2009). *Comparing children's online opportunities and risks across Europe: Cross-national comparisons for EU Kids Online*. Deliverable D3.2 for the EC Safer Internet plus programme (Second edition). London: EU Kids Online, accessed 01/01/2010, http://eprints.lse.ac.uk/24368/ .

ICANN (2009). *Affirmation of commitments by the United States Department of Commerce and the Internet corporation for assigned names and numbers*. Washington, DC: Internet Corporation for Assigned Names and Numbers, accessed 03/01/2010, http://www.icann.org/en/documents/affirmation-of-commitments-30sep09-en.htm .

International Telecommunication Union (2009). *Child online protection*. Geneva: International Telecommunication Union, accessed 03/01/2010, http://www.itu.int/osg/csd/cybersecurity/gca/cop/cop-brochure.pdf .

Internet Safety Technical Task Force. (2008). *Enhancing Child Safety and Online Technologies: Final Report of the ISTTF to the Multi-State Working Group on Social Networking of State Attorney Generals of the United States*. Cambridge, MA: Berkman Center for Internet and Society, Harvard University.

Jessop, B. (2002). *The future of the capitalist state*. Cambridge: Polity Press.

Lessig, L. (1999). *Code and other laws of cyberspace*. New York: Basic Books.

Livingstone, S. (2009). *Children and the Internet: Great expectations, challenging realities*. Cambridge: Polity Press.

Livingstone, S. (2009a). A rational for positive online content for children. *Communication Research Trends*, 28 (3), 12-17.

Livingstone (2011) 'Regulating the internet in the interests of children: Emerging British, European and international approaches', in Mansell & Raboy (Eds.) *The handbook on global media and communication policy* (Oxford: Wiley-Blackwell).

Livingstone, S., & Lunt, P. (2007). Representing citizens and consumers in media and communications regulation. *The Annals of the American Academy of Political and Social Science, 611*, 51-65.

Livingstone, S., & Haddon, L. (2009). *EU kids online: Final report*. Deliverable D6.5 for the EC Safer Internet plus programme. London: EU Kids Online, accessed 01/01/2010, http://eprints.lse.ac.uk/24372/ .

Madge, N., & Barker, J. (2007). *Risk & childhood*. London: The Royal Society for the Encouragement of Arts, Manufactures & Commerce.

Millwood Hargrave, A., & Livingstone, S. (2009). *Harm and offence in media content: A review of the empirical literature* (Second edition). Bristol: Intellect Press.

PricewaterhouseCoopers (2009). *European framework for safer mobile use by younger teenagers and children*. London: PricewaterhouseCoopers, accessed 01/01/2010, http://www.gsmeurope.org/documents/PwC_Implementation_Report.pdf.

Rose, N. (1996). Governing 'advanced' liberal democracies. In A. Barry, T. Osborne & N. Rose (Eds.), *Foucault and political reason: Liberalism, neo-liberalism and rationalities of government* (37-64). London: UCL Press.

Schulz, W., & Held, T. (2006). Together they are strong? Co-regulatory approaches for the protection of minors within the European Union. In U. Carlsson (Ed.), *Regulation, awareness, empowerment: Young people and harmful media content in the digital age* (49-65). Göteborg: Nordicom.

Smith, P. K., Mahdavi, J., & Carvalho, M. (2008). Cyberbullying: its nature and impact in secondary school pupils. *Journal of Child Psychology and Psychiatry, 49*(4), 376-385.

Szoka, B., & Thierer, A. (2009). COPPA 2.0: The new battle over privacy, age verification, online safety & free speech, *Progress on Point, 16*(11), accessed 03/01/2010, http://pff.org/issues-pubs/pops/2009/pop16.11-COPPA-and-age-verification.pdf.

Tambini, D., Leonardi, D., & Marsden, C. (2008). *Codifying cyberspace: Communications self-regulation in the age of Internet convergence*. London: Routledge.

Thierer, A. (2009). *Parental controls & online child protection: A survey of tools and methods*. Washington, DC: The Progress & Freedom Foundation.

United Nations (1989). *Convention on the rights of the child*, accessed 29/1/2008, http://www2.ohchr.org/english/law/crc.htm.

Van Dijk, J. A. G. M. (2006). "Law", in J. A. G. M. Van Dijk (Ed.), *The network society: Social aspects of new media* (127-155). London: Sage Publications.

Vandebosch, H., & Cleemput, K. V. (2009). Cyberbullying among youngsters: profiles of bullies and victims. *New Media & Society, 11*(8), 1349-1371.

World Summit on Media for Children Foundation. (n.d.). Children's television charter, accessed 05/8/2010, http://www.wsmcf.com/charters/charter.htm

Attaching Media Education to Human Rights by Socializing Young People to Ethics Online

Competences and E-strategies

Divina Frau-Meigs

With the turn of the third millennium, after years of pioneering work and struggle at the margins, media education has come to the attention of policy-makers. Definitions, curriculum development and training materials no longer are questions of interest for communities of practice alone: they are defining options for the future and require strategies that can be shared, tested and adopted in a spirit of social change that goes beyond school reform and youth employment. Regional initiatives have taken place, such as the European Commission's recommendation that all member states have to provide national assessments on the level of media literacy of their citizens (2007), the First Conference on Media Education of the Middle East in Saudi Arabia (2007), or the First Africa Media Literacy Conference in Nigeria (2008) (Frau-Meigs & Torrent, 2009).

But the conditions of feasibility of such a comprehensive view of media education, as a lifelong process, inside and outside schools, need to be articulated very carefully, for successful implementation. They require to be critical of the current public discourse and policies around it. They also entail to anchor media education within an engaging vision around the master narrative provided by the human rights framework, lest it should be associated with neo-liberal policies exclusively. Finally, they require to take into consideration "the cyberist moment", i.e., the third millennium shift from Web 1.0 to Web 2.0, characterized by a move from a centralized technology that allowed for basic interaction, around e-mails and blogs, to a decentralized network of speedy broadband applications, browsers and social platforms, that encourage broader participation.

In contrast to the Web 1.0 client-server model, where providers supplied tethered applications to consumers, Web 2.0 uses distributed network architecture via peer-to-peer coordination (P2P) and shared resources (such as disc storage or network bandwidth) for users who are both suppliers and consumers of information. In this paradigm shift, from the post-modernist era to the cyberist era, the behaviour of the end-users, as they become contributors and producers of information, tends to move from an alphabetical culture to a visual culture, from media as spectacles to media as services. Education tends to be seen as the means to create the workforce of the Information Society, in the third industrial revolution, built around data mining and processing. The future direction of this paradigm shift is of primary importance for media education as a sense-making process and as a collective practice (Frau-Meigs, 2011a, 2011b).

Criticizing the current public discourse on media education

The sweet candy around the bitter pill

For such is the current context, as deregulation policies seem to consider media education as a panacea, whatever the political spectrum under consideration. In Europe, a series of measures have been taken that point to a Digital Agenda: the European Union's Audiovisual Media Services Directive (formerly Television without Frontiers), that mentions media literacy in its paragraph 37 (2007); the communication of the European Commission on the obligation to follow-up and report on national policies (2007); and the European Parliament resolution that relates media literacy to digital access, inclusion and participation (2008). Some countries like France have added media literacy to ICT (Information and Communication Technology) education as one of the core competences in schools. Media education seems to be a concession granted by the neo-liberal forces to mitigate their commercial conquests over state regulation (less emphasis on quotas, more inclusion of product placement, ...) – the sweet candy around the bitter pill. For such policies promote self-regulation and place the responsibility of media risks on the individual. They tend to disengage the public sector and the private interests, as they place control in the hands of intermediate entities, such as the media regulatory bodies. The leading example is Ofcom (the independent regulator and competition authority for communications industries) in England that spears the movement as media literacy has become part of its missions, since the UK Communication Act of 2003 (Lunt & Livingstone, forthcoming).

Hence, the risk for the implementation of media education policies lies in their being used as a lever to weaken market regulations, in particular those concerning the protection of children, consumers and personal data, historically acquired by the public after heated debates on manipulative advertising or harmful content. Since it has become acceptable to place products, it seems fair enough to teach about advertising; since consumer protections are lowered, it has become tolerable to teach about consumption practices. The implied idea is that education is not a deterrence to consumption; the other implied idea is that protection is no longer a citizen right but a paid-for service (Frau-Meigs, 2011a).

Under the buzzwords of participation and empowerment, two other phenomena are happening, relatively unquestioned in the public sphere: the self-regulation of the audience and the semi-privatization of media education. The audience is consistently constructed as a consumer, not a citizen and is therefore expected to treat media as services and to adjust to the self-regulation of the market vindicated by the media companies. In this context media education is construed as self-regulation by the audience, which has to deal individually with the privatization of risk online and offline. Self-regulation is supposed to foster self-help solutions, in the form of privacy-enhancing technologies and security tools for instance, provided by the market, for a price. Furthermore, media education is being privatized, partly because it is not fully acknowledged in public school curricula therefore leading to package deals prepared by private publishers or operators and partly because of the unquestioned acceptance of the technological control of media devices over human agency, especially when supported by market-dominated e-learning strategies, where media education is confused with ICT education and is run via proprietary platforms, even in public schools.

Privatization of risks, rights and services

To these trends, an additional one has to be adjoined, privatization of rights, as a secondary, unexpected effect of deregulation, with the attendant risk that inequalities and info-poverty related to access and content may increase the digital divide. Indeed, the challenges raised by the new communication services as to respect of rights carry beyond the nevertheless essential questions of pluralism, freedom of expression, privacy or protection of minors. The new digital services present the overall risk that the rights which are protected in the public domain of the real world are subcontracted to private interests in the virtual sphere, thus compelling individuals to buy them as services, instead of enjoying them as free, unalienable civil liberties (Rifkin, 2000; Rotenberg, 2000). Such is the case of protection of minors that comes today integrated in “Internet security packages” that include anti-virus and anti-spam, such as the ones offered by Norton or McAfee (Frau-Meigs, 2011a).

Due to the new dichotomies of the cyberist moment around access and ownership vs. the preservation of privacy and freedom, the actual fight for media education promoters and activists may be in preventing fundamental universal rights from being turned into mere commercial services. This all the more so as globalization facilitates trade to the detriment of rights (making services migrate to countries that have little respect for them). This kind of blind spot in the public discourse is partly due to the fact that such new media services are developing within the context and mindset of the United States, where most of them are being invented and legally located. For both legal purposes and pragmatic commercial problem-solving, rights have been and still are construed as property, as exemplified by the American privacy model, where personal data can be sold to third parties or be part of a stringent Digital Rights Management system. As Daniel Solove acknowledges, “Loss of property seems to be more readily recognized by courts today than the amorphous feelings of embarrassment or loss of dignity” (Solove, 2008: 156). And yet, in a European Human Rights perspective, the challenges of new media and services in cyberspace strongly link rights to dignity and as such they are unalienable.

The privatization of rights and services is also connected to a budding cyberist society that has internalized the digital networks' production of risk. There is no ethical questioning of what happens to individuals forced to engage in self-protection when enormous corporations are endowed with legal and political lobbying capacities to crush their attempts at protest or independence. There is no consideration for class inequalities and information asymmetries as only people with considerable wealth at their disposal will be able to maintain their dignity and integrity, whereas poor people or young people will fall prey to all sorts of abuse. A failure to consider the problems attendant upon the privatization of risks and rights can entail the failure of the whole social fabric that media education proponents and activists have been fighting for since the pioneering stages.

The risk thus is not where expected, as often with the media. This situation implies to take a new perspective on rights as "values" that are both normative and generative in the Digital Agenda of the so-called "Information Society". In social and cognitive terms, values provide common references that can be shared and tested in a given society and are associated with the representation of reality in its collective mind. They also have implications for the interpretation ascribed to an event or a piece of information as well as the creation of a public debate when there is an ethical doubt or a cognitive conflict (Tomasello, 1999; Harrison & Huntington, 2000).

Putting human rights development in a generative perspective does not go without challenges, as the Universal Declaration of Human Rights celebrated its 60th anniversary in 2008. It is not fully stabilized internationally but it is one of the most encompassing collective frameworks yet (and, arguably, like democracy, the least worst of all evils). The cyberist moment holds the potential of developing, at the international level, a regulation of media that is not connected to commercial media law, but to universal human rights. The cyberist moment is a unique opportunity to do so, as those rights are reaching some maturity and are meeting the development of ICT-driven media that could allow their proper application at international level.

This approach has been underplayed or even rejected in the past by media education promoters and activists, understandably so as they were primarily preoccupied with establishing its legitimacy within schools and curricula. And yet there is a stronger and stronger trend to associate media education to citizenship, so as to construe the user as something more than just a consumer, as exemplified by the Council of Europe's Recommendation on *Empowering Children in the New Information and Communications Environment* (2006). Yet associating human rights to media education implies to move away from a normative vision of human rights as rather abstract, top-down moral principles, and to move to a more operational, bottom-up ethical values. Such a perspective promotes autonomy and cooperation so as to ascertain the consequences of one's actions in everyday life and to evaluate what is good and equitable for all according to the situation. This felt experience of rights as values is what can allow, in the long term, real and effective empowerment and participation (Frau-Meigs, 2011a).

Due to the nature of new digital media and communication services, their focus on codes, sites, cases, simulations, representations and networks, there are options for such implementation of media education. As more and more people join cyberist activities, and as more and more cyberist activities have real-life effects (intended and unintended), there is a need to associate media education and human rights in a heuristic and generative process. Such a process can help stir media education away from just being self-management within the market sphere and self-defence within the political sphere.

The felt experience of ethics and socialization to rights and risks

In such a context, part of the weight of responsibility for change eschews on to communities of practice in the civic sphere, where civil society initiatives at the grassroots may use this critical discourse to propose viable alternatives that articulate rights and values. The community of researchers is producing an increasing amount of studies on the emergence of online social norms, though the social use of ethics by young people tends to be understudied. Paying attention to incidence of risk is less common but a year-long virtual ethnography of a French game platform called Feerik suggests several characteristics about the online ethical practices of young people. Incidence of risk is mitigated by the presence of various mediators such as "self-designated monitors", "clan leaders", "group moderators" and "last resort authorities". Several types of actions and behaviours afford a variety of learning events such as "codes of conduct", "warnings", "preventive strategies" and "peer arbitration" (Frau-Meigs & Meigs, 2009).

Such research suggests that the felt experience of ethics, through practice and interaction with "ethically-minded" others, can be developed online and offline, in spite of the incidence of risk. Young people especially can be drilled to be wary of the dangers on the Internet. They can integrate this knowledge via their network practices, to the point that protective behaviour becomes more and more implicit. In fact, self-regulation is reinforced by self-protection, partly due to public awareness campaigns in the media (which suggests that protection policies also may yield positive results).

The socialization process

The much-touted peer-to-peer monitoring seems to be in fact a combination of peer-moderating and peer-protecting, which implies a high level of awareness of both risks and norms. This combination is very important for building trust and then engaging in friendly interactions. It confirms the bottom-up approach to ethics as initiated and enforced by participants who are on an equal footing because they are players first of all, whatever their age and their position of authority (which may include game developers or site operators). The meaning of the word "peer" becomes enriched: it doesn't refer to people of the same age necessarily, but rather to people who partake of a situation willingly, the situation thus establishing the "peerness" – a process that also suggests that people look closely at each other, constantly (the meaning of the verb "to peer").

Research on the ethical practices of young people on the networks also tends to show that ethics can be a means to experience human rights principles, as an explicit series of values and behaviours. It seems that the non-ethical attitudes that occur are not so much transgressions (wilful breaking of the norms) or dis-engagement from these norms because they do not seem to apply in virtual reality, but rather a result of the absence of transmission of these norms. When they are transmitted, they tend to be accepted. This also suggests that ethics act as a kind of heuristics that facilitate transmission. Transmission then is a process that cumulates over time, where the interaction with the technological tool is taken together with the mediation of others, in such a way that it is the norms and not so much the risks that are assimilated by young people.

In this cognitive light, socialization appears as a process of internalization where several pieces of information are recycled, remixed and re-used in the context of communication, to be put together into a dynamic repertoire of strategies for ethical conduct. Socialization sensitizes young people and adults alike to norms more than to risks, and prepares them not to accept just any norms, unquestioned. The process can be seen as having multiple steps, as a series of specific cognitive assessments that may reinforce positive attitudes to ethics and values:

1. Engagement: is part of the motivation to use ICT-driven media, as they solicit attention and participation via moral dilemmas and cognitive conflicts.

2. Anticipation: is also part of the felt experience of ethics as people build expectations increasing the feeling of agency and self-control over the situation.

3. Interpretation: is part of the process of appraisal, as people evaluate the situation, the agents, the interactions and their consequences. It is also important as it builds skills for evaluating the reliability of sources and of helpers, which consolidates trust.

4. Reflexivity: is connected to practices accumulated through time. Recounting of the observations to others increases self-awareness about the process of self-protection and of self-expression.

5. Performance: is encouraged by the media as they facilitate possibilities for people to assume other identities, via avatars and pseudos. They can have thus a better understanding of social roles and expectations about attitudes and values.

6. Co-construction: is an added value as people can buttress each other's knowledge and bring in their cultural context; they do not just rely on individual empowerment but also use some elements of social account-

ability and collective responsibility. This alleviates the stress of ethics put on the sole responsibility of the individual, be it of children or adults.

7. Revision: is part of socialization as one becomes aware that values and ethical positions need to be reviewed and sometimes revisited. For instance, the whole notion of protection is being revisited online: it is being affected by the debate on parental control and filtering and endorsed by the different actors at stake, in an empowerment framework (Frau-Meigs & Meigs, 2009).

The reality of this hyper-connected socialization process needs to be fully integrated when dealing with media education in the cyberist moment. Young people are indeed "digital natives" as Mark Prensky (2001) has said, but they are helped along the way by digital immigrants so as not to remain digital naïves.

The repertoire of e-strategies

The growing presence of virtual environments as locations and means for communication also needs to be taken into account when defining online competences. The Web 2.0 allows for play, simulation and augmented reality to foster cultural remix and multimodal circulation, as young people can navigate the web looking for help or additional resources. Researchers all insist on embracing their cognitive capacities to help them improve their tacit knowledge of the media and to attach them to a repertoire of e-strategies that are embedded in the tasks that the dynamic platforms have designed in a very user-friendly manner:

- Play can be related to problem solving;
- Simulation can help test dynamic models of real-world processes;
- Content-aggregation encourages the endorsing of alternative identities for self-discovery and self-assembly;
- Sampling shows understanding via the sampling and remixing of media outputs;
- Multitasking supports interaction with a variety of media tools and options;
- Pooling contributes to distributed intelligence by aggregating knowledge and media resources for common goals;
- Transmedia navigation favours control over the knowledge that is available in the public domain and beyond;
- Networking facilitates search and distribution of information;
- Peer-to-peer coordination fosters negotiation and can take place across communities, for alternative processes and generation of innovative solutions (adapted from Jenkins, 2009; Frau-Meigs, 2011a).

Such an approach, according to Jenkins (2009), may lead to participatory cultures but the notion of "participation" is being trivialized and loses some of its dynamic edge if it is to be reduced to the use of one-click services on pre-designed platforms. The performance of users runs the risk of being more and more machine-controlled as the designers of graphic interfaces put as the basic principle for interaction the fact that "the users cannot cause unexpected events or become disoriented by the system behaviour" (Marriott & Meyer, 1998: 361). Their expectations of usability, reliability and robustness do not necessarily match the purposes of the teachers and learners in media education, even though new user-centered designs try to placate the needs of users as regards participation (Wickens et al., 2004; Sears & Jacko, 2007).

The critique of the neo-liberal political discourse on media education thus requires also a critique of the techno-discourse that comes along with it, as cognitive tools and strategies also need to be examined analytically as the presence of the designers of such services and their hidden agenda cannot be ignored in a literacy context. The freedom of choice afforded the users is mostly reduced to consumer choices based on purchasing power. Such embedded user-oriented designs need to incorporate some of the demands of human rights in terms of privacy, agency and freedom of expression, if they are to foster wellbeing, trust and connectedness. Such uses reveal the thrust of collaborative exchanges to be taken into account when devising new policies and rights in the digital age, for the right scale of interaction to take place (Frau-Meigs, 2011a).

Proposing an alternative discourse for media education as a Global Positioning System (GPS)

To ensure that media education is not just turned into a neo-liberal tool for the employability of young people but as a sense-making mechanism and an opportunity for meaningful participation online and offline, several elements need to be taken into account: specific competences, cyberist opportunities and an integrated rationale beyond cultural studies.

Articulating the 7 C's and human rights

The e-strategies and socialization steps need to be put in congruence and compatibility with the off-line competences developed by educators, including in their articulation with the human rights framework, as is developed, for instance, in UNESCO's *Media Education Kit* (2007) and its follow-up "Training the Trainers" programme (2010) or the Council of Europe's Recommendation on *Empowering Children in the New Information and Communications Environment* and its follow-up Pestalozzi Programme "Trainer training modules on media literacy development" (2010). The different models for competences that circulate in Europe and other regions of the world seem to share three main over-arching competences. Recurrently, these models insist on developing abilities for Comprehension, Criticism and Creativity. They are the 3 Cs of media education Competences, at the core of the school system. When non-formal school activities are considered, four more abilities tend to be added that provide mastery over participation: Consumption, (Cross-) Cultural Communication, Citizenship and Conflict. All in all, they can be packaged as the 7 Cs, whose main strength lies in the fact that they cannot be reduced to workplace skills.

- Comprehension refers to the capacity to call upon the felt experience of matrices, scripts and representations to engage with the ICT-driven media spectacles, services and situations.
- Criticism implies the capacity to evaluate the reliability of the contents, attitudes and values proposed by the media
- Creativity evokes the capacity to use media so as to understand better social roles and activities while also solving problems and fulfilling cultural expectations.
- Consumption takes into account market events as commercial strategies that need to be decoded before deciding to engage with them or not.
- Cross-cultural communication consists in the capacity to place spectacles and services within their cultural networks and evokes the possibility, especially with transborder media, to become more tolerant because of increased access to content from various cultures.
- Citizenship refers to the capacity to test dynamic models of the world and, in so doing, to strengthen civic participation and ethical practices connected to human rights.
- Conflict hints at the double capacity to solve the cognitive conflicts created by media spectacles and services, especially in terms of harmful content and risk of harm, and to revise positions and values by using the pluralism of the media during situations of real conflict (riot, war, genocide). (Frau-Meigs, 2011a)

These 7 Cs reintroduce 'value' in education and in media while showcasing 'values' inherited from the human rights heritage. They can serve as a socialized cognitive framework to train young people in democratic participation. Just as in the United States, the First Amendment of the Bill of Rights – on the fundamental liberties of religion, expression, reunion and petition – is considered as the vector of the other individual rights (privacy, justice, representation,...), in many respects media education can be seen as the indispensable condition for the existence of the other lifelong educational areas that are evolving in the digital humanities, such as education to health, environment, etc., as so many of them are mediated by media and are experienced via media.

These values, in the cognitive meaning of the world, are less rules for behaviour than frames for action, that can create a sense of membership in a given culture, while allowing for their revision, if need be. The 7 Cs can modify young people's behaviour towards the media and the others, by making them sensitive to dignity, respect, mutual tolerance, responsibility and the common good. They hold the potential to turn the current civic apathy into agency as the young people become producers and creators of contents on the digital networks. They can empower them to resist the tenets of the privatization of risk in the cyberist moment, by creating new benchmarks for social justice, that differ from those promoted by the neo-liberal policies.

The 7 Cs as over-arching competences can be materialized with a number of actions and e-strategies, with attitudinal change as an output: to manage (risk, on-line postings, etc.), to read (decode, analyse, etc.), to deconstruct (the context, the culture, the history, etc.), to solve problems, to search and share content, to evaluate (critically, while understanding the others' opinions, etc.), to create (adopt fictional identities, remix media contents, etc.), to use media responsibly (mainstream and alternative), to share knowledge and to contribute to democratic debate.

The 7 Cs, combined with e-strategies and in step with the process of socialization can foster the deep appreciation of human rights. In such a case, they can produce an increased awareness about ethics: awareness of media constructs as regards interests, values and rights; awareness of media as tools for human rights appropriation (freedom of expression, pluralism, cultural diversity, etc.); awareness of media as commodities (objects, services, goods, etc.); awareness of the hidden agenda (sources, gatekeepers, etc.). Awareness can then lead to such cognitive steps as engagement, interpretation, performance, co-construction and revision for full participation in the democratic debate.

Harnessing the disruptive potential of the cyberist moment

Such an approach has gained in complexity with the recent evolution of Web 2.0 and it needs to integrate the cyberist moment as an opportunity for attitudinal change. The cyberist moment, with its transition from analogical to digital modes of data input and output, is an accelerator of change that displaces the prominence of such a value as transmission in education to promote co-construction of knowledge and collaborative intelligence. In so doing, it can transform any spectacle or service into a learning event, be it in formal or non-formal settings.

The cyberist moment is also characterized by the progressive mutation from alphabetical culture to visual culture. The potential for disruption of such a cultural shift is real in itself but it also has implications as a learning shift. Visual culture is akin to material culture and implies a change in the socio-material conditions of the production of culture. This is evidenced by the transition from a notion of media as mostly texts and spectacles (for news as well as entertainment) to a notion of media as services (for decision-making and action), as manifest in the very title of the European Audiovisual Media Services Directive. If nothing is done to prevent it, services will always be paid-for services, as the principle of public service value on the networks has clearly been evacuated from political discourse, on the left as much as on the right.

The learning shift implicit in such a process needs to be verbalised and rationalised so that its disruptive potential is integrated and appropriated by the body of teachers and learners. Focusing on user-generated content reinforces the need for new media literacies (about the image, information, internet, games,…) and even "trans-literacies", as the ability to read and write extends across a range of media platforms and networks (Thomas, 2006). New cognitive and intellectual tools can thus be made available to teachers. What current research shows is the importance of cognitive distribution in the new learning environments built around ICT-driven media. When applied to education, media can serve both as means for understanding our interactions with the environment and engaging with it, be it via spectacles or services, and for determining the organization and nature of the learning events facilitated by such situations. In that sense only can learners move from information to actual knowledge, as this one emerges through social negotiation and through the evaluation of individuals and groups that apply it to their situation.

A lot of the new research and pedagogical models that can be applied to media education evolve around such constructivist views, as addressing one of the major issues of cognition, problem-solving. Such "instructional principles" tend to be designed around an authentic task and to give the learner the ownership over the process of developing solutions (Savery & Duffy, 1995). It becomes clearer and clearer that pedagogical stances need to move away from teacher-as-source to teacher-as-resource, from set-texts to mobile-texts and from traditional didactic transmission to a view of knowledge as co-construction of meaning, the students contributing to it as well as the teachers.

A researcher like Aminata Sen reinforces this perspective for development, as his "capability" model is based on "functionings", i.e., the competences a person needs to achieve his or her goals within local living conditions (Sen, 1993). The opportunities afforded by media education then encompass their civic agency as well as their employability. Sen insists on the fact that such literacy allows for the conversion of commodities like media into functionings that serve basic needs of poverty and deprivation as much as fundamental needs for freedom and social justice.

The cyberist moment implies accumulated ways of expressing one's identity and one's sense of others, as expressivity and performance are particularly solicited in Web 2.0 applications for spectacles and services. New roles are being made available to them, for which they need to be prepared. They can be "prosumers", i.e., consumers who are also producers; they can be "gamers" and players, if not gamblers; they can be "netizens", whose vote is constantly solicited for non political participation (page ranking, video marking,…); they can be "netcroppers", i.e., workers who do not realize that their free play time is in fact hidden labour; they can also be "cyborgs", cybernetic organisms like avatars, whose ownership they cannot be assured of… (Frau-Meigs, 2011b). These roles solicit the 7 Cs constantly, as young people need to be critically aware of their consumption practices and of the legitimacy of the tasks they are encouraged to perform on pre-designed platforms whose "terms of service" are not always respectful of their rights.

Moving beyond cultural studies

Such complexity and such paradigm shifts call for a comprehensive framework for implementing media education policies and training tools. Historically, the countries that are advanced in the field, particularly in the English-speaking world, have benefited from the development of cultural studies in the research field, from the onset with Richard Hoggart's influential *Uses of Literacy* (1957). Cultural studies have provided a relatively coherent framework for understanding the construction of media texts around the representations of genre, race and ethnicity in postcolonial settings. They have also incorporated the audience as social subjects whose multiple subjectivities allow them to work with the media for their own interest while accommodating commercial ones (Hall, 1980; Fiske, 1989). They have thus enabled teachers to introduce the media practices and popular culture of their learners in the school process, without neglecting the contribution of the media "reality" in the class. They have made it possible for teachers to design learning events with a hands-on approach without a heavy scientific apparatus.

However, this rather amorphous field of studies, that has incorporated media studies and visual culture, needs to be criticized and upgraded. It needs to be criticized because of its focus on reception rather than on production, a blind spot that has not allowed for the political economy of media to be given a proper place. As a result it is a field that does not prepare well for the new roles of the learner, for the critical analysis of labour in the cyberist moment, for the political implications of risks, rights and services. With their current emphasis on market culture as a given, cultural studies have disengaged themselves from the critique of political discourse, and as such they tend to encourage an attitude that is more about "coping" with the media than actually proactively "mastering" the media. They do not seek out alternative views to the neo-liberal system and can be seen as having been abducted by it.

Cultural studies need also to be upgraded, if they are to be used at all. As a fifty year old field, born in the 1960s, some of its key notions and concepts no longer encompass the reality of the media environment in the cyberist moment, when the digital humanities are transforming the meaning of all classical disciplines and research areas. The notion of 'text' is rather weak when faced with 'spectacles' and 'services', both of which cannot be separated from power and control relationships. The notion of 'representation' no longer applies just to social events but also to mind theory and social cognition. Gender, race and ethnicity remain valid perspectives on the varied nature of the audience but their on-line extensions need to incorporate other identity constructs such as avatars and cyborgs. The notion of 'risk' has emerged with force because it is a way of constructing social problems for public issues that have been carefully evacuated by cultural studies, particularly media effects around violence, advertising or even addiction. Finally, globalization has shaken the micro-analysis perspective favoured by cultural studies, with phenomena that require methodologies ranging from virtual ethnography to digital mapping and visualization.

New approaches then need to be provided, informed by recent developments in the research field, around social cognition in particular, with such notions as social intelligence and cognitive modelling that reconfigure issues of attention, memory, engagement, attribution and action while affecting values and attitudes (Goleman, 2006; Fiske & Taylor, 1991). Notions proposed by other fields of research also offer renewed perspectives, like sociology with its critique of information and risk (Lash, 2002; Beck, 1992), political economy with its special focus on postcolonial and postcommunist transformations (Rifkin, 2000), anthropology with its focus on flows and diasporas (Appadurai, 1996), urban studies with its focus on networks and infrastructures (Castells, 1997) and even law with its extensions into digital identity and privacy (Solove, 2008). All these propose an analytical framework that shifts research on media from traditional linear cause-effect analysis to more reticular, process-oriented approaches that incorporate the governance of globalized media.

Socialization, as a framework buttressed on such an extended view of social cognition, can offer a relatively clear, coherent and articulated view of how the media function in society while at the same time providing levers for action in such a society. Such a framework offers a rationale that does not oppose uses and effects, risks and gratifications, high culture and low culture, rights and responsibilities, protection and participation. It fosters preparation over protection and participation; it promotes competences over uses and effects. It conceives of media education as a lifelong process, propitious to transliteracies that can prepare young people for dynamic learning in a changing international media environment, that needs to be mastered, not simply managed without resistance. As such it can be buttressed on human rights as a political framework, as long as they are not construed as an ideology but as a generative vision (Frau-Meigs, 2011a, 2011b).

The current context of the "Information Society", with its emphasis on knowledge-management via communication spectacles and services, holds powerful economic implications for the support of a media literate workforce. It may be attractive to public policy decision-makers as well as the industrial sector, even without an established business model, because employability is key in such a neo-liberal view. Though this perspective cannot be discarded in relation to the future of young people, it needs to be enriched and augmented by a vision of media education that prepares them to lifelong sustainability in all dimensions of life, not just the economic one. The long-term viability of the democratic model in the cyberist moment then claims a change from the original 19th century motto of education as "free, lay and compulsory" into a 21th century motto of media education as "open, participatory and ethical".

Note

A shorter version of the first section of this article was published in Pinto, M. and Sousa, H. (eds). (2011). *Communication and Citizenship: Rethinking Crisis and Change*. Coimbra: Gracio Editor.

References

Appadurai, A. *Modernity At Large. Cultural Dimensions of Globalization*. Minneapolis: University of Minnesota Press, 1996.

Beck, U. *Risk Society: Towards a New Modernity*. London: Sage, 1992 (first published in 1986).

Buckingham, D. *Media Education: Literacy, learning and contemporary culture*. Boston: MIT, 2007.

Castells, M. *La era de la información. Economía, sociedad y cultura. La sociedad red*, vol. I. Madrid: Alianza, 1997.

Council of Europe. *Internet Literacy Handbook*. Strasbourg: Council of Europe, 2006.

European Parliament Resolution on Media Literacy in a Digital World. 16 December 2008 http://www.europarl.europa.eu/

Fiske, J. *Understanding Popular Culture*, London: Routledge, 1989.

Fiske, S.T. & Taylor S.E. *Social Cognition*. New York: McGraw Hill, 1991.

Frau-Meigs, D. *Media Matters in the Cultural Contradictions of the Information Society. Towards a Human-Rights-Based Governance*. Strasbourg: Council of Europe press, 2011a.

Frau-Meigs, D. *Penser la société de l'écran. Dispositifs et usages*. Paris: Presses de la Sorbonne nouvelle, 2011b.

Frau-Meigs, D. & Meigs, D. "Socializing Young People to Ethics via Play Experience: Browser Games and Parental Concerns for Safety Online". *Global Media Journal* 2 1 (2009): 89-106 available at: http://www.gmj.uottawa.ca/0901/v2i1_frau-meigs%20and%20meigs.pdf

Frau-Meigs, D. & Torrent, J. (eds). *Mapping Media Education Policies Worldwide: challenges and visions*. New York: UN Alliance of Civilizations, 2009.

Goleman, D. *Social Intelligence*. New York: Bantham, 2006.

Hall, S. "Encoding/Decoding" (1973), *Culture, Media, Language: Working Papers in Cultural Studies (1972-79)*. London: Hutchinson, 1980,128-138.

Harrison, L.E. & Huntington, S.P. *Culture Matters: How Values Shape Human Progress*. New York: Basic Books, 2000.

Hoggart, R. *The Uses of Literacy*. London: Pelican, 1957.

Jenkins, H. et al. *Confronting the Challenges of Participatory Culture. Media Education for the 21st Century*. Cambridge: MIT Press, 2009.

Lash, S. *Critique of Information*. London: Sage, 2002.

Lunt, P. & Livingstone, S. *Media Regulation: Policy, Publics, Audiences*. London: Sage (forthcoming).

Marriott, K. & Meyer, B. (eds). *Visual Language Theory*. New York: Springer, 1998.

Pestalozzi, European Modules for Trainer Training. (2008). Training resources in Intercultural Education (ICE) available at http://www.coe.int/t/dg4/education/pestalozzi/activities/modules/ice/ice_intro_EN

Prensky, M. "Digital Natives, Digital Immigrants". *On the Horizon* 9 5 (2001): 1-6.

Rifkin, J. *The Age of Access. The New Culture of Hypercapitalism Where All of Life is a Paid-For Experience*. New York: Putnam, 2000.

Rotenberg, M. *Protecting Human Dignity in the Digital Age*. Paris: Unesco, 2000.

Savery, J.R., & Duffy, T.M. (1995). "Problem Based Learning: An instructional Model and its Constructivist Framework". *Educational Technology* 35 (1995): 31-38.

Sears, A. & Jacko, J.A. (eds.). *Handbook for Human Computer Interaction* (2nd Edition). New York: CRC Press, 2007.

Sen, A. "Capability and Well-being", Nussbaum, M. & Sen, A. (eds). *Quality of life*. New Delhi: OUP, 1993.

Solove, D.G. *Understanding Privacy*. Cambridge, MA: Harvard University Press, 2008.

Thomas, S. "The End of Cyberspace and Other Surprises" *Convergence* 12 4 (2006): 338-391.

Tomasello, M. *The Cultural Origins of Human Cognition*. Cambridge, MA: Harvard University Press,

1999.

UNESCO and Council of Europe. *Media Education: Advances, Obstacles and New Trends Since Grünwald. The Paris Agenda or Twelve Recommendations for Media Education*. Paris, 22-23 June 2007.

UNESCO, IFLA and National Forum on Information Literacy. *The Alexandria Proclamation on Information Literacy and Lifelong Learning, Beacons of the Information Society*. http://portal.UNESCO.org/ci/en/

Wickens, C.D., Lee, J.D., Liu, Y. & Becker, G. *An Introduction to Human Factors Engineering*. Upper Saddle River (NJ): Pearson Prentice Hall, 2004.

Youth and the Paradoxes of the Indian Media Situation

Considerations for a Socially Responsible Youth Media Policy

Manisha Pathak-Shelat

'India has more cell phones than toilets', screamed headlines all over the world in April 2010. The story that followed was based on a report by United Nations University:

> Recent UN research in India, the world's second most populous country, shows roughly 366 million people (31 percent of the population) had access to improved sanitation in 2008. Other data, meanwhile, show 545 million cell phones are now connected to service in India's emerging economy. The number of cell phones is expected to reach 1 billion by 2015 (UNU-INWEH, 2010:1).

This observation reflects the irony of the structural and cultural paradoxes in India, which also shape its media situation. We cannot talk about the Indian media situation without taking into consideration the larger context. India is a difficult country to gauge and summarize. The cliché 'when you say something about India, the exact opposite is also always true' is still an excellent way to describe the country. The following figures serve as examples of the Indian paradox. On one hand, 24 Indians are among the world's richest people; in the world happiness survey, India's Net happiness is at 40 percent, with 47 percent reporting being quite happy; the GDP with real growth rate is 9 percent; India tops the world in newspaper circulation and film production; India has well-respected leaders in science, spirituality, art and industry, a strong non-government sector and a large number of highly educated, vocal, active women. On the other hand, 40 percent of the world's poor live in India; India is ranked 133 out of 156 countries with its 60 percent literacy rate; child labor is a persistent issue with an estimated 20 to 50 million children in the labor market, many in hazardous industries; severe water and power shortages affect quality of life for a large number of Indians and numerous instances of gender-based discrimination and abuse occur daily (www.indiastat.com, www.nationmaster.com, www.sajaforum.org).

This structural divide makes it almost impossible to pin down who is an 'average' Indian youth. There are several complicating factors such as class, caste, geography, gender, and language skills that would determine the life experiences of a young person, including access to and participation in the media. There are young people who are urban, affluent, educated, and proficient in English with access to state-of-the-art technology and world-class skills and efficacy. There are young people from the middle classes, who are eager to catch up, innovative and trying to make the most of limited media and technology resources that they often share with family and peers at school. There are young people in villages and small towns who work while pursuing studies and who would have access to new technologies if only such technologies were institutionally supported. And there are numerous young people in remote villages and urban streets who are poor and struggling to get the basic necessities like food, shelter, health care, fuel and clean drinking water. They face discrimination on the basis of class, caste and gender, and have no access to technologies. There is also variation in each of the above over-simplified categories, and the categories themselves are not watertight or stable in a rapidly changing country like India.

My argument is that a socially responsible media policy for India cannot afford to ignore any of these groups. Here again, it is important to understand the tricks that India's large population plays on how reality is perceived. With over one billion people, even a small percentage of the population translates into millions of people. On the other hand, a seemingly huge number would be a minuscule percentage of the Indian population.

Globalization, transnational media flows and rapid technology transfer in the digital age are some other factors complicating Indian youth's interaction with the media. Liberalization of the Indian economy, digital technology and globally spread Indian diaspora have brought about many changes in India, and yet so many deep-rooted structural and cultural aspects have changed very little. Under these circumstances, it is dangerous to hastily pronounce a celebratory verdict regarding the achievements of 'tech savvy' Indian youth, but at the same time it is equally dangerous to view these young people only as 'victims' of global economic forces. Both conditions coexist, many a time in the same situation, in the same individual.

The world famous or infamous call centers would be a good example to discuss here. Bringing India the 'honor' of being the world's back office and coining new phrases like 'a job being Bangalored', call centers have helped many middle-class Indian young men and women climb the economic ladder and break out of the grind of poorly paying menial jobs, and the accompanying economic and social deprivation. And yet in India, call centers are fundamentally the result of the colonial legacy. We cannot overlook the colonial history and the economic disparity it created between the global North and the global South that is at the heart of out-sourcing. Even today, more than the night-shift working, easily replaceable and constantly watched young workforce, it is the powers in the parent Western companies that tend to benefit the most from the call centers. Divya McMillin's (2008) nuanced study of call center workers explores these contradictions.

Similar contradictions are found with respect to media. The booming electronic media have opened many new career choices for young people and televised contests have provided new platforms for talented young people from small towns. At the same time, a new kind of 'child labor' in the advertising and entertainment industry has emerged. Early eroticization of young girls, sexual abuse and exploitation are some of the accompanying problems. Easy access to mobile phones at a younger and younger age can mean liberation, on the one hand, but also increased possibilities of parental or self-surveillance, on the other. Being recognized as a target market itself means being both empowered and exploited. Along with the power of more choices, more exposure and opportunities for experimentation, there is the threat of manipulation and imposition of the hegemonic culture.

Fisherkeller (2009: viii) succinctly summarizes this contradiction:

> On the one hand youth are regarded as vulnerable and impressionable, and thus susceptible to the ploys of the contemporary market, a stance that simultaneously perceives of youth as passive consumers and media as overpowering producers. On the other hand, youth are regarded as discerning and savvy, and thus resistant to or at least skeptical about their being consumer targets, a stance that perceives of youth as active and media as often ineffective in hitting their intended mark.

Actually, both these phenomena very often occur simultaneously.

India's digital revolution has captured worldwide attention, and not without reason. The following figures on cell phone growth in India are indeed impressive. Until the mid-1990s in India, one had to wait six to seven years for a landline phone. Today, 3 to 4 percent of the population has landlines and the same applies to computers. 0.37 per 100 people have broadband. Compare this to the statistics on mobile phones in India. Mobile phones have shown a rapid growth from 100 million in 2006 to 400 million in 2009 to 525 million in 2010. These figures are only indications, because it is estimated that India adds four new mobile subscribers every second (mobileYouth, 2010). The figures have important implications for those targeting youth, as nearly half of all Indians are under 30 (approximately 550 million, which is equivalent to the number of youth in Western Europe and USA together). By 2011, one in five of the world's mobile-phone-owning youth is likely to be living in India. Even rural youth is catching up with 100 million rural cell phone owners out of the 600 million strong rural population (mobileYouth, 2010).

These impressive statistics, however, dim when you consider per capita figures and other aspects of development. India is ranked fourth out of 185 countries in number of TV receivers and second out of 89 countries in number of broadcast stations. Its rank slides down to 148th out of 209 countries when you look at percentage of households with a TV (www.nationmaster.com). The same applies to personal computers, mobile phones and other media. For corporations and industries, the number of people using a service or technology is a sufficient parameter for gauging market success. If the required number adopts their goods or services (and with India's huge population even the top 1 percent of the richest would themselves be a big market), businesses do not have to worry about the rest of the people who either do not want or cannot afford these goods and services. Per capita statistics, however, are more important for policymakers and the development sector. Considering per capita figures, India has a long way to go in becoming a leader in the media and technology area.

Media for young people in India: Overview

Just like the larger development patterns in India, the media sector and its development give us ample reason to rejoice, but also to feel concern. On the positive side, Indian youth is exposed to a wide variety of media available in English and in all major Indian languages. With over 900 films produced annually, India is a leader in film production. India's government-owned and -run television and radio – Doordarshan and Akashvani – have had strong educational and developmental objectives as well as special slots for regional content. Apart from Doordarshan, Indian audiences have more than 100 television channels available to them. Many non-governmental organizations all over the country are actively engaged in making young people's voices heard through the media. Also, there are numerous new career opportunities offered by the media, even in small towns.

India has a rich tradition of folk and traditional media, which though gradually diminishing in importance, is still alive in villages and tribal areas. There are vibrant folk theater practices such as Ramlila, Bhavai, Nautanki and Tamasha, to name just a few. There is the art of puppetry, with its great regional variations and also colorful folk dances and songs. In fact, there is such tremendous variety, history and richness here that India, and the world, would be losing a great deal by neglecting to preserve these traditional folk media. There are, fortunately, several urban institutions working for folk media revival in India and artists adapting them to contemporary needs.

These achievements, however, do not do enough to create a vibrant youth media scene. The average TV viewing time of an Indian child is estimated at 4 to 6 hours per day – longer on selected days, for example when there is a cricket match (Joshi et al., 2002). At the same time, programs produced especially and thoughtfully for children form a minuscule portion of the total media programming. There have been some excellent attempts at indigenous programming on television and also book publishing for preschool or primary school age children by private publishing houses as well as by the National Book Trust, but by and large, very little indigenous media content is available in India for tweens and young adults.

Here it is important to introduce the positioning of television as a 'family medium' rather than an individual medium in India. Television started more as a medium for education and development than for entertainment in the 1960s when community viewing was introduced as a viable option, especially in schools and villages. The entertainment aspects of television gained dominance in the 70s and more strongly in the 80s. Television became a family entertainment medium. When television sets were not easily affordable, it was not uncommon in Indian cities and villages for people to gather at a neighbor's place to view favorite programs. India's socialization practices for children also differ from those of their Western counterparts. Very few homes in India have a strict 'bedtime', or for that matter a separate bedroom, for children. Children are very much present when adults watch television, dropping off to sleep when their bodies can no longer keep up. A direct consequence of this is that Indian children grow up watching a disproportionate amount of adult content. At a very early age, they are regularly exposed to crime, violence and obscenity through the media. Despite the persistent work of some voluntary organizations and academics, parental discretion and media literacy programs are still not particularly common in India. The same is the case for cinema. Despite boasting the largest number of films produced in a year, only a minuscule number of them can be called children's films in any true sense. There is very little available that is specially produced for adolescents and young adults. Ironically, young people have gained recognition as an important target market for lifestyle products, but not as an important niche audience for television and cinema, because it is expected and accepted that they will watch programs/films made for adult sensibilities. India has strong regional cinemas, but laudable efforts in regional cinema rarely reach the mainstream audiences. Hence, Bollywood movies, 24x7 news and daily soaps, with their adult themes and issues, remain a staple diet of India's young people. Our fieldwork in the state of Gujarat in 2010 revealed another interesting facet. School-going adolescents in Gujarat, especially those from small towns, take a keen interest in reading newspapers, but the newspaper industry has yet to respond to this interest in creative ways.

Young people's exposure to inappropriate sexual content does not only occur through films and television. Internet and cell phones are the two new channels through which pornography is emerging as a big business. Scandals involving youth and these two relatively new media never fail to catch media attention, causing panic reactions in policymakers, teachers and parents. These reactions often overshadow any acknowledgement of the constructive and empowering role of media use. At the same time, the gravity of situations arising from abuse of the Internet and cell phones cannot be ignored. MMS scandals involving cell phones and cyber bullying are two relatively new issues facing youth and their guardians. There are legal provisions for Internet misuse in India, but again, unfortunately, the final responsibility for protecting children from media abuse falls only on parents and that too with little assistance or cooperation from the other agencies involved.

Youth media policy in India will also need to address two issues about which parents and policymakers do not think as seriously as they do about graphic sex and violence. These issues are the confusing messages about gender, sexuality and body image and the limited and often problematic coverage and representation of young people in the media. The long-term subtle influences of hidden messages may have grave psychological consequences for young people.

A brief overview of policy level efforts to focus on young people

The heartening quality of India is that, despite several attempts to repress open discussion, vigorous debates in the public sphere have continued. The media's influence on young people has always been a hotly debated public issue, and some of these concerns have found their way into policy documents – those pertaining to young people as well as those specifically dealing with the media. There have been several specific media-related policies in India, and efforts in this direction started soon after India gained its independence in 1947. In fact, at times it seems as though India was more concerned about quality children's media in those early years than it is at present.

For example, a Film Inquiry Committee was appointed by the Government in 1946, which culminated in the establishment of the Children's Film Society in 1955. It was later renamed the National Center for Children and Young People (NCYP). The main objective was to provide quality entertainment for children. The Joshi Committee, appointed under the chairmanship of social scientist P.C. Joshi, came out with its report titled 'Indian Personality for Television' in 1985. The report included a chapter, 'Children: Victims or Beneficiaries', exclusively devoted to children that specified several measures necessary to ensure quality media for children. The Codes for Broadcasting on All India Radio and Television and the Code of Advertising Practice have several protective measures for children.

Compared to these earlier efforts, the Information Technology Act of 2000 and Communication Convergence Bill of 2001 do not address children as a special category at all, though some of their general protective provisions may cover children and young people. The Government of India laid down a Youth Policy in 1985. The salient features of this policy were instilling respect for the constitution, the rule of law and commitment to national integration, non-violence, secularism and socialism; awareness of historical and cultural heritage, pride in national identity, enrichment of the environment and ecology; development of qualities of discipline, self-reliance, justice and fair play, concern for the public good and sporting spirit and scientific disposition; increased access to education and employment; and awareness of international issues, involvement in world peace and a just international economic order (Joshi, 2006:16). The Indian Government is a signatory to the UN Convention on the Rights of the Child. The National Commission for the Protection of Child Rights Bill of 2005 makes the commission the legal mechanism to implement the National Policy for Children, which sees to child rights. However, it has always remained unclear how exactly the media's role is spelled out in these lofty missions. Besides, to date, no effort has been made to produce a coherent children's media policy or youth media policy in India.

Key issues that a youth media policy in India would need to address

Looking at the overview of the Indian media scenario and national policy, several key issues emerge. Media scholars point out that, thus far, the role of youth media policy has been more regulatory than developmental (Agrawal, 1997; AV-CODE, 2007). Now, policymakers need to focus more on the developmental potential of media, addressing both the hardware and software aspects. Joshi (2006:15) proposes four means for addressing youth media issues: development of communication policy, production of suitable and attractive software, media education and, finally, monitoring and evaluation.

I would add immersive fieldwork to this list, because policy or software development without listening to the end-user and understanding the cultural context of the technology have recurrently failed to have any impact. Again, I would like to give an example from the research carried out with young people in the state of Gujarat in 2009-10. Our data from a school located in an urban slum showed many children with a computer and Internet connection at home. Puzzled by this, we probed further to find that for these low- and middle-income families, investment in computers and Internet was seen as a family investment in a better future, and they took loans to procure them, forgoing other amenities. Thus, young people were the main driving force behind this decision, but at the heart were family aspirations.

Immersive research as the foundation for software development is not a new idea in that sense. The entire Satellite Instructional Television Experiment (SITE) of the Indian Space Research Organisation (ISRO) in the seventies used formative research in developing educational programs, and the Development and Educational Communication Unit (DECU) of ISRO carried forward this tradition in their consecutive projects.

The work being carried out under the MILLEE (Mobile and Immersive Learning in Emerging Economies) project and by Indrani Medhi in development of user interfaces are two excellent examples of contemporary research that best exemplify the philosophical directions discussed above. MILLEE was started in 2004 by Mathew Kahn as his PhD project in Berkeley. Through extensive fieldwork, the MILLEE team recognized several crucial factors in the individual-media-society interface in India. Knowledge of English was observed as the dividing factor between those who have higher educational and employment opportunities, scope for mobility and material success and those who struggle for these things. Once again, India's colonial past and recent forces of globalization collude in producing this condition. Time spent by young people working on farms and in households and cell phones becoming the fastest growing tech platforms in India with their multimedia capabilities were other important considerations. The MILLEE team also used ethnographic research to study the influence of caste and gender. Based on their ethnographic research, MILLEE uses cell phones as a vehicle for complementing the formal educational system and expanding English skills in young Indians. The MILLEE website describes how they use 'a human-centered approach to designing immersive, enjoyable, language learning games on cell phones, modeled after the traditional village games that rural children find familiar' (www.millee.org).

Indrani Medhi's work in developing text-free user interfaces (UIs) for illiterate users is the other good example of use of ethnographic fieldwork in bridging theory and practice. She says in an interview (*Technology Review*, 2010):

> Through an ethnographic design process involving more than 400 subjects from low-income, low-literate communities across India, the Philippines, and South Africa, I discovered that there were a number of usability challenges which people experienced while interacting with traditional textbased UIs, on both mobile phones and PCs [personal computers]. In addition to the general inability to read text, the other major challenge was the difficulty in navigating hierarchical menus in current information architectures. I developed design recommendations for non-textual UIs for low-literate users that use combinations of voice, video, and graphics.

Medhi also pays attention to other nuanced issues like cognitive difficulties, collaboration, cultural etiquette, experience and exposure, intimidation, mediation, motivation, pricing, power relations and social standing.

Media literacy or media education is another important aspect for improving media experiences of youth. The Grünwald Declaration (UNESCO, 1982) called for comprehensive media education programs, but despite consistent efforts by educators and some voluntary organizations, media education never gained its due status in the Indian school system. These efforts have engaged students, parents and teachers in workshops, produced media education kits and initiated a few research projects, but even after two decades of the Grünwald Declaration, there is no consistent government policy, no committed funding agency and no official recognition for media education in Indian schools. Future media policy has to give the media education sector the attention it deserves and support healthy options, such as public libraries that are not just for books, but that also circulate quality children's media and offer media education programs to schools and families.

Three appeals

After surveying the socio-cultural-economic context in which youth media policy in India has to operate, I make three strong appeals through this article. First of all, there is a need to refrain from restricting young lives in the name of 'preserving Indian culture' and to design media policies that go beyond the regulatory measures. The policy has to be sensitive to the importance of maintaining the fine line between protection and repression. Media education has an important role to play here if the policing of young people is to gradually give way to self-discretion.

Again, the whole issue of preserving a national culture is a very complex one. On the one hand, youth consumerism driven by global capitalism – as evident in the burgeoning beauty, fashion and fitness industries and westernized celebrations of the New Year Eve and Valentines Day – raises the issue of a new colonization. On the other hand, the growing influence of youth culture and attention to youth as a niche target group can help young people to experience their unique space in the adult-centered world. They may experience more choice and agency through exposure to cultures other than their own and through experimenting with different lifestyles. The frequent panic attacks about 'losing the Indian culture' ignore the fact that culture is a dynamic process. No nation or culture can bubble wrap itself and ignore the forces of change. Ideally, we must encourage young people of all cultures to question the regressive practices of their own cultures, as fresh ideas are important for any culture to remain vibrant.

An observation by mobileYouth (www.mobileyouth.org) that youth culture in India is a 'local offering with global variance rather than a local variant of a global offering' shows that youth has its own way of filtering different influences. Curtin and Shah (2010:3) observes the dominant perception: 'Not only is power seen as emanating from the West to the rest but so too is cultural influence with media seen as the conduit for Western notions of fashion, taste, politics, and modernity.' The essays in their recent book challenge the modernization theory of the 1950s and 60s and the media imperialism approach that spread in the 1970s

> not because they are wholly inaccurate but rather because Western media are now only one element in the increasingly complex global communication order and the movement of content is increasingly multidirectional (Curtin & Shah, 2010:3).

According to Curtin and Shah, Indian and Chinese television networks, music, publishing, and Internet media now have audiences and viewers around the world, 'where increasingly transnational creativity and circulation foster new cultural forms and new audience affiliations' (Curtin & Shah, 2010:1). Citing an example of the Indian superhero movie Krrish, they discuss the global cultural impact of Indian blockbusters and argue that these movies have a larger global reach than their Hollywood counterparts if one considers the number of people who have seen them.

Here, it is important to consider the role Bollywood has been playing in packaging and perpetuating its own brand of Indian culture. It is true that the cultural symbols, music and imagery of Bollywood films are helping young people of Indian origin the world over create their own brand of youth culture and helping them create a separate identity from the homogenizing Western youth culture. On the other hand, what is touted as the 'Indian culture' by Bollywood *masala* movies and several prime time soap operas in India is their own hybrid and over-simplistic version of upper-class, upper-caste, patriarchal practices and rituals, predominantly Punjabi/North Indian and in some recent cases from Gujarat.

If the youth media policy is to remain relevant for today's young people, it has to question assumptions and respond to the contemporary cultural environment.

My second appeal is the importance of respecting the innovative edge and resourcefulness of Indian youth, who hungrily seek media hardware and software under painfully restricted circumstances. The same 'Indian creativity and resourcefulness' also encourage unethical and disruptive media practices, and cracking down on these practices is also an important task of media policy, but as shown the world over, it is an uphill battle, easier said than done. With due respect to intellectual property rights and the struggle against piracy, I would like to draw attention to the sad fact that a majority of young people in developing regions cannot afford authentic, copyright protected media. So, my appeal is to strengthen the copy-left, open source and creative common initiatives and give them due status in the media policy.

Availability of media in local languages and at affordable prices is a crucial factor that is complicated by Indian diversity. With fourteen official languages and hundreds of minor languages, India still has no single common language, despite Hindi having the official status as the 'national' language and English being the *lingua franca* of the educated. 'Life Tools' by Nokia is an interesting example of how affordable prices and relevant content in local languages can make technology empowering. Life Tools was first commercially launched in India in 2009, with the purpose to provide relevant and enriching information to communities living in remote areas. Agriculture, education, entertainment and general knowledge are the main components offered. The subscription fees are kept within reach of low-income groups. For example, the 'Learn English' component costs Rs.30/- per month and provides simple courses on English in local languages. As mobileYouth (2010) reports, Life Tools subscribers to the education service tend to make a family affair of gathering around the phone and learning new words, phrases and pronunciations. The education service also provides students help with exam preparation in the form of tips and advice for various education boards in the country. Nokia Life Tools in India operates in nine local languages (Marathi, Gujarati, Punjabi, Bengali, Kannada, Tamil, Malayalam, Telugu, Hindi) as well as in English. During its China launch in May 2010, Nokia revealed that the service has around 1.5 million subscribers across India and Indonesia (http://www.mobileyouth.org/post/mytv1-rural).

The scaling up of success stories is my third priority area for youth media policy. India has seen numerous successful experiments in using media and new communication technologies in ways that can enthrall and empower young people. From success stories of local voluntary organizations all over the country (for details see Joshi et al., 2006: 293-313) to some better known, government-funded larger projects like Indian Space Research Organization's (ISRO's) Zabhua Development Communications Project (1996-2000) and the state of Karnataka's Student Internet World 2004 program, to industry-sponsored experiments like the 'Hole in the Wall' by Sugata Mitra (1999 onwards), we now have viable models and guidelines for what works and what does not. Unfortunately, in its preoccupation with regulations and banning of media, policymakers have not given sufficient priority to scaling up these success stories. The large population and resulting resource crunch remain a major hurdle in reaching the large numbers of young people who lack even the minimum level of media access and exposure. But on the other hand, we have many tech savvy, globally connected young people; this is a small percentage of the total population, but a huge force if one considers their sheer number and influence. Youth media policy can maximize available resources by supporting initiatives for private/public, diasporic/local and industry/NGO/university/schools partnerships that use these privileged young people as resources.

Finally, youth media policy in any country needs to take into consideration the needs, opinions and aspirations of young people. We need to facilitate greater youth participation in the public sphere. Media policy can play an important role in creating media environments that are youth-friendly public spheres, where young people not only have a voice, but also peers and adults paying attention to what they have to say.

References

Agrawal, Binod. (1997). Media Policy For Children In India: Is There a Need? Keynote address at the Seminar 'Towards a Media Policy for Children' held at SNDT College of Home Science, Pune, India, 26-28 December, 1997

AV-CODE. (2007). Audio-Video Communicators for Development and Education: Proceedings and Recommendations of the symposium on Broadcast Bill, July 7, 2007. Ahmedabad: AV-Code and Media Society

Curtin, Michael & Shah, Hemant. (2010). *Reorienting Global Communication: Indian and Chinese Media Beyond Borders*. Urbana and Chicago: University of Illinois Press

Fisherkeller, JoEllen. (2009). Foreword, in McMillin, Divya C. *Mediated Identities: Youth, Agency, and Globalization*. New York: Peter Lang, pp. vii-ix

http://www.indiastat.com/default.aspx

http://www.millee.org

http://www.nationmaster.com/red/country/in-india/med-media&all=1

http://www.sajaforum.org/2007/04/stats_figures_a.html

Joshi, Madhavi, Joshi, Sanjay & Jain, Gopalkumar. (2006). Youth Have the Media Advantage, in Joshi, Subhash (Ed.) *Children, Youth and Electronic Media: Prospects and Portents*. Delhi: B.R. Publishing Corporation, pp. 293-313

Joshi, Subhash, Bhatt, Dharmesh & Ayyangar, Gayatri. (2002). *Children's Fare: Indian Media*. Ahmedabad: Development and Educational Communication Unit, Indian Space Research Organization

Joshi, Subhash. (2006). Children, Youth and ICTs: The Indian Scenario, in Joshi, Subhash (Ed.) *Children, Youth and Electronic Media: Prospects and Portents*. Delhi: B.R. Publishing Corporation, pp. 15-16

McMillin, Divya, C. (2008). 'Around Sourcing: Peripheral Centers in the Global Office', in Gajjala, Radhika & Gajjala, Venkatramana. (Eds.). *South Asian Technospaces*. New York: Peter Lang, pp. 249-264

MobileYouth. http://www.mobileyouth.org

Technology Review. TR 35: 2010. Young Innovator. http://www.technologyreview.in/tr35/Profile.aspx

UNESCO-Education Sector. (1982). The Grünwald Declaration of Media Education 1982 (Grünwald, Germany), http://portal.unesco.org/ci/en/ev.php-URL_ID=27310&URL_DO=DO_TOPIC&URL_SECTION=201.html

UNU-INWEH. (2010). Greater Access to Cell Phones than Toilets in India. UNU-INWEH News Release – Sanitation Report, p. 1, www.inweh.unu.edu

Tools to Measure the Levels of Audience Involvement

Content analyses vs. social impact 1998/2010

Tatiana Merlo Flores

in collaboration with Marcelo Petrazzini, Mariana Arraztoa, Gabriela Nahabedian and Elena Vázquez

Due to the paradigm changes media convergence has produced in audiences, especially young ones, our study wishes to explain and measure the necessity of taking into account these new demands from the perspective of young people, based on what they feel, express and do.

During the past twelve years, we have been working in Argentina on two main points:

- content analyses of the narratives in television programs measuring the social responsibility of the media related to the problems young people experience as theirs
- methods for analyzing the social impact of these narratives on young people's everyday life.

The final product is an index of the processes and levels of audience involvement.

We look forward to promoting – through the media – social and human development and respect for children's rights, mainly their rights to be included and to participate, as a clear way to exert their rights as citizens.

Theoretical frame

I would like to list, briefly, the paradigms and methodological steps that allowed us to implement the index.

The approach to social reality that I have been developing for many years considers, as the main methodological premise, the "paradigm of complexity", which Edgar Morin (1984, 1994, 2010) has stated as an aspiration for all the sciences, including the social sciences. He wished to express the complexity and ambiguity of the multidimensional reality, saying at the same time that it is not an "omniscience", which is why it does not eliminate the uncertainty of total reality in its multiple "layers" and nuances.

The "paradigm of complexity" also restores the human being to the natural world as "a being that is part of it", mutually and necessarily involved and associated as interdependent and inseparable. This implies that all social phenomena, although small, specific and concrete, are always "global" or "total", meaning that a phenomenon includes in itself not only specific components of a particular type, but also a very large and variable number of other phenomena of a different nature, which show that the whole is in the parts and vice versa, as Marcel Mauss (1954), among others, holds. This view takes into account the social "nanoscience" elements as they are recognized in physics and biology (the DNA substance) and which are very difficult to put into practice in social research.

This is just like how children read, for example, television images, and it is here the individual view is deeply holistic. Listening in depth to the narratives of children's favorite shows, and looking at their performances and drawings, one may discover children's own biographies, family histories, what happens in their society and their different cultures, and interwoven with all these stories, mythical tales and the search for meaning appearing across children's responses and pervading their views, perhaps as an innate impulse that seeks to add balance and meaning to life.

Listening deeply to children, we find that the individual and the whole are there (the "hologrammatic" concept of Morin), receiving feedback, finding what I call "conceptual knots of consistency". We understand theoretically that, in the systemic networks of which we are part and which we try to look at in an objective way in order to understand and explain them, we can speak of these "conceptual knots".

Where there appear related items – expressing combinations of quantitative and qualitative variables, including minimum facts of "nanocause" significance that are reiterated in the multi- and interdisciplinary view, with different expressions – they always refer to the "nuclei" that are fed and remain dynamically, even if they change their forms and expressions, being part of the processes, in continuous transformation, but remaining the "knots" or the roots that hold the mesh network system together. Without them the network would fall, senselessly. Based on these roots it is possible for theory to progress (see also Figure 1).

Our research, with its different approaches and results, helped us to understand that the paradigm of complexity was the only frame that allows us to integrate and understand the dynamic and many contradictions of the whole, among children and youth living in a society permeated by the image. The theoretical and methodological framework does not depart from the paradigm of complexity, but it was imposed as it complicates multidisciplinary approaches and methodologies that try to look beyond the facts.

Figure 1. Methodological premises

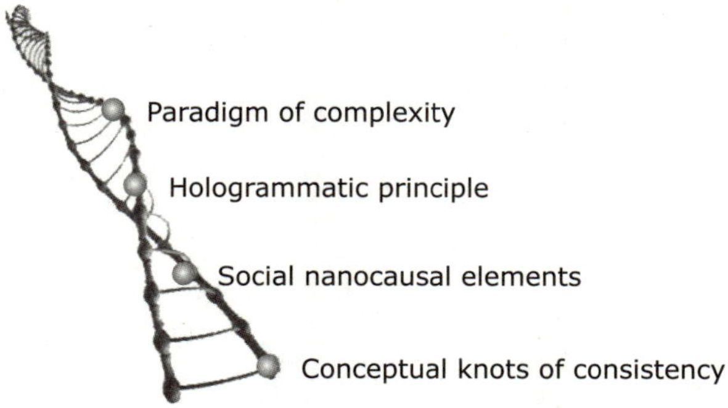

Source: Tatiana Merlo Flores, IDIEM (Instituto de Investigación en Medios, Media Research Institute), Buenos Aires, Argentina, 2010

MIT – Measure of the social impact of television

Why is research that leads to action so important to us, as Latin-Americans? There are several elements that always underlie our research processes:

1. The problems of social and human development that entail many global inequalities, particularly among the children and young people of our continent.

2. The worldwide acceptance, at least theoretically, that development cannot be measured solely in economic terms.

3. The cultural paradigm shifts that have affected primarily children and young people and have a close relationship with the media environment in which they were born and are growing up. The changes in the cultural paradigms are reflected in complex and interrelated ways: the generation gap, a new holistic point of view, the primacy of emotional instead of rational ways of knowing and learning, horizontal communication, recognition of the adult world and its problems from an early age, as well as self-recognition of the duality of human nature, the mythical thinking that pervades the responses of children in their own narratives. And most importantly, the consequences of these changes in children's daily lives: feelings of loneliness, lack of role models, clear awareness of social inequalities, concern for environmental degradation, and so on.

4. The proposals that emerge as international initiatives such as the Millennium Development Goals and the United Nations' Global Compact.

To aid us in our search and to find an answer, MIT – a measure of the social impact of media on children – was developed in co-operation with Buenos Aires

University. Many other organizations have joined us on the way. During the past twelve years, we have analyzed virtually every fiction television production of our country, how their contents have made an impact on children and young audiences, and the ways in which the incorporation of new technology has been changing these processes. What are the demands and how do these new audiences express them? Do the media have the ways and means to respond to young people's demands?

The progress of our research led us to analyze the correlation between, on the one hand, the media's level of responsibility or commitment in their treatment of social problems that concern children and young people and, on the other, the levels of involvement of the audience. Involvement means the engagement of the audience with the media content and is analyzed as a cumulative process – as opposed to audience ratings, which only pay attention to contact. The corollary was, thus, the creation of indicators that could measure the ethical commitment in the television contents in the treatment of social issues, and its relationship to the levels of audience involvement.

Having clarified this methodological umbrella, let us look at the specific techniques used for collecting and analyzing the data that led to the creation of the indexes.

Morin's perspective is oriented toward a bio-anthropological conception of the world, where the psychological, physical, and social levels of human existence are not watertight compartments, but are linked and integrated. This perspective caused us to combine different multi-disciplinary views, mixed with appropriate techniques for researching the dynamic complexity we are trying to understand.

The methodology applied to the content analysis was:

- A general description (of the TV material)
- Description of specific program grids (according to typologies such as family, gender, occupation, age groups, etc.)
- In-depth interviews with scriptwriters, producers and responsible persons
- Unit analysis:
  - Main topic
  - Field
- Application indexes:
  - Index MIT Commitment to an Ethics for Development
  - Indicators of experts

The methodology applied to construct the Index of Level of Audience Involvement was:

- The investigation (1995/2010) "Young people and their daily lives" carried out by the institute IDIEM (Instituto de Investigación en Medios, Media Research Institute), Buenos Aires
- General questionnaire

- In-depth interviews
- Focus groups (with specific targets)
- Representations (young people's acting)
- Specific questionnaire
- Narrative analysis
- Content analysis (social networking 2.0)
- Secondary data

Problems facing teens: "Young people and their daily lives"

According to the above, we applied from 1995 to date (every two years) a questionnaire survey (each one to 1,200 young people) through which we tried to understand their expectations, problems, family relationships, daily activities, models, the importance of formal education, and much more. We successively incorporated new technologies as part of the daily lives of children and adolescents. Following this process over time has been very enlightening. The questionnaire surveys have been the basis for understanding the issues that youngsters experience as their own and that concern them most. These data, together with many other studies, allowed us to construct the Index of Level of Audience Involvement.

The graphic in Figure 2, for example, synthesizes one open question that allowed teens to express the problems they consider their own.

Drugs/alcohol have been ranked highest in all the surveys, and it is interesting to compare the years, because in 2001 our country suffered a huge crisis, similar to the one that currently exists in Europe and the United States. After the crisis, teens' concern for their studies and work appear as a problem that was mostly not considered in previous years.

The agenda of adolescents does not generally coincide with the agenda of the media and even less with the topics selected to be developed in the narratives of television fiction productions.

These findings, very briefly explained, and the results of other studies we have carried out over many years, led us to question what social commitment television has to addressing the most important issues and concerns among children and adolescents, and what impact the media treatment of social problems has on child and adolescent audiences. From 1998 to date, we have analyzed dozens of fiction programs on national television and the social impact they have on children and adolescents. By impact we mean, as mentioned, the engagement the audience has with their favorite programs (not only the contact in terms of audience ratings).

The engagement or involvement is exactly how children read television images, and it is here the individual view is also deeply holistic. Listening care-

Figure 2. What problems do teenagers experience as their own? (percent)

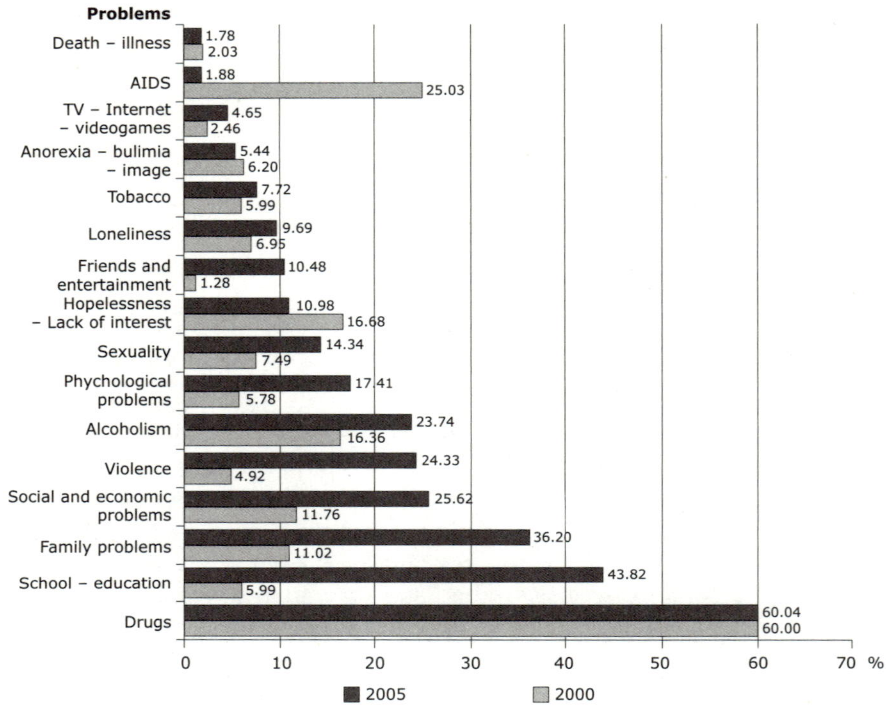

Source: Survey IDIEM 2000 (N = 1,200) and 2005 (N = 1,200).

fully to children's narratives about their favorite television programs, and their performances and drawings concerning the contents of the stories, one may discover young people's own biographies, family histories, what happens in their society and in the different cultures, and, interweaving all these stories, the mythical thought appears, the search for meaning, perhaps as an innate impulse that seeks balance and meaning in life.

The result of this work was the creation of two complementary indexes: one index that accounts for the ethical commitment to social development in the television content, and another index measuring the levels of involvement of young people with these programs. To both indexes were added, for each specific problem, Expert Indicators, which were worked out with the help of Save the Children. Together we invited national and international experts on the most important development issues to create indicators to measure each problem. A book summarizing all this research, conducted over time, is now in press (Merlo Flores, in press).

MIT: Measure of Television Social Impact

I will present a paradigmatic case. The case concerns a fiction program called *Vidas Robadas* (*Stolen Lives*), which developed the subject of human trafficking, based on a true story that happened in Argentina. We applied to the content analyses of this fiction program the Index of Commitment to an Ethic for Development (see Figure 3), as well as the Expert Indicators related to specific problems (see Figure 4). *Vidas Robadas* obtained the highest MIT scores among the programs reviewed during the past twelve years. The index was applied to a corpus of nearly 2,300 scenes in the program. The score on the indexes measuring children's and youth's levels of involvement was also the highest.

Content analysis

Figure 3. MIT Index: Commitment to an Ethic for Development

Dimensions	Categories	Score max. possible	Score Obtained	Dimension Score MIT
CREDIBILITY a. and b.: on characters, c. on stage existence (taking into account corpus TSE-EE)	a. Rules b. Characterization c. Setting-atmosphere	5 5 10	4,5 4,5 9	18
COHERENCE LEVEL (considering corpus correspondence between EE and TSR-EE-)		15	14	14
CONTEXTUALIZATION on TSR (Main topic)	a. Procedures b. Information on the plot: b1. Mention b2. Access c. Information outside the plot: c1. Shared c2. Exclusive	6 2 4 2 4	6 2 4 1 2	16
PROBLEMATIZATION (Main topic)	a. Causes b. Consequences c. Expert Indicators d. Pluralism	7,5 7,5 7,5 7,5	7,5 7,5 7 7,5	29,5
CITIZENSHIP CONSTRUCTION (main topic)	a. Recognition b. Participation c. Commitment d. Mobilization e. Demand of rights	3 3 3 3 3	3 3 3 3 2,5	14,5
Content Idex "Stolen Lives" Corpus 2256 scenes				**92**

Source: IDIEM (© 521550).

Problematization is the hinge dimension with four categories in the index of ethical commitment. We understood problematization as being the narrative blanks in the program that allow discussion and public opinion formation. Its intention is not linear education. Problematization enables a diversity of opinions, a pluralism that takes place not only in the media content but also in the audiences. The opposite is the naturalization process.

A naturalization process was very clearly expressed in another TV fiction called *Patito Feo* (*The Ugly Duckling*), produced in Argentina and sold to over 40 countries, where the action takes place in school and the "delightful" or "divine" kids mistreat and discriminate against "ordinary" kids in all conceivable ways, also with songs and dancing. In the case of *Patito Feo*, which was the highest audience-rated fictional program for two years, the issue of discrimination was never problematized in the narrative. There was no plurality of voices, unlike in H.C. Andersen's Danish tale, which the program was supposed to be based on. The discriminating divine kids were always the popular and successful characters, and not even the end was what we all expected, because it was not the ugly duckling who became the winner of the singing and dancing competition.

In the fieldwork, we found that 90 percent of the girls in the audience wanted to be "a divine" because they are pretty and popular and always win. When asked if the divines were not in fact bad, the answer was "yes, but it's not so bad to be bad". Discriminatory actions in schools increased by 60 percent. We call this process "naturalization of a social problem" and socialization through imitation. The social consequence is a further deterioration of children's problems in daily life.

Simultaneously and cross-sectionally, the Expert Indicators, produced in cooperation with technicians from Save the Children and The Network Stop Trafficking, were applied to the content analysis of *Vidas Robadas* (Figure 4).

Figure 4. Dimensions and indicators on trafficking, and commercial sexual exploitation

1. PURPOSE Objectives pursued by traffickers in the exploitation of victims.	– Exploitation (sexual and labor) – Pornography – Sex tourism – Economic benefit of sexual trafficking	
2. ACTIVITY Modes of operation of traffickers linked to the recruitment, posting and receipt of the victims.	Catchment	Deceivement Work Seduction Studies Foul consent
	Displacement Migration Reception	Local National International
3. TOOLS Means of traffickers to influence the suppression of the will of the victim and the deprivation of their liberty in order to exploit it.	Forms	Coercion Force Fraud Threat Deceivement Abuse
	Control	Debt Confiscation of documents Addictions Seduction Manipulation of information

Source: Save the Children, Argentina, and RATT, Argentina, for IDIEM in 2008.

Audience involvement

The Index of Levels of Audience Involvement (Figure 5) is a cumulative scale. Some of the indicators are related to non-conscious processes. "Problematization" is again the hinge dimension. When problematization is not well developed, naturalization of the problem and its subsequent worsening in everyday life become the process taking place in the audience, as explained in the *Patito Feo (The Ugly Duckling)* case.

Figure 5. MIT Index: Audience levels of involvement

Vidas Robadas (Stolen lives)
Obtained Score: 92/100

Recognition
Association
Socialization
Problematization vs. Naturalization
Knowledge Integration
Conduct/Attitude
Conflict resolution tools
Bias for action
Cross-sectional analysis
Expert Indicators

Dimensions	Categories	Max possible score	Score obtained	Dimension MIT score
Recognition	• Problem Identification	5	5	5
Association	• Identification and projection	10	10	10
Problematization vs. Naturalization	• Imitation of models • Questioning • Causes – effects • Critical Opinion • Expert Indicators	25	25	25
Previous Knowledge Integration	• Comparison • Reflection • Opinion Formation • Proposals	10	10	10
Personal attitude/ Behavioral changes	• Attitudes • Tools/Contributions • Behavioral Changes Attitudes	15	12	12
Toward citizen action	• Tools/Contributions • Participation/ Association • Demand of Rights	25	20	20
Audience INDEX MIT "Stolen Lives"				**92**

Source: IDIEM (© 521550)

In a second instance, a cross-sectional analysis is performed with the Expert Indicators to see how they are recognized, socialized and integrated with prior knowledge that can lead to later citizen action.

The fiction program *Vidas Robadas* received 16 audience rating points, but 92 points on the MIT Index. This shows what is possible when the media are committed to addressing children's real demands, that is, when the production develops themes that are sensitive to the child audience and in doing so takes into account the needs of this audience.

The index of levels of involvement takes a new look at an old problem. It emerges as the analysis of both conscious and unconscious processes that occur in children and young people when they are in front of the screen. I have dealt here with narrative fiction because it often implies strong processes of socialization, but the index can be applied to all genres.

Secondary data related to *Vidas Robadas*, as part of the research work, increase and reconfirm the high involvement of the audience, the exercise of their citizenship and their demand for rights:

- In many schools across the country, children and adolescents made prevention campaigns and brochures on human trafficking to be distributed in their neighborhoods (in Tucumán, Mendoza, Pergamino, La Plata, and so on).
- There were headlines in the local and even national press, providing feedback on the ethical commitment of the media.
- Social networks were the site of action and integration that added thousands of teenagers and younger people to the campaigns.
- The teens created blogs "to be vigilant and defend each other". We interviewed them and, interestingly, they identified with the victims and thought that, because human trafficking is a mafia business, they could at least do something to defend themselves, including acquiring the in-depth knowledge that is essential for any action.
- In the surveys, awareness of human trafficking raised to almost 90 percent and was related to what the soap opera *Vidas Robadas* had conveyed about children's lives.
- Newspaper reports grew by 250 percent according to our comparative analysis (between two years) of the theme's presence in three major national newspapers over a period of 180 days.
- The phone calls denouncing cases of human trafficking increased by 300 percent (*source*: RATT, Red Alta a la Trata y al Tráfico/The Network Stop Trafficking, an Argentine non-governmental organization).
- A law on human trafficking was enacted that had previously been postponed for years.
- *Vidas Robadas* received an award from the National Parliament for its cultural contribution, which is also shown in the present research results.

Conclusion

Our data clearly show that television committed to an ethic of development is possible, and that the consequences for child and youth audiences can be *involvement as a process – with participation, inclusion, media education, empowerment, citizen action, and demand for rights – that modifies reality*. The voice of children and young people achieved visibility and was listened to by media makers and all stakeholders.

When we try to understand the phenomenon of media and the cultural change they represent, there is a need to consider as many variables and levels of analysis as possible in order to take into account the apparent contradictions between factors that are combined in different ways. The paradigm of complexity is necessary when facing an era that may seem chaotic and that is already showing a new dynamic equilibrium.

Paradigm changes are confirmed and specified and are not only understood from a phenomenological or technological perspective, but also with regard to the internal processes of man. The individual, social, cultural and global features intersect and complement each other. What seems different or local is also a global phenomenon with specific glocal characteristics.

Based on these internal human processes, produced spontaneously by young people, we want to take action to promote and follow the establishment of a contract for an ethics of development between the media and audiences.

Indexes of ethical commitment will be the basis of participation, as they have emerged from children's own demands. Regulation will be a process that starts in the base, in children's and youth's opinions and participation.

In a suggestion for a further Media Social Responsibility Index, we have as a final goal to add indicators to the Global Reporting Initiative related to the platform Global Compact of the United Nations.

Lastly, I would like to stress the necessity of bringing knowledge into action. There are three key elements for an ethical commitment to development:

- recognition of the weaknesses of the present reality,
- the will to help this reality change, and
- faith in the future.

These are also the three main components of hope, which is the highest demand for children and young people…

"Hope is passion for the possible", as Søren Kierkegaard put it.

References

Mauss, Marcel (1954) "The Ethnological Theory", *American Anthropologist*, 56: 58-71

Merlo Flores, Tatiana (in press) *Las demandas de las nuevas audiencias. Medición del Impacto Televisivo*. Buenos Aires: La Crujía

Morin, Edgar (1984) *Science avec Conscience*. Barcelona: Edit. Anthropos (Editorial del Hombre)

Morin, Edgar (1994) *Introducción al pensamiento complejo*. Barcelona: Gedisa

Morin, Edgar (2010) *¿Hacia el abismo? Globalización en el siglo XXI*. Ibérica: Paidós

Youngsters' Expressions of Responsible Citizenship through Media Diaries

Sirkku Kotilainen, Annikka Suoninen, Irma Hirsjärvi and Sara Kolomainen

For young people in the West, acting with the media, e.g., in online communities, can be part of everyday practices. However, even in Western countries, researchers have found "digital divides" among the young concerning the quality of online activities. The lack of an Internet connection, or a low-speed connection, or less up-to-date software all mean unequal access to opportunities for participation online. Other discriminatory factors among users include poor media literacy skills or even media illiteracy (Livingstone & Helsper, 2007; Jenkins et al., 2009). What could the picture be if we also look to the East and to the South?

Thomas Tufte and Florencia Enghel (2009) point out social realities that construct the life worlds of the young in the global context: "unequal living conditions and disparities, marginal and vulnerable rural livelihoods in poor areas of the globe, illiteracy, inadequate education, unemployment, and apathy and disengagement vis-a-vis political participation" (p. 12). In this situation, following Naila Kabeer's (2005) definition of inclusive citizenship, they consider important aspects of young people's responsible citizenship as follows: justice, recognition, self-determination and solidarity. Within this framework, they highlight youth-centred communication in debates on social change and social justice, for example, young people communicating for their rights through participatory media production. So, what significance do the media have for socially responsible activities in life and society from the viewpoints of young people?

We are highlighting this question based on media diaries that have been collected in five countries, Argentina, Egypt, Finland, India and Kenya, during the first half of 2010. The collection of the diaries has been one of the research activities in an ongoing comparative project entitled "Global Research on Youth Media Participation (YMP)". The project provides knowledge about the means and conditions of youth media participation through questionnaires, interviews and diaries among 11- to 18-year-olds.

The emphasis of the project is on the active role of children and youth in all media and in societies. Young people are considered not only as a single cultural phenomenon, or as an audience, but also as multiple groupings and actors who are shaped by sociocultural differences. For example, different age groups probably show out different kinds of participation with media. Youngsters under 18 years are living adolescence, and their desires and practices, including media use, are on the move (cf. Kotilainen & Rantala, 2009; Mannheim, 1928/1952).

The media are considered to include all information technologies that offer public spaces and presentations for interacting with people as audiences, for example, radio, television, newspapers, the Internet and mobile phones. Media are approached as embedded within social relationships and possibilities to participate in societies, as well as local and global communities (cf. for example, Jenkins et al., 2009).

Societal and cultural participation in relations with media

Rossana Reguillo (2009) names three media-related participatory and political activities of the young that take place on a global scale: claiming their rights and intervening directly in national politics, strengthening the blogosphere as an alternate space for communication, and participation in movements with a global reach. She states that, through blogs, young people's "subjective, personal, emotional, every day matters shape politics" when there is a possibility to publish one's own problems and events. In general, she thinks that having access to and the skills to use communicational technology strengthen young people's social participation, which weakens when "participation calls for the body" (Reguillo, 2009: 31-34).

Sirkku Kotilainen and Leena Rantala (2009) point out that youths, even those younger than 18 years of age, can use an activist identity when faced with an important issue for which action in the public media is necessary. Thus, the fluid borders of the public and private in youth civic cultures are evident. According to the writers, these kinds of mixed positions and modes of participation, even if culturally oriented, can be seen as important structures in young people's lives. They argue that the modes of cultural participation of youths in relation to media should be considered more as a resource for developing new modes of civic engagement and political participation.

Peter Dahlgren (2006) states that it is important to get over the traditional divides between the rational public and the emotional private spheres in order to understand the motivations, identities and passions that launch people into the public sphere. He calls for a cultural turn in our understanding of civic agency: citizenship should not only be seen in formal terms, but also in regard to meaning, practices, communication and identities – more in terms of civic cultures. In this way, we consider the media diaries of the youths collected in five countries (see above) and see them as expressions of citizenship in different local cultures.

Henry Jenkins et al. (2009; cf. Knobel & Lankshear, 2007) list the cultural competencies that young people should acquire in order to be full participants in the emerging participatory culture online, where the key elements are sharing and taking part. For example, play and simulation are current media literacy skills that enable participation in communities online. Furthermore, other important competencies include judgement (the ability to evaluate the reliability and credibility of different information sources) and negotiation (the ability to travel across diverse communities, discerning and respecting multiple perspectives). But what about having the courage and motivation to take part in public discussions, criticizing and calling for social change (cf. Tufte & Enghel, 2009)?

The study "Global Research on Youth Media Participation" is being conducted mainly in Finland, Argentina, Egypt and India (the state of Gujarat) among youngsters between 11-18 years of age. We are exploring, among other things, the kinds of media literacies that are activated in relations and engagements in literacy events with media or access points for media literacy, for example, while playing, watching TV, reading newspapers and in diverse activities online (cf. Street, 2003; Kotilainen & Arnolds-Granlund, 2010). Special attention is being paid to media participation, i.e., youth engagement with public media.

In the present article, we are looking for expressions of young people's citizenship in relation to media mostly from the viewpoint of social responsibility: What kinds of sociocultural issues come up in the media diaries and what kinds of responsible and ethical attitudes or positions emerge concerning solidarity and recognition of youngsters as actors in society (cf. Kabeer, 2005)? Social issues might vary from societal to neighbourhood relations including family and friends. Moreover, we focus on media literacy practices, for example, taking a critical attitude towards media as a source of information, i.e., judgement (cf. Jenkins et al., 2009).

One day with media around the world

As part of the Youth Media Participation project, we collected media diaries from 14-year-olds in five countries during spring 2010. In addition to the four countries taking part in the YMP project (Finland, Argentina, Egypt and India), diaries were also collected in Kenya in collaboration with Nokia Research Centre.[1]

The purpose of this "One Day with Media" collection was to get a picture of how media uses are embedded in the everyday life of youngsters in different cultures. The youth were encouraged to write about the purposes of their media use and what kinds of thoughts and feelings the media and media contents aroused in them.

In Argentina, there are great differences in access to and use of different media between urban and rural areas and between social classes. This divide was best seen in regard to access to and use of the Internet, which played a central part in the lives of urban teenagers, but was rarely used in rural areas. In Argentina, the overall expressions about media were often very emotional: The media fill the emptiness, prevent loneliness or boredom; they are a good friend when real friends are not available. Media are for socializing and for entertainment, and are not seen as giving information or acting as a medium for civic participation to such a great extent. The most important media are television, mobile phones and in the urban area also the Internet, which is also used mainly for communication with friends.

In Egypt, too, the "digital divide" between urban and rural areas and different social classes is very clear. In Egypt, a wide range of different media are available also in the native language Arabic, but all national media are supervised by governmental authorities. In their media diaries, the Egyptian youngsters emphasized the role of media in seeking and getting information about different subjects for school work and about their own interests as well as current affairs. The Internet and mobile phone also appeared as important tools for communicating with friends and relatives. Radio and newspapers seemed to play an essential role.[2]

In Finland, new media technologies are part of the everyday life of youngsters both in urban and rural areas, as three fourths of all Finnish households have broadband Internet and there are more mobile phones than inhabitants. In their diaries, the Finnish children expressed their surprise at how much they used media themselves on a daily basis. Using media was part of everyday leisure activities both in school and at home, and the media were seen as an essential tool for socializing throughout the day. Finnish youngsters used different types of media during the day, and several media simultaneously.

In the Indian media diaries, using media gives a strong sense of belonging to both the local and global community. The news was followed carefully; it aroused strong emotional feelings of joy and sorrow and was talked about with friends and family members. Learning through media was highlighted in numerous diaries. Comments on ethical issues were also common. Especially rural teenagers had very limited access to different types of media (above all the Internet), and radio played a central role. In addition, the importance of audiovisual media for illiterate people was mentioned repeatedly in the diaries.

In Kenya, those teenagers taking part in the diary collection had very limited access to most of the electronic media. Their media use consisted mainly of radio and newspapers. The use of media among the Kenyan youth is selective; the youngsters often decide ahead of time to use a certain media for a certain purpose at a certain time. In the Kenyan media diaries, media are seen more as providing educational information and national and global news than as devices or a platform that enables peer-to-peer interaction, self-expression, or content creation.

Reflections on responsible citizenship

The youngsters were not asked to write particularly about responsible citizenship, but contents related to this theme could be found to some extent in diaries from all participating countries. The main ways in which responsible citizenship was described in media diaries were the young people's *expressions on solidarity* and *involvement in societal issues through media*:

- How young people use media for taking care of others
- How young people feel about being looked after through media or in connection with their media use
- How young people can be involved in and informed about societal issues through and by media
- How young people see the role of media as one major player in society.

Expressions of solidarity

In their diaries, youngsters wrote about various ways of taking care of others and expressing solidarity with family members, relatives, friends or schoolmates. Different kinds of communicative media were used for contacting friends and family, respectively, and all kinds of media could be used together with other people in order to spend time in the company of others.

> Yesterday I watched a programme that tells about the news in a humoristic style. It was a good way to share some moments with my mum, after a long day of work and school. [...] I also used the regular telephone to call to my grandparents, because they had been to the doctor and I wanted to know how it went. I also called a friend in another city – I do it once a week. It's a need I have because she's a lot of fun and we have two very different lives. (Argentina, boy)

> I used the mobile phone to communicate with my younger sister who lives in the countryside. I'm very happy to have the mobile phone because you can very quickly find out what's happening. (Kenya, girl)

> In our family everyone reads a lot. The smallest ones, those who cannot read, listen to fairy tales from CDs and we read a lot to them, too. [...] A friend of mine called me during the school hour and asked how I am. I answered her during the recess. (Finland, girl)

The young teenagers also described their concern over other people's media uses, and expressed their hopes about protecting other people from the possible harmful effects of media. The young people could also describe the kind of media contents they found recommendable. The people they were concerned about could include younger siblings or children in general, but also teenagers and adults with limited media literacy skills. Taking care of others through media use could also be quite literal, as in this excerpt from an Indian media diary:

> Yesterday in one person's house the gas cylinder exploded and the whole family died in the blast. On reading this, I took the newspaper to my grandfather and

> made him read the news. I also called my brother, father and mother and made them read the news. I told my brother to use the gas cylinder very carefully [...]. Thus, because I had read the news in the newspaper, I made my family members aware. (India, boy)

Young people did not only take care of other people or their media usage, but they felt that they themselves were taken care of as well. Parents and friends contacted them to see how they were doing. Friends could offer them possibilities to use some media they would not otherwise have access to, or give help and advice about using different media technologies.

> Since my friend has a computer at his house, I went to his place to learn to use the computer. There were many programs on the computer, like PowerPoint, Excel, PC logo, Paint, etc. My friend had taken a course to learn all these programs and so he knew them very well. Then my friend gave me information about the Internet and email on the computer. I understood all the information he gave me and told him that we would find information about the work done in other countries, like the animals, plants and trees, by opening the website in the computer. (India, boy)

Involvement in societal issues through media

In their media diaries, the youngsters also wrote about their thoughts and feelings concerning different kinds of societal issues, such as environmental issues, human rights, the cultural rights of different minorities, their notions and opinions about domestic and foreign politics and policies, and their concerns about social injustice both at the local and global level. In many diaries, these kinds of issues came up as short remarks in between the more general descriptions of media use.

> The biggest news of the online newspaper was about the volcano in Iceland and the consequences of the spreading ash cloud. In connection with that I joined the "Send the Foreign Ash Clouds Back Abroad" group in Facebook. [This group makes a parody of anti-immigrant groups and movements] (Finland, girl)

> Later in the evening, I watched TV for a moment, and just before writing this diary I read a book about boys in Afghanistan. It made me think. I realized that what is normal to me is unfamiliar to millions. I felt privileged. (Finland, boy)

> I also watched a programme about the government officials, which told stories about people in power and how they work for their own sake and not for the sake of the country. (Egypt, girl)

> Through media, different thoughts appear in my mind and I become more social and attached to society [...]. With the help of media, citizens can keep updated on the prevailing conditions in the world, as well as in our country. [...] in my view the electronic media are the best. There are many illiterate people in our country who can't read properly. So for them the most developed electronic media act as a friend to help them stay updated. (India, girl)

Especially in India and Kenya, societal issues and reflections about them could form the main part of the diaries. Young people could reflect on the social inequalities in their own country or globally and think about the role of media in spreading knowledge about these issues and – possibly – playing an active role in finding solutions to these problems.

> It was on a Saturday morning the 28th of March when I took my father's Daily Nation paper. I started reading it from the first page. It said "How the Post-Election Violence Has Affected Women in Kenya". Especially those women in slums who had cast their votes. Women and girls were raped, impregnated, infected with HIV/AIDS, killed, abandoned, discriminated by their tribes. [...] In my own experience: the media groups are trying very hard to counsel Kenyans to promote peace, especially the youths who are being used during election campaigns, because they need development, employment, change. They sometimes become very desperate about life, leading to suicide. The media try their best to go where the clashes occur, sing songs based on challenges youths and teenagers are facing, encouraging them not to lose hope. The media really make it clear that the justice does not realize in Kenya. But Kenyans try to fight corruption because they need human rights. Without people, no development can take place, not only in our country but around the whole world, for whatever happens. (Kenya, girl)

Reflective and critical tones towards media

Youngsters in all countries also wrote generally about the great role the media play in the everyday life of people all over the world – especially in developed countries. As mentioned, particularly the Finnish youths often expressed at the end of their diaries their surprise at how many different media they had used during the day and how dependent they were on media. However, the medium they personally felt they were most dependent on – or even addicted to – was the Internet.

> Media is a crucial part of life all the time [...] I could not live without it. I use media in my home, at my friends' places, in school and also while I'm outdoors. Most of the time I'm on Facebook and use Messenger. If there is something wrong with the Internet connection, I get angry and start terrorizing the computer. I think that I have been without Messenger only for a couple of days, maybe once a month. (Finland, girl)

> Nowadays the media are around us all the time. With an Internet connection, almost all the information in the world is available to us on our computers and mobile phones. We can't even think about the world without Internet. (Finland, boy)

Generally it seems that when access to media is limited, media are seen very positively. In the Indian and Kenyan diaries, media were mainly given praise for educating people and spreading information about national and international news. But the youngsters felt that, given this power, the media should also assume responsibility for their actions. The media should be responsible and give people the right information, because today the media are by far the most important source of information.

> So I turned on the radio. They were talking about the school holiday that pupils and students were about to start. How they should behave at home, what kind of friends they should have and walk with. I was happy for Citizen FM and for their good work. You really have to hope that young people know the right thing to do at the right time. (Kenya, girl)

> In the same way, when a bomb has been placed on a bus, plane or in a multiplex, then we learn about it through the media. When this happens, relatives of people who are there in the malls, bus or plane get very anxious and start inquiring about their near and dear ones. At the same time, these media people, like the newspaper people, TV and radio announcers, give news in a very sensational manner and then it turns out to be that the thing was just a rumour. Though this doesn't happen every time, but media people should not spread any news and information without complete accuracy. Many people's blood pressure shoots up and many suffer from heart attacks when they hear such news. Media people should keep this in mind when they broadcast news and advertisements. (India, boy)

When access to and use of different media increase, critical tones appear when writing about media in general. Media are seen to be giving one-sided information and therefore maybe building up or even creating political or cultural tensions. Young people also thought about whether the media provide a truthful picture or whether their news pictures are biased in any way.

> But in my opinion, we should use media so that awareness is created in the country. And our country keeps progressing in this way. But friends, many unlawful activities are also carried out through media that can harm the reputation of the country. [...] Today's children use the Internet, mobile phones, etc., and also use the hacking software to destroy people's businesses. [...] Because of this, the citizens of our country are not permitted to go abroad. The people of other countries also refuse to do business with us.
>
> Terrorism is the root cause of this. If there is a solution to the problem of terrorism, then it should be brought about. That way we could stop the fighting between countries. The blame for the terrorist attack falls on the one who has not done it. (India, boy)

> I visited – again – the online newspaper and read some interesting news. Many of the news items were about the chaos caused by the ash cloud [from a volcanic eruption in Iceland]. When reading about Finnair [the Finnish airline company] I couldn't avoid thinking whether the media were treating it in a unfair manner; after all the company had tried to get the stranded passengers to Finland, for example by sending buses to Germany; they had not left them totally without help.

> The media sometimes exaggerate things, and they can change the original meaning to something totally different. Sometimes it's extremely difficult to say, for example when reading gossip magazines, what is true and what is exaggerated. (Finland, girl)

> I read an article in the newspaper about the new iPad from Apple. This product was given praise and it was called a "media consumption device". That phrase caught my eye and I was quite irritated by it, even though it is true. Do we really need one more "media device" in addition to the existing ones? But iPad has been a success in the U.S., so it seems that other people find it quite necessary. (Finland, boy)

Discussion

We have presented some preliminary results from a collection of media diaries from youths in five countries around the world, looking at how they express responsible citizenship. First of all concerning access, digital gaps seem to get wider when the picture broadens from the West and North to the East and South. Based on the diaries, young people living in rural areas of developing countries seem to have no choice in media use and limited possibilities to participate through media compared to those living in city areas or developed countries.

However, young people's expressions of responsible citizenship, i.e., solidarity through media and an interest in societal issues via media, do not seem to be dependent on the technical device. Where Internet connections are not available, radio, television, newspapers and magazines inform youngsters and promote discussions among them. The difference seems to be the mode of participation: When a 14-year-old in Finland is able to enter an international political movement online, youngsters of the same age in rural areas of India and Kenya reflect on national political themes via (traditional) mass media with their friends, family or by themselves. Anyway, we can ask whether 14-year-olds take further political action without the Internet, for example by participating in demonstrations (cf. Reguillo, 2009; Kotilainen & Rantala, 2009).

While the Internet in particular is a medium through which even young people can make their opinions heard or visible, it seems that our method has worked in this way, too. Youngsters experienced the media diaries as a channel through which they could express their opinions and make their voices heard, being recognized as themselves (Kabeer, 2005). For example, many of the Kenyan youngsters wrote the media diaries as if they were writing directly to decision-makers, media representatives or even their favourite athletes.

In the present material, media literacies appear as reflections on one's own media uses and as criticisms of the media, or 'judgements' according to Jenkins et al. (2009). These judgements include youngsters' concerns about other people's media uses and express their hopes about protecting other people from possible harmful effects of the media. Moreover, the young people are willing to participate in renewing the contents, when they describe the kind of media contents they have found recommendable.

The media diaries show how youngsters in different parts of the world implement their responsible citizenship through the media, while expressing solidarity with others through communication devices and getting involved in social themes through the media. Worldwide, the media should take young people's willingness to participate seriously.

Notes

1. In Argentina, Egypt, Finland and India (Gujarat), the diaries were collected in schools both in urban and rural areas and areas with different socio-economical conditions. In Kenya, all but two of the diaries were written at a school in a low-income, informal urban settlement. In Argentina, we collected a total of 175 diaries, in Egypt 100 diaries, in Finland 144 diaries, in Gujarat 160 diaries and in Kenya 48 diaries.
2. The media diaries from Egypt were under translation and analysis while we were writing this article, which is why only a few diaries were available in English.

References

Dahlgren, Peter (2006) Doing Citizenship. The Cultural Origins of Civic Agency in the Public Sphere, *European Journal of Cultural Studies*, 9(3), pp. 267-286

Jenkins, Henry et al. (2009) *Confronting the Challenges of Participatory Culture: Media Education for the 21st Century*. MacArthur Foundation. An occasional paper on digital media and learning, www.digitallearning.macfound.org

Kabeer, Naila (Ed.) (2005) *Inclusive Citizenship. Meanings and Expressions*. London: Zed Books

Knobel, Michel & Lankshear, Colin (Eds.) (2007) *A New Literacies Sampler*. New York: Peter Lang

Kotilainen, Sirkku & Rantala, Leena (2009) From Seekers to Activists: Characteristics of youth civic identities in relation to media, *Information, Communication & Society*, 12(5), pp. 658-677

Kotilainen, Sirkku & Arnolds-Granlund, Sol-Britt (Eds.) (2010) *Media Literacy Education. Nordic Perspectives*. The International Clearinghouse on Children, Youth and Media at NORDICOM, University of Gothenburg, in cooperation with the Finnish Society on Media Education

Livingstone, Sonia & Helsper, Ellen (2007) Gradations in Digital Inclusion: Children, Young people and the Digital Divide, *New Media & Society*, 9(4), pp. 671-696

Mannheim, Karl (1928/1952) The Problem of Generations, in *Essays on the Sociology of the Knowledge*. London: Routledge & Kegan Paul, pp. 276-322

Reguillo, Rossana (2009) The Warrior's Code? Youth, Communication and Social Change, in Tufte, Thomas & Enghel, Florencia (Eds.) *Youth Engaging with the World. Media, Communication and Social Change*. The International Clearinghouse on Children, Youth and Media at NORDICOM, University of Gothenburg, pp. 21-42

Street, Brian (2003) What's "new" in New Literacy Studies? Critical approaches to literacy in theory and practice, *Current Issues in Comparative Education*, 5(2), pp. 77-91

Tufte, Thomas & Enghel, Florencia (Eds.) (2009) *Youth Engaging with the World. Media, Communication and Social Change*. The International Clearinghouse on Children, Youth and Media at NORDICOM, University of Gothenburg

Panel Session on Communication for Social Change

Introduction

Florencia Enghel and Thomas Tufte

Communication for social change is a challenging notion, both in terms of how to conceptualize it and in terms of how to implement it strategically through concrete initiatives. The challenge is apparent in efforts by non-governmental and civil society organizations to mainstream communication for social change, or communication for development, into initiatives involving, e.g., bilateral donors, United Nations agencies or The World Bank. In the academic field, the challenge is reflected in the ongoing interest in citizenship, participation, voice and public engagement – and in the role of communication and media in enabling social action. In this context, critical scrutiny of the concept of communication for social change is both pertinent and timely (Wilkins, 2009), and we need to embed such an examination in the actual real-life experiences of people. Our articles in this Yearbook are intended to contribute to such critical scrutiny.

The contributions focus on youth, and particularly the ways in which they engage with the world through communicative action (Tufte & Enghel, 2009). The overall purpose is to explore the role of communication and media in the relationship between youth and social change critically, moving away from optimistic/pessimistic approaches to analysis and highlighting the importance of understanding processes of communication in the context of the social relationships in which they take place (Schiller, 2007).

Three of the four articles in this session inform the role of communication and media in the relationship between youth and social change from an empirical perspective, focusing on countries that are experiencing significant processes of social transformation – Belarus in East Europe, Turkey on the European borderline to Asia, and Malawi in Southern Africa. The articles provide three different entry points to the study of youth engaging with media, communication and social change. First, Iryna Vidanava's article 'On Disc and Online: Expanding Digital Activism in Belarus' discusses *a youth-driven media initiative* – a digital youth magazine in Belarus – and its strategies for opening a discursive space for debate, critique and citizen activism within the constrained political environment of Europe's last dictatorship. Second, in 'Strengthening Civil Society – a Communication for Social Change Agenda?' Mette Grøndahl Hansen and Lise Grauenkær Jensen introduce us to *an NGO-driven development programme based on youth participation* in community communication centres in Malawi. Their article speaks to the difficulties encountered by people attempting to articulate civil society development through community media, and particularly to orchestrate communication for social change institutionally. Third, in 'Being Read by a DJ – Youth Interaction via Radio and Cell Phones in Southeast Turkey', Ece Algan presents *a media ethnographic study of how Turkish youth make use of mobile phones*, focusing on how gender identities and sexualities are manifested and experienced via mobile media in a small town bordering on Iran. The article looks critically into claims made in certain media scholarship that the mere existence of media induces social change.

Finally, in our own article, entitled 'Citizenship Practices among Youth – Exploring the Role of Communication and Media', we consider the notion of citizenship in the context of *globalization*, looking into communication and the media's role as a resource enabling citizenship practices among youth. Our discussion is framed in the context of the socio-economic and cultural realities of youth worldwide (Reguillo, 2009).

References

Reguillo, Rossana (2009) "The Warrior's Code? Youth, Communication and Social Change", in Tufte, Thomas & Enghel, Florencia (Eds.) *Youth Engaging with the World: Media, Communication and Social Change*. Yearbook 2009. The International Clearinghouse on Children, Youth and Media. University of Gothenburg: NORDICOM, pp. 21-39

Schiller, Dan (2007) *How to Think about Information*. Champaign, IL: The University of Illinois Press

Tufte, Thomas & Enghel, Florencia (2009) "Youth Engaging with Media and Communication: Different, Unequal and Disconnected?", in Tufte, Thomas & Enghel, Florencia (Eds.) *Youth Engaging with the World: Media, Communication and Social Change*. Yearbook 2009. The International Clearinghouse on Children, Youth and Media. University of Gothenburg: NORDICOM, pp. 11-18

Wilkins, Karin (2009) "What's in a Name? Problematizing Communication's Shift from Development to Social Change", *Glocal Times*, No. 13 (November), http://www.glocaltimes.k3.mah.se/viewarticle.aspx?articleID=173&issueID=20

On Disc and Online

Expanding Digital Activism in Belarus

Iryna Vidanava

Belarus is a country known mainly for its dictator, Alexander Lukashenka, and the 1986 Chernobyl Disaster. With its Lenin statues, KGB (State Security Agency), and collective farms, time seems to have stopped in this part of Europe. But many young Belarusians refuse to be left in the past. Behind the country's closed borders and hidden from the secret police, a dynamic youth scene is alive and active, underground, in dorms, clubs, informal groups, artistic communities and cyberspace. The story of the country's opposition and counterculture youth, the future of a free Belarus, is being told on Internet-based, independent media. And the political and cultural activism of these youth is being aided and abetted by cutting-edge "new media".

Being young and active in "Europe's last dictatorship" is no easy task. Youth leaders are imprisoned, activist students expelled from schools, and youth NGOs (non-governmental organizations) closed down. The situation of independent media is also grim. Human rights groups regularly rank Belarus near the bottom of media freedom lists. Independent newspapers, radio stations and newspapers have been shut down and journalists have been beaten, jailed, murdered and made to disappear.

Creative responses

In this climate, the free media have been forced to be more inventive. The result has been a flowering of alternative media, embodied by *samizdat* (underground publishing), email newspapers, information websites, blogs and online social networks. While the free press has almost ceased printing, the readership of new media news sources is growing. The web versions of independent papers have become more popular than their state counterparts. Statistics indicate that the opposition dominates the online information space.

Young activists have embraced new media that can be produced at home and easily disseminated. In Belarus, youth are the creative force behind new media. Young people make up most of the techies responsible for producing online sites, and they are the driving force of innovation in this field. Young people are also important users and purveyors. They have taken their struggle online, merging activism with the Internet. After protests in 2006 were brutally put down, young activists retreated to various online communities. Like the kitchen, which was the refuge of their Soviet dissident parents, the Internet became a virtual meeting place, where young activists cooked up new forms of real-world resistance, such as flash mobs, campaigns to assist persecuted young people, and other forms of cyber-assisted activism.

Virtual activism has become an inseparable part of Belarusian reality, especially for young digital natives. In one survey, students cite virtual activities as second in popularity only to going to discos, clubs and movies.[1] While most young users surf the Net as an entertainment source, they can hardly avoid news posted on Belarusian web portals. A purported state survey at two universities found that more than a third of respondents listed the Internet as their primary source of information.[2]

From thought to action

Despite ongoing repression, some youth media have been able to develop successfully. One of the most interesting new media stories is *34*, formerly *Студэнцкая Думка* (*Students' Thought*), the country's premier youth publication.[3] *Students' Thought* first appeared as a Belarusian newspaper in 1924. Re-started in 1988 by students during the USSR's (Union of Soviet Socialist Republics) *glasnost* period, it became the bulletin of the Belarusian Students' Association. At first, the publication was small, unprofessional, irregular and not very lively. But in 1999, it was re-launched as an independent youth magazine, became a monthly and grew from 16 black-and-white to 40 color pages. By 2005, circulation went from 500 to 5,000 copies and readership was estimated at 10,000. The magazine covered topics such as cultural diversity, corruption at universities, youth employment and new technologies.

The worsening political situation pushed the magazine to be more innovative and activist. In 2003, it launched the country's first Internet civic campaign. The goal of "Become.A Self-Made.Person" was to paint a portrait of a new generation as seen through the eyes of young people, and to convince them that it is possible to make a difference by being active. Youth were asked to design their idea of the Belarusian dream. More than 160 teams submitted concepts for a video spot. The campaign attracted broad public attention: 600 young people took part, thousands voted online for their favorites, and millions saw the winning spot on state TV.

It is not surprising that the authorities, nervous of the tiny publication's impact, reacted by trying to close it down. At the end of 2003, two weeks after the campaign's award ceremony, the Ministry of Information cancelled the magazine's registration. Forced underground, *Students' Thought* continued publishing. Unable to use the state-run subscription service, it created an alternative distribution system using places popular among youth, like Internet cafés and music stores.

In 2005, a second campaign – "Become.A Self-Made.Person.ACTION!" – was held. This time, youth were asked to identify a challenge facing their local community and propose an action plan to raise awareness of and address the problem. Finalists were provided with resources to implement their social campaigns. The activities were so creative and interesting that state television featured several on the news.

The publication was making its mark. One commentator wrote that: "*Students' Thought* is something new, something unseen before among Belarusian-language publications."[4] Due to its growing influence, the November 2005 issue was seized by the police on the pretext of being printed with "poisonous ink". The magazine was banned, a criminal case was launched against the editor-in-chief, and publishing houses refused to print it.

Collage of *Students' Thought* magazine covers, including final issue confiscated by police

Source: 34mag.net, September 2010. Reproduced with permission from *34 Multimedia Magazine*

Going digital

The publication's response was to transform itself into a multimedia edition on compact disc.[5] The editors exploited a loophole in the media law, which did not regulate materials on CDs. In January 2006, the magazine reappeared under the title of *CDMAG*.[6] Like the original magazine, *CDMAG* targets students and youth aged 16-25.[7] The bimonthly reports on social, political, economic and cultural issues important to youth, such as problems of higher education, students' rights, information on youth NGOs, Belarusian youth subcultures, and European youth life.

The shift to new media helped the magazine become more attractive to youth, who love CDs and computers. Each issue focuses on one topic relevant to youth. In addition to text and illustrations, the digital format allows the use of video, audio, music and flash animation. Original video materials – short spots, reports and interviews – make up 50 percent of every issue. The CD also allows a more substantial publication; while the last print issue included .87 MB of text (44 pages with illustrations), an average issue of *CDMAG* contains 600 MB of multimedia content. Because the CD can be read and replicated on any computer, multiple copies can be burned and passed on. *CDMAG*'s slogan is "Make Your Own Copy!". Referring to the appearance of *CDMAG*, one youth website noted: "by banning and persecuting independent media, the state forces it to produce even better and more competitive products."[8]

That summer, the magazine showed what the new format could do. It produced a special issue on the March protests following the rigged election. "Open Air Revolution" told the story of the revolution that took place in the hearts and minds of young people who experienced the 2006 events. It was the first multimedia chronicle of the demonstrations, protesters' "tent city", Independence Day March and crackdown that followed, in which more than 1,000 people, mostly youth, were beaten and jailed. The story was told through four hours of the words, music, pictures, poetry, videos, protest art and text messages of young participants. It offered interviews, including those smuggled out of prisons, with youth activists and gave a voice to their excitement, hope, disappointment, fear, suffering and commitment to freedom and democracy. In recognition of its groundbreaking work, *CDMAG* was awarded the Gerd Bucerius Prize for "Free Press of Eastern Europe" in 2007.[9]

Forever young

A key principle of the magazine is that it is produced by young people for young people.[10] In 1998, students founded the original *Students' Thought*. They have since developed into a professional team of eight. About 30 young activists, mainly students, also contribute. With no requirement that a contributor be a trained journalist, any young person with creative ideas is welcome. Together the editorial team and contributors develop topics and materials for future issues. The input of contributors, who are the same age as the magazine's audience, helps the editors team to accurately reflect new trends and stay on top of youth developments. The editorial team intensively interacts with its audience via email and social networking communities. Each week, it receives feedback in the form of hundreds of online comments and emails. The team encourages its young readers to participate in producing the magazine.

While not overtly political, *CDMAG* encourages young people to think and make informed choices. It remains the only national publication to introduce key ideas, events and people to a youth audience. It links political youth with young members of the counterculture, strengthening youth activism and the democratic movement as a whole. The magazine has evolved over the past decade, but the goal remains the same: to inform, educate and encourage young people to be more active. Born in an authoritarian state, the publication helps young people think for themselves and make their own choices, whether it is the candidates they vote for or the music they listen to. Despite its success, *CDMAG* is not a mass publication. Knowing its limitations, the magazine focuses on Belarus' young elites. It tries to expand the mentality of students and youth leaders, believing that the vanguard of a new generation will play a crucial role in transforming Belarus into a European democracy.

Writing about resistance

Like kids everywhere, young Belarusians are crazy about the Internet and popular culture. But unlike in the West, the Belarusian authorities attempt to restrict anything that smacks of free thinking. Youth activists are detained, expelled from universities, fired from jobs and forcibly conscripted into the army. Youth NGOs and publications are closed down. The regime tries to control youth because it fears any independent ideas, home-grown or from the West. The authorities try to restrict, repress and impose, but they cannot dictate what young people listen to, read or watch. What is forbidden becomes even trendier and more desirable. Young Belarusians are no different from other youth who respond to restrictions with creative forms of dissent. Thanks to the regime, a counterculture is alive and well in Belarus. Young activists stage flash mobs to ridicule the authorities' absurdities. Youngsters go to underground clubs and across borders to listen to banned bands. Young artists and photographers show in alternative art galleries and post works online. Writers and journalists publish in independent newspapers and blogs. These are the trends covered by *CDMAG*.[11]

In Belarus, where the regime would like youth to be a passive grey mass that obeys the leader's decrees, *CDMAG* encourages its readers to be individuals: "Don't be like the others, be yourself!" Always searching for new faces and trends, each issue blends serious and fun materials about Belarus' creative hippies, revolutionaries, rock stars, youth leaders and other nonconformist heroes. Many well-known musicians and artists were first featured in *CDMAG* at the start of their careers. One way of helping youth overcome the fear of being different in a dictatorship is to feature their peers who have already achieved something special and share their opinions on important issues.

While trying to "keep it real", the editors understand that it can be dangerous for authors and subjects to appear in an underground publication. In such cases, the multimedia concept shines. When choosing the format of each piece (a mix of video, podcast, slideshow, comic or flash cartoon), the editors decide on the best fit for the form, content, style and wishes of the featured person. If appearing on camera is too risky, a flash cartoon using the actual voice from an interview is utilized. Interactive comics are also used to protect activists.

Special covers and art work are also unique features that make the magazine stand out. Each disc is designed and programmed to reflect the topic of the issue. For example, the "Univer's" issue, which focuses on higher education, resembles a student's notebook, with ink doodles serving as pathways to the materials.[12] "Music under Pressure" looks like a concert stage filled with the silhouettes of famous musicians and uses their different microphones as entry points for the contents.[13] Designing each issue differently keeps the audience interested and makes the magazine fun to explore.

CDMAG is a unique youth publication that has already made an impact on several generations by creating an alternative public space for nonconformist youth dissatisfied with a stifling regime. In "Europe's last dictatorship", the magazine is a breath of fresh air and a beacon of hope. As one independent

Unique art design for disc and sleeve of *CDMAG* "Univer's" issue on higher education

Source: 34mag.net, September 2010. Reproduced with permission from *34 Multimedia Magazine.*

newspaper declared, "reading it is like traveling to another Belarus".[14] *CDMAG* responded to difficult political and economic challenges by successfully transforming itself from a print to a multimedia magazine. In both format and content, the publication continues to be at the forefront of new media. After a decade, it remains one of the most interesting and innovative independent publications in Belarus.

Disc dilemmas

In 2006-2007, repression against youth rose to new heights. Due to the pressure from the secret police, the magazine was again forced to be more underground in its activities. As a result, it was re-named *34 Multimedia Magazine*[15] in fall 2006. More edgy than its predecessor, *34* is an underground publication that is produced and distributed at some risk.

While the compact disc format[16] has proven successful, makes the magazine unique, and helps *34* avoid persecution, it also poses atypical challenges and has certain limitations. Operating in conspiratorial conditions hinders development. The team must work anonymously and cannot openly build a community around the publication. Producing a CD edition is demanding. Each multimedia component requires significant time and effort to assemble; issues having 600 MB of data need a one-month production cycle. CDs require access to a computer and cannot be read on the go. A bimonthly does not allow for a timely response to breaking issues, which is a drawback given the short attention span of young people and the brief life-span of youth trends. The CDs must be distributed through private channels, limiting issues' size, coverage, impact and readership. Even if each disc is shared by multiple users, the CDs can at best reach about 15,000 readers.[17] It is difficult to insure that the CDs get to subscribers and the target audience.

Recognizing these challenges, it was only a matter of time before *34* launched a website.[18] Like the CD magazine, the new site employs a multimedia format and a similar style. Both take advantage of new media's explosive growth and the lack of its regulation in Belarus. The message of the publications is the same: be active, creative and unique. The website not only includes a downloadable archive of all past CD issues,[19] but also gets readers to contribute to forthcoming issues. However, the content of the two publications is very different. While each CD issue focuses on a specific question, the website is updated daily and covers a broad range of topics and breaking events.

At the right time

It was the right strategy for the underground magazine to go online. Belarus is experiencing an Internet boom. Unlike in other repressive states, the Internet's expansion has been encouraged by the regime. Despite the state monopoly over service providers, the number of users has grown rapidly. In a country where the state controls just about everything, Internet connectivity is among the highest in the CIS (Commonwealth of Independent States). In 2010, users in Belarus numbered over 3 million – 30 percent of the population – with 71 percent using the Internet daily.[20]

The regime's Internet-friendly approach[21] was probably based on its easy subjugation of traditional media. Perhaps propaganda bosses believed that subsidized, state websites would easily trump those of a poor and disorganized opposition. Most likely, these post-Soviet men did not understand the unique nature of the Internet or the young people using it. For young people whose classrooms and workplaces are controlled by the state, cyberspace has become a refuge for those seeking an independent, alternative existence. About 70 percent of Internet users in Belarus are aged 15-34. By profession, the largest single group of users is students, more than 20 percent.

Since 2006, the rise of online social networking in Belarus has been remarkable. It too is driven by young people. More than 78,000 Belarusians have blogs on LiveJournal, the most popular blogging platform; Belarus is one of the smallest of the 15 countries with the most LiveJournal blogs.[22] Each day, there are more than 2 million unique visitors from Belarus on Vkontakte, the most popular networking site in the former Soviet space. Facebook grows ever more popular, counting over 190,000 Belarusian users by January 2011; 50 percent of the Belarusian Facebook population is 15-24 years old.[23]

Similar but different

While it made sense for the country's only youth magazine to follow its audience online, *34*'s editors were also aware that there was a niche to fill.[24] Although independent news and information websites make up half of the country's top 30 most popular Internet media outlets, research showed that young people are not keen on consuming news online. There is a generation gap in Belarus' Internet audience; while young people make up the majority of users, they are a minority among visitors to news sites, whose primary audience is 35-55 years of age.[25]

With the new site, the *34* team targets surfers under 26, hoping to hook young people on independent information through a multimedia format and provocative content. 34mag.net is not an ordinary website but a unique online magazine, a webmag focusing on youth. Like the CD publication, it presents the underground and counterculture scenes in a broad sense, as anything excluded from the official information landscape. The goal is to expose this alternative reality and introduce it to broader circles of youth. Instead of just reporting news, the webmag helps shape youth trends in Belarus, reports on Western youth life, and offers columns by young creative figures. Like the CD edition, it does not reprint materials; all content is original.

The webmag focuses on events taking place under the radar screen and features those who are misunderstood by Belarus' conservative society. It continues the tradition of the print and CD magazines, which had a reputation for breaking stereotypes and promoting tolerance. The webmag does not focus on unusual youth just to be different. It spotlights those who are civically active, struggling for freedom of expression, promoting independent culture, self-organizing and trying to foster positive change. For example, in solidarity with Tatsiana Shaputska, who was expelled from university for taking part in the Eastern Partnership's Civil Society Forum, the webmag ran "No Need to Study".[26] The article offered examples of people who were kicked out of school but nevertheless became successful and well-known. It not only poked fun at the authorities, who fear activist students, but offered hope to young people brave enough to stand up for what they believe.

Like the CD magazine, the online version employs a multimedia format, including video, audio, music, flash animation, photos and text, resulting in a distinctive coverage of issues. One example is "Books on Fire", which appeared after the novel *Paranoia*, by the young Belarusian author Viktor Martinovich, was banned in Belarus.[27] The anti-censorship piece[28] included short texts on historical cases of book burning in Belarus, collages illustrating those events by a young artist, and a podcast by the author himself, sharing his views on freedom of expression.

One example of the site's innovative methods of getting young people interested in political events is the weekly podcast "MC News", which highlights important news of the week in the form of original hip-hop songs.[29] It has already caught readers' imagination; one declared "this is what real rap should be – sharp and politically hot!". The site's most-read materials include a mix of political materials (i.e., "The Stupidest Post-Soviet Rules"), entertainment posts (i.e., "The Coolest Belarusian Music Video") and student information (i.e., ratings and reviews of students' haunts). Like the print and CD publications, the webmag is connecting with its target group.[30] According to independent analysis, over 80 percent of visitors are 16-25 years of age.[31]

Reaching out

Launched in August 2009, 34mag.net is not Belarus' oldest, most popular or best-funded website, but its audience is growing rapidly. In its first year, the site cracked the country's Top 30 most popular news and information sites. While it has yet to surpass the top youth site, Generation.bY, 34mag.net has existed for a shorter time and is not far behind. During its first six months, the site had about 10,500 unique visitors. By the end of the second half of 2010, traffic had almost tripled to 30,000.[32]

The site is also building an audience by using popular social networks. *34* communities on LiveJournal, Vkontakte, Facebook and Twitter unite almost 6,000 members.[33] Rather than just sharing information, the site's editors actively engage

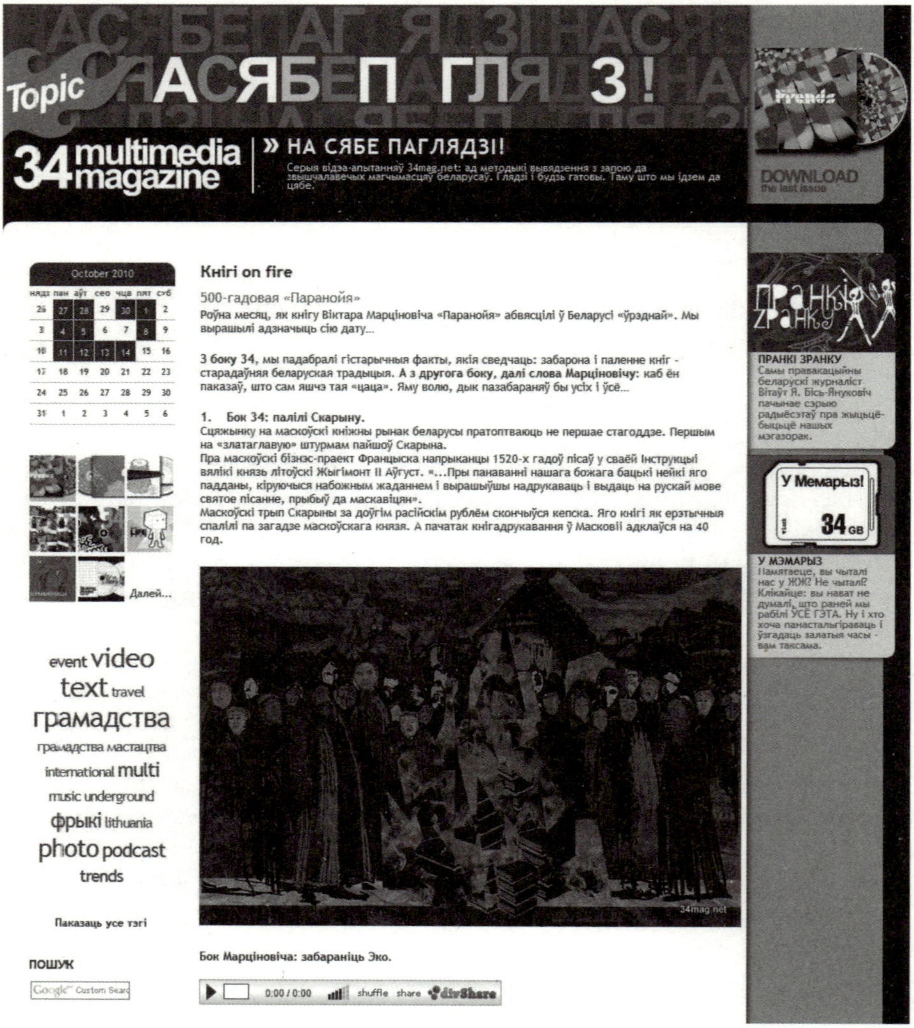

Anti-censorship "Books on Fire" article, art collage and audio interview on 34mag.net

Source: 34mag.net, September 2010. Reproduced with permission from *34 Multimedia Magazine*.

with readers. It uses Twitter as a teaser to bring audiences to the website and as a mobilizing tool for youth-related events. As a result, the webmag's account has become one of the most popular Belarusian-language communities on Twitter. The Vkontakte community is a truly interactive platform, where members comment on the site's design, post announcements of interesting events, leave links to other Belarusian groups, and share feedback about the CD issues.

In addition, materials from 34mag.net are regularly reprinted. In 2010, more than 80 posts appeared on Gazetaby.com, a Top 10 independent news site.[34] Hundreds of young people download *34*'s exclusive podcasts. To date, 252 original video clips posted on YouTube have been viewed by more than 120,000 people.[35] The editorial team is taking full advantage of the Internet to broaden the site's audience, expand its communities and engage young people who were not previously interested in traditional news sites.

Discard the disc?

Despite the Internet's growing popularity and *34*'s successful expansion online, it would be premature to stop the CD version. The regime knows that it is losing the online war. After years of rumor and anticipation, Decree #60 on "Improving the use of the Internet" came into force in July 2010.[36] Designed to regulate the Net, the law contains vague definitions and broad requirements. All Belarusian Internet systems, information resources and networks must be officially registered. Internet cafés need to log users' personal data, time spent online and traffic. Belarusian news sites must move to the domestic .by domain, bringing them under state jurisdiction. Paragraph #8 requires providers to block access to certain sites at users' request, specifically listing sites promoting extremism, trafficking, pornography "and other acts banned by the law".[37]

While the consequences are not yet clear, there is little doubt that the decree will be used to control and suppress independent online resources, especially after the flawed 2010 presidential elections and the demonstrations that followed. It will also strengthen self-censorship. Because it is the most active segment of society, the authorities will probably target youth-related media. It is therefore important to maintain as many channels of independent information as possible.

In Belarus, the "new media" are a powerful tool against dictatorship. They attract "the best and brightest" of Belarus' opposition and nonconformist youth. In contrast to an oppressive regime, Belarusian cyberspace is full of energy and ideas. A core group of creative and committed young people are helping new media win the online information war. From its groundbreaking print magazine to its unique CD publication, and through its multimedia webmag and online social networks, *34* is playing its part to preserve and expand the space for freedom of information and democratic reform in Belarus.

Notes

1. *Ценностные ориентации и гражданская активность белорусских студентов. Результаты социологического исследования*, BISS, 2007 [The Value Orientation and Civic Activism of Belarusian Students: Results of a Sociological Survey, Belarusian Institute for Strategic Studies. Minsk, Belarus, 2007].
2. "*Новая информационная война. Эпизод второй*", *Белорусский Партизан* ["The New Information War: Episode Two", *Belarus Partisan*] http://www.belaruspartisan.org/bp-forte/?newsPage=0&page=100&news=18614 and Luft, "*Война по законам подлости*", *Live Journal* [Luft, "War without Rules", *LiveJournal*]. http://community.livejournal.com/lulu_gov_by/163808.html.
3. For an electronic archive of *Students' Thought* print issues, see http://www.kamunikat.org/studenckaja_dumka.html.

4. Interview with Siarhai Sakharau from "*Студэнцкая Думка: часопіс, не падобны да іншых", Центр экстремальной журналистики* ["*Students' Thought*: A Publication Like No Other", Center for Extreme Journalism]. http://www.library.cjes.ru/online/?a=con&b_id=571&c_id=6757.
5. For a more detailed history of the *Students' Thought* print and *CDMAG* compact disc versions of the magazine, see Vidanava, 2009.
6. The letters C and D in Belarusian are the first letters of the two word title of *Students' Thought* (*Студэнцкая Думка*), as well as the English abbreviation for "Compact Disc".
7. A survey contained in one issue indicated that 82 percent of the audience is 18 to 25 years old, 12 percent is older than 25, and 5 percent is younger than 17.
8. *Мартинович, Виктор, "Пробило на "Думку", Белгазета*, No.14 [Martinovich, Viktor "Getting *Dumka*", *Belgazeta*, No. 14]. http://www.belgazeta.by/20040412.14/430460142.
9. The Gerd Bucerius Prize is awarded annually by Germany's ZEIT Foundation and Norway's Freedom of Expression Foundation to publications in the region which strive to promote press freedom and freedom of expression in the face of threats and censorship.
10. As a 20-year old journalism student wrote in a college research paper: "Youth media are in decline and extremely underdeveloped in Belarus. There is not a single influential and popular publication for youth. The only exception is *CDMAG* – the country's brightest and most progressive youth magazine. *CDMAG* sets very high standards of journalism. Its editors and authors are creative and original. No other media has spoken about the problems covered in *CDMAG*. Like youth itself, *CDMAG* is always avant-garde, experimenting with its content and formats. It targets creative, curious and proactive young people." *Канцэптуальны аналіз часопіса Студэнцкая думка* [A Conceptual Analysis of the Publication *Students' Thought*]. http://www.referat-911.ru/referat/journalism/2_object6685.html.
11. For a more detailed description of some of the topics and issues covered by the magazine, see an earlier version of this article, Vidanava, 2009.
12. See at http://34mag.net/content/education-cd1.
13. See at http://34mag.net/content/music.
14. *Мартинович, Виктор "Пробило на Думку", Белгазета*, No.14 [Martinovich, Viktor "Getting *Dumka*", *Belgazeta*, No. 14]. http://www.belgazeta.by/20040412.14/430460142.
15. The new title links the publication to its two predecessors. The numbers 3 and 4 are a nod to the third and fourth letters of the Latin alphabet, C and D, which refers to CD*MAG*. In turn, the letters C and D in Belarusian are the first letters of the two word title of *Students' Thought* (*Студэнцкая Думка*), as well as the English abbreviation for "Compact Disc". As well, *34* refers to the number of the article in the Belarusian Constitution that guarantees freedom of information.
16. The magazine has experimented with other formats. In 2009, it released an issue on digital video disc (DVD). "Stand.BY" ("BY" is the international abbreviation for Belarus) was the magazine's first attempt to create a television-style show on CD. Since the issue was produced in DVD format, instead of using the standard flash technology, the video materials were of a higher quality and could be watched on big screen TVs, making the issue look like a real TV show. The show's goal was to portray the unusual subjects that could not be shown on Belarusian state TV, the regime's main propaganda mouthpiece.
17. The print run of each CD issue is 5,000 copies. A survey included in one issue indicated that 61 percent of respondents watched the issue alone and 23 percent with two or three people. 16 percent declared that they had copied the issue onto a home computer network.
18. Perhaps re-launched would be more accurate, since it had been one of the first publications in Belarus to create a website in 2003. But the original site was only a static version of the print magazine, and not nearly as innovative or successful.
19. Found at http://archive.34mag.net/archiu.
20. See http://www.e-belarus.org/news/201004051.html.
21. According to government plans, broadband access will triple and wireless access double by 2014.
22. See http://www.livejournal.com/stats.bml.
23. See http://www.facebakers.com/countries-with-facebook/BY.

24. While a few youth-oriented sites have become relatively popular, such as Generation.bY and Moladz.com, they focus on narrower topics, such as Belarusian language, music and culture.
25. *Соколова, Марина "Белорусские медиа онлайн: аудитория, структура, регулирование", Наше Мнение,* [Sokolova, Marina "Belarusian Media Online: Audience, Structure, Regulation", *Nashe Mnenije*] http://nmnby.eu/news/xlibris/2648.html.
26. Found at http://archive.34mag.net/content/1052.
27. See http://www.opendemocracy.net/natalia-leshchenko/belarus-love-and-paranoia.
28. Found at http://archive.34mag.net/content/1083.
29. Found at http://34mag.net/rubrics/newsmc.
30. Not all of the reviews of the CD magazine and website have been positive. A critical piece on *34* was published in the fall 2010 issue of the Polish journal *Res Publica* and can be found at http://publica.pl/archiwum/5269.
31. Gemius, Gemius Audience, July, 2010, http://www.audience.by.
32 About 65 percent of visitors return to the page, indicating that the site is building a loyal audience. *34*'s statistics are open and can be viewed at http://stat.akavita.com/stat/stat.pl?id=36389&lang=ru.
33. Links to all of *34*'s online social networks can be found at http://34mag.net/.
34. Found at http://gazetaby.com/fnd.php.
35. See the videos and statistics at http://www.youtube.com/34video.
36. For the text of the decree, see http://president.gov.by/data/press83054.doc.
37. For a more in-depth analysis, see http://www.i-m-s.dk/article/razor%E2%80%99s-edge, http://www.tol.org/client/article/21531-trying-to-close-pandoras-box.html and http://i-m-s.dk/article/price-internet-regulation.

References

"*Канцэптуальны аналіз часопіса Студэнцкая думка*" ["A Conceptual Analysis of the Publication *Students' Thought*"] (2008) http://revolution.allbest.ru/journalism/00029706_0.html

Luft (2008) "*Война по законам подлости*", *LiveJournal* [Luft, "War without Rules", *LiveJournal*]. http://community.livejournal.com/lulu_gov_by/163808.html

Мартинович, Виктор (2008) "*Пробило на 'Думку'* ", *Белгазета*, No.14 [Martinovich, Viktor "Getting *Dumka*", *Belgazeta*, No. 14] http://www.belgazeta.by/20040412.14/430460142

"*Новая информационная война. Эпизод второй", Белорусский Партизан* (2008) [The New Information War: Episode Two, *Belarus Partisan*]. http://www.belaruspartisan.org/bpforte/?newsPage=0&page=100&news=18614

Соколова, Марина (2010) "*Белорусские медиа онлайн: аудитория, структура, регулирование", Наше Мнение* [Sokolova, Marina, "Belarusian Media Online: Audience, Structure, Regulation", *Nashe Mnenije*], http://nmnby.eu/news/xlibris/2648.html

Сяргей (2008) "*Мэдыя-часопіс* CDMAG – *глыток свабоднай інфармацыі*" [Siarhai "The Media Publication CDMAG – A Breath of Free Information"]. http://gayby.org/naviny/belarus/medyya-chasopis-34-glytok-svabodnai-infarmacyi.html

"Студэнцкая Думка: часопіс, не падобны да іншых", Центр экстремальной журналистики [*Students' Thought*: A Publication Like No Other, Center for Extreme Journalism], http://www.library.cjes.ru/online/?a=con&b_id=571&c_id=6757

Ценностные ориентации и гражданская активность белорусских студентов. Результаты социологическогоисследования, BISS (2007) [*The Value Orientation and Civic Activism of Belarusian students: Results of a Sociological Survey*, Minsk, Belarus: Belarusian Institute for Strategic Studies]

Vidanava, Iryna (2009) "From Pages to Pixels: Belarus' Unique Youth Multimedia Magazine", in Tufte, Thomas & Enghel, Florencia (Eds.) *Youth Engaging with the World: Media, Communication and Social Change.* Yearbook 2009. The International Clearinghouse on Children, Youth and Media. University of Gothenburg: NORDICOM, 81-100

Vidanava, Iryna (2010) "On a razor's edge – new law stifles online media in Belarus", June 21, 2010, http://www.i-m-s.dk/article/razor%E2%80%99s-edge

Vidanava, Iryna & Potocki, Rodger (2007) "Out with the Old", *Belarusian News and Analysis*. http://www.data.minsk.by/belarusnews/122007/208.html
Vidanava, Iryna & Potocki, Rodger (2010) "Trying to Close Pandora's Box", Transitions Online, June 10, 2010, http://www.tol.org/client/article/21531-trying-to-close-pandoras-box.html

Strengthening Civil Society

A Communication for Social Change Agenda?

Lise Grauenkær Jensen and Mette Grøndahl Hansen

The present article illustrates how the development approach Communication for Social Change is operationalized in a specific planned development intervention – the Action for Social Change programme[1] – that seeks to empower community groups to be active agents for change, who are able to act and interact on the civil society arena in a developing country with its specific context – in this case Malawi in southern East Africa.

Thus, the article is not a meticulously structured research project that isolates its object of study with methodology and theoretical aspirations, but an attempt to illustrate how the development and implementation of a full-blown development programme born in the midst of development aid conditionalities, the need for measurable objectives, donor-beneficiary power relations, and the boundaries of organizational capacity and resources still relate to and are informed by research and different theoretical conceptualizations – and by one study in particular.[2]

We will discuss the development programme's strategic approach in relation to the research findings and lessons learned that have informed the programme design and its operationalization of a Communication for Social Change approach.[3]

Action for Social Change – the programme

The Action for Social Change programme is funded by Danida – the Danish government's development aid agency – and implemented by ADRA (Adventist Development and Relief Agency) Denmark and ADRA Malawi. The programme is planned to begin in January 2011, six months after the writing of the present article.

The programme is conceived of as a nine-year development programme consisting of three consecutive phases and it focuses on livelihood and food security issues, on the one hand, and health – particularly HIV prevention and

AIDS mitigation – on the other. More importantly, though, this programme falls within the civil society paradigm that currently guides Danida's allocations of development aid to NGOs (non-governmental organizations), and the overarching development objective of the programme:

> A strengthened vibrant locally rooted Civil Society in Malawi which can be a dynamic actor in social, political and economical development processes in areas of health and food security/livelihood. (Action for Social Change Programme document, p. 32)

While the Action for Social Change programme is the first intervention for both ADRA Malawi and ADRA Denmark in which they pursue explicit civil society development, both organizations have considerable experience working with and within communities to strengthen public life.

The organizational setting[4]

ADRA Denmark has existed in its current form since 1987 and is a middle-sized development and humanitarian aid NGO that receives most of its funding through Danida, but also through the European Union's aid institutions and through private donations. The organization was set up by the Seventh Day Adventist church to carry out its humanitarian work around the world.

Since 1992, ADRA Denmark has worked with ADRA Malawi on several development projects addressing HIV/AIDS and food security.

For the past five years, ADRA Denmark and ADRA Malawi have implemented an AIDS project, which utilizes a Communication for Social Change strategy with a media vehicle that promotes community dialogue through dialogue sessions, on the one hand, and addresses relevant issues on a national level through radio and television programmes, on the other[5] – with the new programme this strategic approach is applied even more rigidly.

Communication for Social Change (CFSC)

The following is a brief description of the conceptualization of CFSC that has informed the Action for Social Change programme. The conceptualization embraced in the development programme's strategic approach and the research study informing the programme originates from the Communication for Social Change Consortium.[6]

CFSC – which is part of the participatory communication for development paradigm – can be, and has been, conceptualized in various ways. The overall aim of participatory communication is a bottom-up approach to making 'local' people and communities central and influential to development by involving local knowledge and perspectives, thereby increasing people's decision-making over their own lives (Kothari, 2001:5). In this way, communication becomes an integrated part of development initiatives, where people have access to relevant channels; they know how to use these channels "and the ensuing communication environment in improving the quality of their lives" (Waisbord, 2002:562).

In this approach, communication is seen as power and essentially what shapes our world every day. Through horizontal CFSC dialogue processes, people learn to

> identify obstacles and develop communication structures, policies, processes and media or other communication tools to help them achieve the goals they themselves have outlined and defined (Parks et al., 2005:4).

The understanding of communication as dialogue can also be related to Paulo Freire's concept of true communication as dialogue based on subject-to-subject relations (Freire, 1974:40,81), which has resulted in a paradigm shift from "a view of our counterparts as development 'beneficiaries' ('objects') to that of development 'partners' and 'colleagues' ('subjects')" (Cadiz, 2005:147; Freire, 2005:40-45). This understanding has also informed the development programme's approach and furthermore resulted in a practical shift from focusing on individual beneficiaries to collectives and changes in societal processes and structures.

Lastly, CFSC is action-oriented – it is not just about providing a space where people can air their problems and discuss information disseminated to them, but instead Communication for Social Change seeks to promote deliberation, collective decision-making and collective action (Parks et al., 2005:3).

Ideally, the processes initiated when applying a Communication for Social Change approach will strengthen civil society, because they empower individuals and groups to speak up for themselves, build networks and relations, and act collectively to challenge existing structures by politicizing daily issues and problems. In other words, community-based groups and organizations are empowered to mobilize resources and to influence decision-making processes on different levels.

However, the reality is often not as clearcut as the intentions. First of all, true communication is not as easy as it sounds, and community members do not leave their social status and relationships at the door when attending community dialogue sessions. Thus, problem identification itself is often hindered by the same marginalizing structures that need to be challenged, and even once the problems are identified and agreed upon, they are difficult to address due to lack of capacity, organization and resources.

For instance, one of the areas that is very much a part of the current development agenda is gender equality. However, the norms, roles and relationships that are responsible for gender inequality are very much a part of the individual's own identity, and thus changes could mean a potential loss of identity.

Before looking more closely at the Action for Social Change programme, let us take a detour and look in more detail at the aforementioned study that informed the Action for Social Change programme. Every mention of 'the study' in the present article will refer to the study described below.

Study in a Malawian youth club

The study and its findings are described in more detail in Grauenkær Jensen et al. (2008 and 2009).

The study explored youth empowerment within a Communication for Social Change framework and specifically looked at the potential of anti-AIDS youth clubs to drive social change processes to empower a community's ability to manage AIDS – not only on the prevention side, but also in mitigating the negative consequences of AIDS.

The empirical material was gathered through 7 workshops held in an anti-AIDS youth club established by ADRA Malawi in their Danida-supported AIDS project.[7]

The activities undertaken in the youth club were designed with inspiration from the integrated model for Communication for Social Change (Figueroa et al., 2002), and Brazilian educator Paolo Freire's thinking on critical learning and critical consciousness (Freire, 1974, 2005).

A theoretical framework was developed that would not only allow an analysis of the processes taking place in the youth club, but also an exploration of the potentials and challenges in using Communication for Social Change strategies to empower youth clubs to play a role in their communities and on the civil society arena and actually catalyse social change processes.

The theoretical framework was developed with a focus on the central elements in the CFSC approach: *empowerment, social change, collective action, and communication as dialogue.* Underlying the framework is the assumption that in order to address structural issues, individuals have to be empowered to challenge hegemonic discourses, which legitimize social norms, roles, relations, and behaviour.

The framework offers analytical tools through the conceptualizations of horizontal dialogue, civil society, social movements and community media. In this way, the youth club or community-based groups are framed as collective actors, who contribute to public debate on social structures in civil society.

Overall, the analysis explored whether or not a linkage of the concepts of horizontal dialogue, civil society, social movements and community media could frame and explain empowerment processes by moving the perspective from small- to large-scale empowerment. In this movement, conscientization and critical learning constitute the entry point to large-scale processes, which were framed within the concepts of civil society, social movements and community media.

Findings informing Action for Social Change

Overall, the findings show that, in the youth club, an empowerment process determined by critical consciousness and learning was initiated. However, it was evident that the critical consciousness created was limited to some degree, as the club members only superficially identified problematic power relations and never really challenged legitimizing structures of social norms, roles, relations, and behaviour in their community.

This became even more apparent when the members expressed a collective identity that was very limiting to their collective action. The empirical data were collected during a short period of time – seven weeks – and the fact that the youth club members did begin a process of critical thinking and quickly developed a collective identity, however limited, indicates that such groups do have some potential to work as a nucleus for CFSC processes. But it also shows that learning critical thinking and building a collective identity takes time, and that it is not done solely through engaging in dialogue, but action and support in group organization and management are also relevant components to consider when operationalizing CFSC.

The group was also limited in their collective action because they had difficulty identifying possible channels through which they could address these issues. On the other hand, the findings also showed that the youth club provided the members with a platform from which they could enter into decision-making processes and address issues of social inequality on a local level. Based on this, the development programme seeks to provide the groups with both communication platforms from which they can express their interests and address issues, as well as to build the groups' organizational capacity to such an extent that they are and feel capable of addressing different issues.

Using the theoretical framework set up in the study, it was possible to describe in words the potential such groups have for contributing to change processes.

The group contributes to change processes on both an individual and social level by constituting a *social movement* that identifies everyday problems and politicizes them. The power and importance of social mobilization in addressing issues are recognized in the programme's strategic approach, in which it is stressed that the groups have to be empowered to mobilize resources both in the form of support and financial resources.

The analysis also showed that the youth group contributed to change by providing alternative ideas and meanings to public negotiation of social meaning just as a *community medium* does – or *citizen medium* as it has been called by Colombian media scholar Clemencia Rodriguez (Rodriguez, 2001).

Normally, the concept of community media or citizen media refers to the production of mass media owned and produced by the community, such as radio, television, newspapers or other print media. However, the communication activities the youth club used – community drama, singing, dances, poems, photography – while being of a more interpersonal nature, and as such not mediated, still produced processes similar to those normally ascribed to mass mediated community media.

By providing the youth club with a platform from which members could express their opinion on the issues they had politicized, the youth club increased access to and participation in the collective processes of decision-making – access the club members did not previously have.

The local group makes this contribution in a setting that can be described as the informal *civil society* arena. This is an arena of community meetings, demonstrations and rallies, where they can interact with local chiefs, traditional authorities, church leaders, educators, district councillors and members of parliament and an arena where social structures take form and where collective community decisions are made.

Lastly, it was found that one of the main challenges for the groups was to act and interact in a formalized setting with actors who were seen as more powerful than themselves. This understanding of authorities as unapproachable and one's right and ability to question their power – or lack thereof – is very prominent in the Malawian society (Maina, 1998:136).

Come together – groups and networks

The Action for Social Change programme focuses on establishing and building the capacity of locally based interest groups to advocate for their own interests and take an active role in civil society.

The framework or strategic approach to achieving this is largely inspired by findings from the study, which emphasized the role small local groups can play in facilitating development processes by challenging the existing state of society and expressing local interests. The core of the programme is to support and strengthen these groups so that they can play that role. As new civil society groups, they will now be the ones securing their communities services, rights, resources, etc.

As mentioned above, the success and ability of locally based groups to become part of and define a locally rooted and vibrant civil society is determined by many factors. The risks and challenges are many, and the leap from theory to practice is too often very wide. One of the salient points is the ability of the implementing staff to mobilize the groups and support them in building the necessary capacities, not only within communication, but also within different technical areas, not least by shifting the groups' expectations from being beneficiaries to being actively involved in their own development. It is not enough that the groups are able to identify problems if they do not have the support system required to help them act on the issues and, in particular, develop the collective efficacy to believe they are able and entitled to act.

It is to some degree questionable whether or not people will act because they have an improved ability to do so. The programme aims to provide the groups with both an organizational and communicative platform, from which they can challenge structures of social inequalities, and to support them in their efforts. In the end, this is still determined by the groups' motivation and existing impeding social, cultural, economic and political factors – factors and structures that take time to change.

The Action for Social Change programme attempts to accommodate some of the challenges identified in the study by putting a strong focus on key elements of the communicative capacity the groups need to mobilize their community and effectively put problematic issues on the agenda. To empower the groups as actors in civil society, the programme will work to strengthen their organizational capacity, provide access to resources, strengthen their sense of citizenship, and not least develop their ability to advocate and build linkages with other relevant stakeholders, creating a platform from which to enter into decision-making processes.

But the findings also showed that a simple youth group could and wished to communicate with their community and address relevant stakeholders. In this way, the youth club members were, in fact, enacting their citizenship and taking political action.

The theoretical framework of the study revealed that groups, such as the youth club in Mpemba, have the potential to extend their influence way beyond the scope of the local community and take part in social change processes on a much larger scale. The Action for Social Change programme has taken several steps to formalize these dynamics.

Community dialogue goes national

As a first step, a structure is set up, in which local dialogue processes feed into a national dialogue process, which in return feeds into and fuels further local dialogue processes.[8]

Most of the programme activities take place within a geographical community setting – a village community – but no such community is isolated from other communities. Not only do members of the community often belong to other geographical communities – e.g., work in the city – but they are also part of mediated communicative processes, which can be regional, national or even global in nature.

The local negotiation of meanings and social norms, values, etc., is part of a continuous negotiation of meaning that increasingly takes place on a global level, but it is – at a minimum – intricately entwined with a national mediascape (Appadurai, 1990: 298-299). The dominant social structures in a geographical community are thus not only defined by the communication within said community, but also by regional, national and even global communication.

Besides facilitating dialogue within the communities and promoting critical thinking, decision-making and action at a community level, the Action for Social Change programme sets up a national platform for dialogue and advocacy with professionally produced radio and television shows.

These media platforms are not new, but have been part of ADRA Denmark/Malawi's HIV and AIDS projects since 2005. One is a soap opera that has been running on both national television and radio using edutainment to address sensitive issues faced by ordinary Malawians in their daily lives. The other is a talk show that invites policy-makers, administrators and civil society leaders into the studio to talk with listeners/viewers on selected issues.

These programmes have been used as catalysts for community dialogue sessions, and furthermore the issues on the shows have been inspired by issues identified in the community dialogue sessions. In this way, the issues raised by people in the local communities have been taken to the national level on shows targeting an urban population and policy-makers.

Local ownership of national dialogue

However, in the new programme, these media platforms will not only take up issues that are of interest to the communities, but will to some extent move ownership of the media production itself to the community and thus to the end-users of the media products (Parks et al., 2005: 4). The idea is to empower the local groups and give them platforms and the communicative capacity to promote and catalyse change processes:

Parts of every show will be produced in the communities by ordinary people – amateurs – from the established groups. Professional producers will still be working on the show, but access to and participation in the production of national shows have been increased significantly – and, thus, access to setting the agenda of the public debate at a national level.

This is possible because the programme sets up four Community Communication Centres (telecentres), where members of the local groups will participate in the production of community radio and also have access to telecommunication equipment, internet, telephones, fax machines, copy machines, etc. The telecentres have been criticized for lack of sustainability, dependency on donor funding, and not providing sufficient management training, but they also provide people with communication channels they would not otherwise have access to and have proved useful in giving ownership to those affected by the problems (UNIDO, 2003).

The national media shows are not only another platform from which local interest groups can voice their opinion – they are a platform where local interests are linked and become national.

Communication for Social Change projects are supposed to be grounded in the community and be so-called bottom-up projects, but often they tend to remain on a localized level and never scale up to a level where they can influence societal structures. The Action for Social Change programme attempts to scale up the dynamics of the community dialogue by linking it to a national dialogue process.

Concluding remarks

Communication for Social Change, as a process, will in theory strengthen community-based organizations, enabling them to become actors on the civil society arena. It does this by empowering groups to attain a critical consciousness, engage in problem-posing dialogue, and politicize daily issues and address them at the relevant levels of society. But as we have tried to illustrate, theory and practice are two very different things and sometimes they are difficult to combine. There are several – known and unknown – challenges and risks that will influence the success of any approach or strategy, and during the course of a development programme, adjustments will have to be made. However, the fundamental idea of CFSC – that it is those affected who will determine what the problem is and how they can solve it – remains the same as well as the assumption that communication is essential when promoting and catalysing social change processes.

Notes

1. One of the present authors has had a leading role in the development of the programme as programme coordinator at ADRA Denmark, and will furthermore be involved in implementation of the programme. She is still employed at ADRA Denmark. The other author has also previously been employed at ADRA Denmark, but has not taken part in development of the Action for Social Change programme.
2. For a description of the mentioned study, please see under the heading *Study in a Malawian youth club* further on in the text.
3. The Action for Social Change programme is informed by the Consortium for Communication for Social Change's conceptualization of Communication for Social Change as can be found in Figueroa et al. (2002), but essentially develops its own approach (see also www.communicationforsocialchange.org)
4. More information on the ADRA organizations: ADRA Denmark's website: www.adra.dk, ADRA Malawi's website: www.adramw.org, ADRA International's website: www.adra.org
5. ADRA Malawi has advocated for issues related to HIV/AIDS prevention and mitigation through two advocacy programmes featured on national radio and television. Both programmes have been very successful in terms of achieving changes in policies, understandings and practices, as well as in terms of the audience that has followed and participated in the programmes regularly (Lassen et al., 2005).
6. The mission of the Communication for Social Change Consortium is to help people living in poor communities lift their voices, stories, ideas, and beliefs in order to bring about the changes they need in their societies and their lives. It was founded in 1997 by Denise Felder-Gray as an association under the Rockefeller Foundation. It was chartered in 2003 to work globally as a registered public charity. It cooperates with partner organizations such as UN agencies, World Bank, IADB (Inter-American Development Bank) and universities in the North and South and The Centre for Communication Programme at Johns Hopkins University. The developers of the integrated model of CFSC are affiliated with this university and the model was developed for the Rockefeller Foundation.
7. For detailed descriptions of the workshops, see 'Voice of Mpemba – an analysis of empowerment processes in a Malawian youth club' (Grauenkær Jensen et al., 2008: 78 and Appendix 10).
8. In the programme, these dialogues will take the form of advocacy activities with the specific aim to influence decision-making processes on the national and local level.

References

ADRA Denmark (2010) *Action for Social Change programme document – ADRA Malawi programme 2011-2013*. The programme document is available at request from ADRA Denmark, lisgra@adra.dk or adra@adra.dk

Appadurai, Arjun (1990) "Disjuncture and Differences in the Global Cultural Economy", in Featherson, Mike (Ed.) (1990) *Global Culture. Nationalism, Globalization and Modernity.* London: Sage Publications Ltd, pp. 295-310

Cadiz, Maria Celeste (2005) "Communication for empowerment. The practice of participatory communication in development", in Hemer, Oscar & Tufte, Thomas (Eds.) (2005) *Media and Glocal Change– Rethinking Communication for Development.* University of Gothenburg, NORDICOM & Buenos Aires, CLACSO, pp. 145-158

Figueroa, Maria Elena, Kincaid, D. Lawrence, Rani, Manju & Lewis, Gary (2002) Communication for Social Change: An Integrated Model for Measuring the Process and Its Outcomes. Communication for Social Change Working Paper Series, No. 1, The Rockefeller Foundation and John Hopkins University's Centre for Communication Programs

Freire, Paolo ([1970] 1974) *Pedagogy of the Oppressed.* New York: Seabury Press

Freire, Paolo ([1974] 2005) *Education for Critical Consciousness.* London: Continuum

Grauenkær Jensen, Lise, Grøndahl Hansen, Mette & Kromann-Larsen, Stine (2008) *Voice of Mpemba: An analysis of empowerment processes in a Malawian youth club fighting HIV/AIDS.* Roskilde University, available at http://hdl.handle.net/1800/3087

Grauenkær Jensen, Lise, Grøndahl Hansen, Mette & Kromann-Larsen, Stine (2009) "Young Voices Driving Social Change", in Tufte, Thomas & Enghel, Florencia (Eds.) *Youth Engaging with the World: Media, Communication and Social Change.* Yearbook 2009. University of Gothenburg: NORDICOM, The International Clearinghouse on Children, Youth and Media, pp. 137-154

Kothari, Uma (2001) "Power, Knowledge and Social Control in Participatory Development", in Cooke, Bill & Kothari, Uma (Eds.) *Participation. The New Tyranny?* London: Zed Books, pp. 139-152

Lassen, Sophie, Mwale, Kwanjana, Olesen, Inger, Staugård, Frants, Tufte, Thomas, Usi, Michael & Övretveit, John (2005) *Combined review of the Integrated HIV/AIDS programme phase five Malawi 2003-2006 and Let's Talk, Malawi 2005-2006*, ADRA Denmark and ADRA Malawi. The document is available at request from ADRA Denmark, lisgra@adra.dk or adra@adra.dk

Maina, Wachira (1998) "Kenya: The State, Donors and the Politics of Democratization", in Van Rooy, Alison (Ed.) *Civil Society and the Aid Industry.* London: Earthscan Publications Ltd, pp. 13-167

Papa, Michael J. et al. (2000) "Entertainment-Education and Social Change: An Analysis of Parasocial Interaction, Social Learning, Collective Efficacy, and Paradoxical Communication", *Journal of Communication*, Autumn, Vol. 50, No. 4, pp. 31-55

Parks, Will, Gray-Felder, Denise, Hunt, Jim & Byrne, Ailish (2005) *Who Measures Change? An Introduction to Participatory Monitoring and Evaluation of Communication for Social Change.* South Orange, NJ: Communication for Social Change Consortium

Rodriguez, Clemenzia (2001) *Fissures in the Mediascape: An International Model of Citizens' Media.* Cresskill, NJ: Hampton Press

UNIDO (2003) Review of Telecenter Sustainability Criteria for the Establishment of Sustainable Rural Business Resource Centers, available at http://www.unido.org/fileadmin/user_media/Publications/Pub_free/Review_of_telecenter_sustainability_criteria_for_establishment_of_sustainable_rural_business_resource_centers_for_SMEs_in_DCs.pdf

Waisboard, Silvio (2002) Excerpt from "Family Tree of Theories, Methodologies and Strategies in Development Communication", in Gumucio Dragon, Alfonso & Tufte, Thomas (Eds.) (2006) *Communication for Social Change. Anthology: Historical and Contemporary Readings.* South Orange, NJ: Communication for Social Change Consortium

www.communicationforsocialchange.org

Being Read by a DJ

Youth Interaction via Radio and Cell Phones in Southeast Turkey

Ece Algan

What difference are new communication technologies and newly emergent broadcast media making in the lives of young people who live in the periphery? Can we simply assume that "the mere fact that communication media exist induces social change" (Schulz, 2004, p. 89) regardless of larger socio-cultural and economic triggers? Do new media and communication technologies dictate particular global uses with a certain set of outcomes across both the developed and developing worlds as well as in urban and rural areas? Or are there unique local applications of new media and technologies that give us important clues, not only about the multiplicity of media use in everyday life, but also about the ways in which social change takes place? These are some of the questions that emerged from my fieldwork research, which I conducted in 2001 and 2007 on the role local radio and cell phones play in the lives of marginalized youth in the city of Şanlıurfa, located in the mostly rural Southeastern region of Turkey.

In the present article, I will examine how cell phones are used in conjunction with local radio to maintain a youth community in a city that puts enormous pressures on youth interaction and self-expression. Since their emergence in 1993, local radio stations have functioned as a social space for youth to discuss issues that matter to them, share their poems, songs, etc., with each other, play games, and send songs to their loved ones via call-in shows (Algan, 2005, 2009). In 2003, local radio stations stopped airing young people's direct telephonic communication mostly for economic reasons and, instead, encouraged their audience to express themselves and to send their song requests via SMS messages, which were then read verbatim on the air by disc jockeys. Even though this has limited young people's interaction on the air, radio and cell phones continue to provide a transformative and expressive space for them that has many implications for social change, though not the type of change that can be easily measured by socio-economic signs of development. Therefore, the article aims to problematize the relationship between new communication technologies and social change by situating young people's interaction via local radio and cell phones within a larger context of socio-economic change as experienced in everyday life in Şanlıurfa and in Turkish society in general.

Cell phones, youth and social change

Recent findings on mobile communication and development encourage us to be cautious about the limits and nature of social change that is seen as a result of the introduction of new media or technology, while not denying the important role they play within the larger socio-cultural, economic and political change experienced. Investigating whether mobile phones play a transformative role in economic development in Sub-Saharan Africa, Aker and Mbiti (2010) suggest that mobile phones have the potential to benefit consumer and producer welfare, and perhaps contribute to broader economic development. However, they argue that "even if mobile phones can enhance access to resources and information, they cannot replace investments in public goods such as roads, power, and water. In fact, they are less effective without them" (p. 228). Like Aker and Mbiti (2010), Donner (2006) also concludes that mobile phone ownership clearly provides significant economic and social opportunities in Rwanda. However, he sees the role of mobile phones as "social and economic amplification" rather than "transformation" in Africa (p. 26). Providing an example of social amplification, Donner (2006) mentions an increase in conversations among family and friends due to mobile phone use, but "found little evidence that users are meeting new family members or friends because they have the mobile" (p. 21).

In her study on cell phone usage among immigrant Jamaicans and their families, Horst (2006) found that "the mobile phone has in many ways altered the perception of mobility among rural Jamaicans who may not have the economic ability or desire to participate in physical movement" (p. 144). By creating what she calls transnational social fields, cell phones enable families to stay in touch, send each other money, monitor their kids, pursue their romantic relationships and "express and communicate love" (p. 144). This mobile communication eases worries about loved ones overseas, while facilitating everyday life and work. Horst's study underlines the fact that mobile phones are instrumental in maneuvering the new global socio-economic conditions and spatial barriers immigrant families are experiencing. This is largely because "the telephone is an inherently spatial technology – its sole function is to allow communication at a distance" (Townsend, 2000, p. 87). Mobile phones, in particular, have modified the norms of being present and absent in social space, and citizens' relation with public space (Fortunati, 2002, p. 526). Therefore, due to their ability to transform our experience of time and space, phones have become an integral part of modern life and urban/rural as well as global/local mediations.

As Townsend (2000) suggests, the increasing decentralization of decision-making and management of everyday life creates new interactions between individuals "that dramatically speed up the metabolism of urban systems, increasing capacity and efficiency" (p. 89). Therefore, the type of change mobile phones cause in cities comes as a result of lower-level interactions among individuals rather than massive physical changes (Townsend, 2000, p. 98). Then the change that mobile telephony induces is "the pace (metabolism) and character of activities being conducted in traditional urban spaces [...] as boundaries between the home, office, automobile, and street are increasingly blurred" (p. 98). According to Tenhunen (2008), the capacity of phones to blur spatial boundaries acts as a catalyst for the reorganization and new interpretations of culturally constructed spheres and boundaries (p. 531). Thus, mobile phones are not necessarily capable of eliminating spatial boundaries all together, but rather they can help reorganize them by enabling and facilitating social relations and personal interactions. Nevertheless, as Spagnolli and Gamberini (2007) write, the mobile phone "is not just a cheap communication medium, but a specific communication mode, characterized by persistency, reciprocation and familiarity" (p. 360).

Townsend's (2000) intriguing assertion, which places the individual as the unit of analysis when looking at the social change initiated by mobile phones in cities, highlights mobile phones' importance in managing and rewriting spatial as well as social and cultural boundaries. When the relationship between social change and mobile phones is redefined in these terms, then any analysis needs to be situated and contextualized in a certain locale. This requires that we not group all adolescents who use mobile phones in one category regardless of their class status, for instance, or generalize the experiences of Western youth as universal. This is exactly the problem with much of the research on youth and mobile phone use today. Most place an emphasis on the phone's role in maintaining social networks, friendships and romantic relationships without situating the youth in their unique environments or without providing adequate context regarding their use (Ling & Haddon, 2008; Skog, 2002; Oksman & Turtiainen, 2004). I agree with Thurlow and McKay's (2003) observation that much academic and lay writing about young people's use and understanding of new communication technologies is "often impressionistic and over-simplistic" (p. 95). They suggest that an overly homogenous, U.S. or Western-centric interpretation of youth culture "falls too easily into the trap of making unsubstantiated (and technologically deterministic) claims for the impact of new technologies" (p. 95). To avoid these pitfalls, my research aims to understand how a small group of underprivileged Turkish teenagers, most of whom live in the ghettos of a city in the more traditional and conservative periphery of Turkey, utilize cell phones in their participation in youth communities and romantic relationships via a longitudinal ethnographic study of media use. It also examines the socio-economic factors behind mobile phones becoming an integral part of interacting via local radio as well as dating.

Youth and the city in a state of flux: Şanlıurfa

The city of Şanlıurfa, which is inhabited mostly by people of Kurdish and Arabic descent, is located 30 miles from the Syrian border in the economically less-developed Southeastern Anatolian region of Turkey. The city, which has a population of around half a million, has undergone very rapid growth and urbanization during the past two decades due to Turkey's integration into the global economy. The government policies on the ethnic conflict in the region between Kurdish citizens and the Turkish state, rural to urban immigration prompted by the conflict and state-sponsored development project in the region (the GAP project), and the increase in wealth due to irrigation-supported agriculture in the province have all impacted the cityscape in many different ways, but these changes left the problems of youth either unanswered or worsened. By bringing irrigation agriculture to the plains south of the city, the GAP project increased agricultural production and profit, initiated industrial development, and caused people to relocate owing to increased opportunities and the construction of a series of dams. As a result, a large number of immigrants from the many rural villages and towns of the region moved to Şanlıurfa. In addition, a number of other forces also contributed to a drastic change in the city's small but progressive urban character, including the increasing power of a new local government with a reactionary, conservative and religious agenda; the disparity in wealth; the increasing power of landlords gained through irrigation agriculture; and martial law that was in effect on and off until 2000.

The increasing power of local religious leaders and political authorities, who have adopted an Islamist discourse and ideology, created numerous constraints on several aspects of social life in Şanlıurfa, especially on women's participation in the public sphere. Establishments that serve alcoholic drinks as well as restaurants and movie theaters where both women and men could go were closed as a result of the social pressure caused by the growing religious sentiment. Moreover, most young girls are not allowed to go to school for more than a few years, if at all, and most boys only attend elementary school. Not only do young people lack social space to experience their gender identities and sexualities, but they are also expected to obey traditional customs regarding education, work, and marriage.

Despite these circumstances and restrictions, since their launch in the mid-1990s both national network channels, especially television, and local commercial radio channels in Şanlıurfa have functioned as a vitally important site for the young people of Şanlıurfa to rethink their place among the larger population of Turkish youth and to vocalize their dissatisfaction with the status quo and traditions. Moreover, many taboos regarding dating and sexuality, such as premarital sex, have been broken in the big cities of Turkey, and this has been widely discussed in the public sphere. Television series on commercial networks show dating, flirting, and messaging as new countrywide trends among teenagers, thus easing the pressure on the youth in Şanlıurfa. When I returned to the city in 2007, my informants told me repeatedly that Şanlıurfa was not the same place anymore and that it had changed a great deal compared to 2001 when I first did my research. One even suggested, "Now it's a place where every week few young couples, who have met in chatrooms, elope!" (Personal communication, July 2007). Therefore, young people's interactions through radio and cell phones should be evaluated within the larger context of the socio-cultural, economic and political change taking place both in Şanlıurfa and in Turkey in general.

Audience interaction on the air via SMS

In Şanlıurfa, both radio and cell phones have come to play significant roles and have meaning in the lives of underprivileged youth since the beginning of the 1990s. Until 1990, broadcasting was a state monopoly with a great deal of cultural programming and news aimed at realizing the official ideology of westernization in Turkey (Algan, 2003). In 1990, pirate commercial radio and TV channels broke the state monopoly on broadcasting and enjoyed an unregulated broadcasting environment, which received an enthusiastic welcome throughout the country until the Turkish Radio-TV High Council (RTÜK) was established in 1995. During this time, many taboo subjects were discussed and the audience was encouraged to express their views through phones and faxes. Soon commercial media became concentrated and big media moguls began working side-by-side with the authorities and within RTÜK guidelines.

While national radio and TV networks' broadcasting have changed their programming content and style drastically after the last half of the 1990s, small local broadcasting channels, especially radio, kept their initial style of audience interaction and song requests for a variety of reasons, including having too small a budget to hire programmers and qualified staff, having to meet continuous audience demands for interactive programming and owners keeping the station to gain political and economic advantage elsewhere (Algan, 2004). Therefore, radio and phones have been used in tandem ever since small commercial local radio stations emerged in Turkey. For instance, in Şanlıurfa, local radio played the matchmaker role and constituted a social space for youth (Algan, 2005), and it accomplished this as a result of audience interaction via phone-in programs. When I first did fieldwork in the city in 2001, young people were calling in to discuss arranged marriage practices, bride prices, *berdel* – the cross-marriage of male and female children of two families – and other traditions that prioritize marriage among relatives, as well as restrictions on women's education. In addition, local radio functioned as a social space for them to experience various aspects of their youth identities by sharing cultural works they created, such as songs and poems, and by pursuing romantic relationships by sending songs and messages to each other (Algan, 2005).

Before the 2000s, most young girls in Şanlıurfa had no access to cell phones and had limited access to land lines at home. Moreover, families that were the newcomers to the city were concerned about their daughters' reputations in a burgeoning and rapidly changing urban environment, which still embodied the semi-feudal kinship and power arrangements as well as tribal traditions of its new inhabitants. Girls, who are kept at home until they are married off, watch a great deal of TV and listen to the radio. Boys, who are mostly sent to their fathers' workplace to help out and learn the job, also listen to the radio frequently. While local media professionals I interviewed did not want their audience to consist predominantly of teenagers due to their belief that listeners' lack of education and maturity prevent them from pursuing 'quality' programming, they continued to cater almost completely to the audience's song requests and text messages. Young people rightfully felt ownership of their favorite radio stations, calling them "ours", hailing the DJs as "one of us", sharing their own stories on the air, and sending their lovers messages encoded in songs via code names. Because young boys and girls were not allowed to date openly, they had a chance to experience platonic relationships through this "local social field" they created over the radio.

Toward the mid-2000s, as girls were inheriting their brothers' or fathers' old cell phones and as the local radio stations shifted audience interaction from call-in participation to exclusively text messaging (SMS) – due to the extra profit it brought to the station – the nature of interaction and functions once attributed to local radio changed. Boys had owned cell phones since the mid-1990s. Now with young girls owning one, they are able to send messages directly to each other without needing the radio or their close friends to carry messages back and forth. The young girls give their cell phone number to boys in the neighborhood whom they like, via friends or sometimes directly through a note with their cell phone number written on it. So, cell phones do not necessarily allow the young people in Şanlıurfa to eliminate barriers to dating, but allow them to experience it in privacy, even if they still cannot go out in public and walk in the parks hand-in-hand. As Townsend (2000) asserted, mobile phones rewrite the spatial and temporal constraints of human communication systems. And as in the Şanlıurfa example, they can help young people overcome the difficulty of expressing their feelings in public and the other constraints of air time, such as not being able to get through to the station or DJs not giving them air time due to high caller traffic, DJs delivering the message inaccurately, playing the wrong song or forgetting to play it (Personal communication with DJ Mustafa Bayram from Harran FM). Because cell phone messages can be exchanged instantaneously between lovers, radio mishaps such as these can be easily remedied.

Just as local radio took over friends' job of matchmaking – those who carried words, gifts, or letters between lovers in rural areas – cell phones have mostly taken over the job of radio DJs, who used to act as matchmakers by playing songs that lovers wanted and giving them air time to deliver their message. Today, according to DJ Erkan Ülgen from Güneydoðu Radyo – one of the oldest radio stations predominantly catering to youth and their song requests via SMS – young lovers still treat DJs as matchmakers after a fight, when both stop sending text messages.

> Instead they send the radio station a text message like this 'I am sending this song to my girlfriend who broke my heart this way...'. Then the girlfriend responds [by sending a txt message to the station]: 'I hadn't done anything to break your heart but I will apologize anyways with this song...' This is how we end up becoming matchmakers. They can also utilize SMS this way. (Personal communication Erkan Ülgen, programmer and DJ, Güneydoðu Radyo, August 2007)

So, as Taylor and Harper (2003) have suggested, "phones have provided young people with new ways to perform old rituals" (p. 294), such as sending a text message to a third person/matchmaker or a DJ to seek reconciliation.

If cell phones remedy the constraints of communication brought about by older media and shift radio's job onto lovers to communicate with each other via their cell phones, then why do young people still send text messages to radio stations? Even though radio ceased to be the main method of pursuing a relationship for young people, sending a song for a loved one is a common gesture and part of what Taylor and Harper (2003) call gift giving. In their ethnographic study, they found that young people use mobile phone content and the phones themselves to participate in the practices of gift exchange. So, practices of sharing the content of messages sent to them with their best friends or exchanging each other's phones are gift-giving practices. While these gift-giving practices also take place in Şanlıurfa, a few others are quite unique to the area and explain why sending SMS to radio stations and requesting songs are still common. Based on my observations of the interaction on the air and both my informants' and DJs' accounts, most of the song requesting that has been taking place since cell phones is intended to show one's love publicly and therefore aims to cement one's relationship by acknowledging it within the public youth social network on the air. Nevertheless, the audience usually states that, for instance, such and such a song should go from person A to person B as a gift. Songs and text messages that accompany the songs are mostly sent to the radio for the love interest, but also for friends and relatives as a gift in order to acknowledge and solidify social relations.

Another example regarding cell phones' function in gift giving that is unique to Şanlıurfa youth is that when young girls use up their phone minutes, they expect their boyfriends to transfer minutes so they can continue conversing. This saves girls from asking for money from their brothers or fathers, who may easily question with whom she has been chatting this much. Instead they send a text message to the radio station explaining that they do not have any more phone minutes left to send another song as a gift for their boyfriends or complain directly that their boyfriends still haven't transferred minutes to their cell phones. This example illustrates a crucial economic dimension of pursuing a relationship via cell phones, which is boys' ability to purchase minutes and send them to their girlfriends generously, as a gift.

Conclusion

As Thurlow and McKay (2003) argued, "the new media landscape is constantly shifting and factors surrounding young people's use of computers and other such technologies are complex" (p. 99). The present article explicated this complexity of media use in a situated and contextualized study among youth in Şanlıurfa. As cell phones have begun to be used extensively in Şanlıurfa, young people not only continued to participate in the "local social field" of radio via text messages, which were read verbatim on the air by DJs, but also pursued their romantic love interests through messaging. In the socially restrictive environment of the city, cell phones became crucial in working within and even renegotiating the boundaries of traditions and tribal cultural practices, which have been weakened since the 2000s. Young people's cell phone use contributed to the transformation of private and public spaces by enabling virtual dating via SMS and by carrying private romantic disputes to the airwaves via SMS so that the DJs – the matchmakers – would solve them and so that their peers – the listening community – could serve as referees.

The study illustrates how young people's cell phone and radio use corresponded with larger social change that has been taking place in the national and local economic realms as well as in the mediascape, which is increasingly commercial and attuned to global imagery, content and style. The tensions between global media-oriented youth culture and local traditions that Kraidy and Khalil (2009) have observed among Arab youth also exist among Turkish youth for quite similar reasons (p. 338). First is the generation gap between the technology-savvy and global media-exposed youth and their parents, who grew up with only state-owned and -controlled broadcasting channels and with no computers until the emergence of commercial and regional satellite channels in the early 1990s. The second is the fact that young people aspire to become a part of the global media-driven global youth culture via consumption and media use such as texting. According to Kraidy and Khalil (2009), this exacerbates the intergenerational gap and "accelerates socio-cultural change to the extent that it reduces parents' influence on their children in favor of increasing their exposure to peer and foreign cultural influences" (p. 338). Indeed, cell phones along with local radio helped young people in Şanlıurfa "differentiate themselves from family or household relations as well as cement their own social networks" (Taylor & Harper, 2003, p. 292). Moreover, the unique way in which the young people of Şanlıurfa developed when using cell phones and radio for dating and for creating a social space served to alleviate the tensions between local traditions and the global media-oriented youth culture. Thus, as this case study has shown, the media alone do not instigate or induce social change, but they can provide people ways to make sense of larger social changes affecting their city and nation and to express themselves and their struggles.

In Şanlıurfa, social change has been taking place as a result of various local and national institutions and state development projects attempting to integrate Turkey into the global economy. Young people's lives are affected by these initiatives both in rural and urban areas. They find themselves deprived of education due to existing patriarchal and tribal structures, but they still expect to compete in a new capitalist economy that they are not even equipped to understand. The use of local radio and cell phones in tandem allows them to express these frustrations and to experience youth identities that are common to others in Turkey. Carrying on romantic relationships via texting enables them to communicate and date without any face-to-face encounters and thus, to obey the local traditions and Islamic restrictions on pre-marital relationships. Moreover, the present study has illustrated how "the appropriation of phones draws from local culture" (Tenhunen, 2008, p. 530) and, in this way, highlighted the importance of placing media use and youth in a specific geographic and historical context in order to understand the transformation of everyday realities and lives in that particular place.

References

Aker, J.C. & Mbiti, I.M. (2010) Mobile phones and economic development in Africa. *Journal of Economic Perspectives* 24(3): 207-232.

Algan, E. (2003) Privatization of media in Turkey and the question of media hegemony in the era of globalization, in Artz, L. & Kamalipour, Y.R. (Eds.) *The Globalization of Corporate Media Hegemony*, New York: SUNY Press, 169-192.

Algan, E. (2004) Development of local radio in Southeast Turkey. *Journal of Radio Studies*, 11(2): 254-267.

Algan, E. (2005) The role of Turkish local radio in the construction of a youth community. *The Radio Journal: International Studies in Broadcast & Audio Media*, 3(2): 75-92.

Algan, E. (2009) "There is no permission to love in our Urfa": Media, youth identities and social change in Southeast Turkey, in Tufte, T. & Enghel, F. (Eds.) *Teens Engaging with the World: Youth, Communication and Social Change*. Yearbook 2009. The International Clearinghouse on Children, Youth and Media. University of Gothenburg, Nordicom, 173-189.

Donner, J. (2006) The Social and Economic Implications of Mobile Telephony in Rwanda: An Ownership/Access Typology, *Knowledge, Technology, & Policy*, 19(2): 17-28.

Fortunati, L. (2002) The Mobile Phone: Towards New Categories and Social Relations, *Information, Communication and Society* 5(4): 513-29.

Horst, H. A. (2006) The blessings and burdens of communication: Cell phones in Jamaican transnational social fields, *Global Networks*, 6 (2): 143-159.

Kraidy, M.M. & Khalil, J.F. (2008) Youth, media and culture in the Arab world, in Drotner, K. & Livingstone, S. (Eds.) *International Handbook of Children, Media and Culture*. Thousand Oaks, CA: Sage, 336-350.

Ling, R. & Haddon, L. (2008) Children, youth and the mobile, in Drotner, K. & Livingstone, S. (Eds.) *International Handbook of Children, Media and Culture*. Thousand Oaks, CA: Sage, 137-151 .

Oksman, V. & Turtiainen, J. (2004) Mobile communication as a social stage: Meanings of mobile communication in everyday life among teenagers in Finland, *New Media & Society*, 6(3): 319-339.

Schulz, W. (2004) Reconstructing Mediatization as an Analytical Concept, *European Journal of Communication* 19(1): 87-101.

Skog, B. (2002) Mobiles and the Norwegian teen: Identity, gender and class, in Katz, E. & Aakhus, M. (Eds.) *Perpetual Contact: Mobile Communication, Private Talk, Public Performance*. Cambridge: Cambridge University Press, 255-273.

Spagnolli, A. & Gamberini, L. (2007) Interacting via SMS: Practices of social closeness and reciprocation, *British Journal of Social Psychology*, 46, 343-364.

Taylor, A.S. & Harper, R. (2003) The gift of the Gab? A design oriented sociology of young people's use of mobiles, *Computer Supported Cooperative Work*, 12, 267-296.

Tenhunen, S. (2008) Mobile technology in the village: ICTs, culture, and social logistics in India. *Journal of the Royal Anthropological Institute*, 14, 515-534.

Thurlow, C. & McKay, S. (2003) Profiling "New" Communication Technologies in Adolescence, *Journal of Language and Social Psychology*, 22: 94-103.

Townsend, A.M. (2000) Life in the real-time city: Mobile telephones and urban metabolism, *Journal of Urban Technology*, 7(2), 85-104.

Citizenship Practices among Youth

Exploring the Role of Communication and Media

Florencia Enghel and Thomas Tufte

In the growing body of research on youth, their uses of media and their communicative practices, increasing attention is being paid to issues of agency and deliberation. Particular consideration is given to the potential for social critique, advocacy, activism and protest through creative uses of the media (for example, Livingstone, 2002; Herschmann, 2009; Olsson & Dahlgren, 2009; Wildermuth, 2008).

The present article reflects upon the role of communication and media in articulating processes of citizenship among youth. Drawing on a broad range of media scholars from Latin America, India, Europe and the United States, two key questions inform the article. First, how is the notion of *citizenship* understood today with regard to the lives of contemporary youth? Second, what role does *communication* play in articulating citizenship among young people?

We will address these questions from two analytical perspectives. First, we will consider the notion of citizenship in the context of *globalization*, looking into communication and the media's role as a resource that enables citizenship practices among youth. Locations of citizenship will be touched upon, including Dutch sociologist Saskia Sassen's references to the urban space of global cities and to electronic networks as strategic sites (Sassen, 2008, 2005) and Mexican social scientist Rossana Reguillo's analysis of the blogosphere as an alternate site for youth's communicative interaction (Reguillo, 2009: 31). Second, we will link our discussion of citizenship to the socio-economic and cultural realities of youth worldwide. Drawing on previous work outlining how youth engage with the world through communication and media (Tufte & Enghel, 2009), we will provide examples of how citizenship practices can manifest themselves through communication and media practices, processes and products. Those examples will also serve as input to the deeper-lying issue of how to define *youth* – as a social, cultural and/or political category.

Citizenship in the context of globalization

> Globalization has raised hopes and expectations of improved well-being in many areas. Young people's consciousness of a world of opportunity, consumption, and popular culture affects how they see their local lifeworlds and the meanings and uses they assign to global goods. (Hansen, 2008: 212)

In a large, 5-year research project in Zambia, Brazil and Vietnam focusing on young people's lives, media use, city experience and education, Danish-American anthropologist Karen Tranberg Hansen (2008) studied the expectations of well-being that globalization has articulated. These raised expectations contrast with the socio-economic and political situation in which many young citizens across the world are caught: situations of unemployment, social and financial marginalization, lack of education, health hazards and the challenges posed by war and climate change.

Polish sociologist Zygmunt Bauman, in a harsh critique of globalization, argues that 'the state is today unable, and/or unwilling, to promise its subjects existential security ("freedom from fear", as Franklin D. Roosevelt famously phrased it)' (Bauman 2010: 65). When the state acts in this way, the individual citizen is left to his/her own resources, unable to obtain existential security, that is, unable to obtain and retain 'a legitimate and dignified place in human society and avoiding the ménage of exclusion' (ibid.). In practice, this means that young people are left to pursue life based on individual skills and resources and cut off from social support networks, in a situation of 'enormous risks, and suffering the harrowing uncertainty which such tasks inevitably include' (ibid.). Examples include the marginalized youth in the slums of Nairobi, the *favelados* in Brazilian mega-cities or the young immigrants in the suburbs of Paris – what Bauman (2010) calls the *'nowherevilles'*.

Hansen reinforces Bauman's emphasis on macro-economic developments leading to what we might call *nowherelives,* constrained by structurally imposed limitations. She maintains that a series of structural conditions are impacting upon the lives of youth, thus making their lives uncertain. In this context, youth can at best experience processes of empowerment and thus feelings of enhanced citizenship, or they will encounter several obstacles, leading instead to frustration, apathy or violence – a paradoxical divide also noted by Reguillo (2009: 22). Hansen (2008: 209-210) refers to the risk of uncertainties in life by stating:

> Many young people's lives are uncertain because of economic changes and shifting household fortunes. Changes in living arrangements, socioeconomic status, schooling and personal relationships complicate many other difficulties that young people may face.

The advent of globalization may produce new opportunities or quite the opposite. In fact, it simultaneously creates *differences*, *inequalities* and forms of exclusion or *disconnections* (García Canclini, 2006)[1] – the social consequences of which seem to affect youth in important ways, according to Reguillo:

> On the one hand, globalization, jointly with technological development, has undoubtedly increased the cultural offers. But on the other hand, it is equally true that the possibilities for access are reduced or restricted. In that sense, the thinking and analysis regarding the relationship between youth, communication and social change must be located precisely in the tension produced by this paradox. I.e., more and better means for communication, increasingly powerful technological devices, "availability" of enormous resources for information and knowledge, in coexistence with the increasing impoverishment of large areas of the planet, the aggravated conditions of exclusion, and the so called "digital divide". (Reguillo, 2009: 22)

Both Hansen and Reguillo reflect upon how globalization may well provide extended resources through access to information and connectivity, thereby raising hopes and expectations of improved well-being. However, they likewise highlight – although to varying degrees – how the lack of resources can be accentuated in times of globalization: increased insecurity and uncertainty, impoverishment and growing divides and inequalities all point towards disempowerment and a weakening sense of citizenship.

In her analysis of how globalization is being produced, Sassen (2005, 2008) proposes an analytical reconstruction of citizenship. She argues that in the context of globalization, the relationships between nation-states and their citizens are being transformed, in a dynamic that produces operational and rhetorical openings for the emergence of new types of subjects and news spatialities for politics.

Sassen notes that what used to be public is being increasingly privatized, in an ongoing process of denationalization of nation-states that reorients their agendas and policy work towards the requirements of economic globalization. The welfare state is shrinking, citizens' entitlements are being eliminated, and the distance between state and citizens is increasing. In parallel, power becomes "increasingly privatized, globalized, and elusive" (2005: 81). This raises several questions. As the organizational architecture for democratic accountability inside states is altered, which informal political actors, practices and vocabularies emerge? What kind of politics does digital technology, particularly public-access Internet, enable? What claims are being made, both in terms of rights and in terms of aspirations? And to which institutions are these claims directed?

Sassen stresses the importance of paying attention to informal practices and to political subjects not quite fully recognized as such, and proposes that "citizenship is partly produced by the practices of the excluded" (2005: 84). This resonates with Reguillo's point that the structural and subjective precariousness affecting a majority of youth worldwide, the widening divide between those with and without resources, the withdrawal of the welfare state and the failure of traditional socializing institutions – the school, political parties, the workplace and labour unions – to guarantee inclusion "shape and materialize the dynamics through which young people become political actors and subjects" (Reguillo, 2009: 27).

The role of communication and media in the articulation of citizenship

We are interested in identifying and analysing the role of communication and media in the articulation of new or changed forms of citizenship practices, particularly what Sassen terms "the production of 'presence' of those without power" (2005: 90). In this respect, Reguillo argues, and we agree, that

> undoubtedly, despite the difficult situation that many young people are experiencing, youth participation is increasing in diverse social processes in which they are speaking up and have seized communication's tools to put them to work in ways that defy the dominant understanding of "politics". (Reguillo, 2009: 31)

Viewed through a communication and media lens, three particular characteristics can be outlined as crucial to consider in the context of globalization.

The electronic mediation of everyday life

The heading above refers to Indian anthropologist Arjun Appadurai's theory of rupture, in which the electronic mediation of everyday life plays a key role (1996).[2] Appadurai explored the relation between globalization and modernity and emphasized two issues characteristic of the transformation of society: mass migration and the electronic mediation of everyday life. He saw these two phenomena as interconnected, and as having an effect on the "work of the imagination" as a constitutive feature of modern subjectivity (1996: 3), and argued that the electronic media "offer new resources and new disciplines for the construction of imagined selves and imagined worlds". Juxtaposed with mass migrations – both voluntary and forced – the result was "a new order of instability in the production of modern subjectivities" (ibid.: 4).

As with other dimensions of their lives, access to the media, and therefore to the possibility to participate in the economic, political and cultural life of the communities they belong to, is not equal for all youth. Data presented at the United Nations Summit on the Millennium Development Goals held in September 2010 noted that

> In 2009, an estimated 26 per cent of the world population, that is to say, over 1.7 billion people, was using the Internet. However, in developed countries, the proportion is much higher than in developing countries (64 per cent and 18 per cent of the population, respectively) [...]. In other words, in 2009, over 80 per cent of the population in developing countries was still excluded from the online world and its benefits. (UN, 2010: 90)[3]

Even in this uneven context, the electronic mediation of everyday life does provide – at least potentially – increased access to symbolic worlds, reinforcing the processes and paradoxes highlighted by Hansen and Reguillo, as discussed above. It has become a resource that informs the everyday life of youth and thus the production and formation of identity.

The articulation of social dynamics through communication

As suggested by Sassen's attention to electronic networks and Reguillo's discussion of the blogosphere, the possibility that social media can open the door to new or changed forms of deliberation is now more widely perceived. However, we still need to better understand the ways and means of deliberation, or of "producing presence" (Sassen, 2005, 2008) and "doing politics", of today's youth. In his latest book, Spanish social scientist Manuel Castells (2009) offers a pathway to explore citizenship practices and articulations of agency by analysing the power of communication within civil society and social movement in connection with the new social media and the network society. In reflecting upon social movements, insurgent politics and the new public space, he states that:

> In a world marked by the rise of mass self-communication, social movements and insurgent politics have a chance to enter the public space from multiple sources. By using both horizontal communication networks and mainstream media to convey their images and messages, they increase their chances of enacting social and political change – even if they start from a subordinate position in institutional power, financial resources, or symbolic legitimacy. (Castells, 2009: 302)

This quote points to the bottom-up communication strategy of social movements and to insurgent politics as a way to enact social and political change – something often seen in youth-led movements. In regard to this, Castells identifies a potential pathway for the practice of citizenship and articulation of social change.

The changing character of the public sphere

A third characteristic of communication and media in the context of globalization relates to how the location, space and character of the public sphere are changing. In his book *Media and Morality – the rise of the mediapolis*, Roger Silverstone developed what German sociologist Ulrick Beck has called "a new cosmopolitan critical theory of the emerging global civil society and its contradictions" (Beck on back cover of Silverstone 2007). Silverstone's understanding of the public sphere, with the logics, dynamics and opportunities of the media at the centre, provides a framework for situating and understanding media and communication practices in the context of the globalized world. He defines mediapolis as:

> [...] the mediated space of appearance in which the world appears and in which the world is constituted in its worldliness, and through which we learn about those who are and who are not like us. It is through communications conducted through the mediapolis that we are constructed as human (or not), and it is through the mediapolis that public and political life increasingly comes to emerge at all levels of the body politic (or not). (Silverstone 2007: 31)

Silverstone is concerned with how mediated spaces represent or constitute public life, to what degree they are inclusive or exclusive, and whether they enable or disable public debate, which relates to our exploration of how citizenship practices can, or cannot, be enhanced by communication and media practices. Silverstone defines the mediated space as a "space of possibility", in which social and political life can emerge as meaningful if and when the communicative practice grounded in it follows certain ethics or principles. Although embryonic and imperfect, the mediapolis, Silverstone argues, is a necessary starting point for the creation of a more effective global civil space. The mediated space of appearance is, at best, a space of potential and of possibility for citizenship practices to develop (ibid.: 33).

The view of Peruvian media scholar and practitioner Rosa Maria Alfaro ties in well with some of Silverstone's ideas. Alfaro's (2001/2008) proposition of alternative communication and alternative public spheres is based on a series of principles: open access to the media; voice and visibility in the media; recognition of mutual differences; and time and space for dialogue and reflection.

Bringing together Appadurai's remarks on the unstable subjectivities produced by the electronic mediation of everyday life, Silverstone's vision of the communicative and deliberative possibilities of the mediapolis, and Alfaro's principles for the emergence of alternative public spheres, we can delineate the contours of communication's potential for the deployment of young people's citizenship practices.

Political economist of communication Vincent Mosco argues that it is more productive to think of the public sphere not as a particular location, but rather in process terms, and therefore to consider the state, the global market and social movements (which he regards as a type of structure that manages to distance itself from both the state and the market) as sites of struggle between people's identities as consumers and citizens – or in other words, as the contested terrains in which the processes of commodification and democracy contend (Mosco, 2009: 153). Because youth is a preferred target of the global market's efforts to sell and at the same time tends to experience an aggravated condition of exclusion from education and work (Reguillo, 2009), the tension between being – or wanting to be, as noted by Hansen – a consumer who can buy and a citizen who can express his or her demands for justice is especially relevant to our discussion.

How do young people produce citizenship 'presence'?

How can we explore how young citizens engage in social and political life and claim their rights? What is the role of communication in such engagement? And what is the impact on communicative practices oriented towards citizenship of the socio-economic divides, the paradoxes of global development and the insecurities of everyday life that we have outlined so far?

In our previous collaborative work on youth, communication and social change, we have approached these questions through four analytical perspectives, each reflecting a manner in which youth exercised citizenship through media and communication: a) memory and identity, whereby youth used the media to communicate for and about their rights; b) the voices of youth: coping, criticizing and calling for change; c) youth as subjects – of content, programmes and regulations; and finally d) youth in processes, primarily gaining a role and some responsibility (in communication for development). These analytical pathways all deliver entry points to answering the questions posed above. Without reiterating here what we have noted elsewhere (Tufte & Enghel, 2009), we would like to insist on the fact that there are multiple and creative ways in which youth are engaging with the world through communicative action and media practices.

The three other contributions in the Research Forum on Communication for Social Change included in this section of the Yearbook all provide examples of how youth engage actively in citizenship practices through their communication and media practices. Turkish media scholar Ece Algan provides an in-depth media ethnographic account of how Turkish youth use radio and mobile telephony as ways and means for young boys and girls to meet, relate and even date each other (Algan, 2011). Beyond the creativity in media use, Algan identifies how these mediated social practices are challenging local community power structures across gender and generations, thereby exemplifying how youth exercise their right to interact with each other. Belarusian media scholar Iryna Vidanava focuses on the right to freedom of expression – providing us with a fascinating account of the challenges faced by a youth-driven underground magazine published and circulated in Belorussia, the last remaining dictatorship in Europe (Vidanava, 2011). Vidanava illustrates how the youth magazine provides social and political critique while tapping into the youth-bound popular culture, from poems and stories to comics and fashion. Finally, Mette Grøndahl Hansen and Lise Grauenkær Jensen[4] provide an account of how a non-governmental organization in Malawi approaches peer education as a strategy for HIV and AIDS prevention (Hansen & Jensen, 2011). Grøndahl Hansen and Grauenkær Jensen argue that the peer club in which face-to-face communication takes place is a citizen medium – a space for dialogue, reflection and deliberation. In their view, the communicative space allows youth to feel empowered and thus promotes more informed and safer choices with regard to sexual practices.

The diversity suggested by these three contributions grounded in empirical research begs the question of how we understand the category of youth.

Who are the youth we are referring to?

Hansen draws our attention to the obvious – i.e., Western – social construction of the predominant notion of youth. She questions what she calls "the development teleology inherent in the western life-stage model", or the Western notion of youth as a simple stepping-stone, linear and automatic, on the pathway to adulthood. Her above-mentioned study allowed her to empirically ground her argument that youth trajectories play out in very non-linear ways:

> The relationship between youth and home is complex and transitions between youth and adulthood are neither one-way nor one-time events. Far from being static, the meanings of youth shift situationally, depending above all on context. (Hansen, 2008: 210).

Furthermore, while in many cultures there are rituals that signify the passing from childhood to adulthood, in the Western life-stage model, youth has established itself as a particular phase. It is a phase that in many ways is gaining volume, spreading over more years of a lifecycle, becoming bigger business for the commercial sector, and in numerous other ways establishing "youth" or "youthful lives" as increasingly central.

Reguillo adds a very critical perspective on how to define youth. She provides a well-grounded critique of the concept as uniform and draws our attention to three core dimensions that must be considered in any serious attempt to think about youth and their potential leadership in contexts of social change: the processes of precarization/informalization of youth's biographies, dynamics, circuits and ideals; the retrenchment of the social state, and the strengthening of the punitive state; and the discrediting of modern institutions – the school, political parties, labour unions, businesses – as guarantors of "successful" socializing (Reguillo, 2009: 25).

Articulating citizenship practices in their everyday lives is often a road paved with obstacles for youth, as outlined by Reguillo. However, despite these constraints, they can be agents of change.

The notion of youth as a particular social group experiencing themselves as social actors and agents of change is a rather recent phenomenon, as noted by Colombian scholar Jesús Martín-Barbero. Martín-Barbero (in an interview by Tufte, 2010) argues that, for the first time in contemporary history, youth have constituted themselves as an independent social group, with some of the opportunities to act that this provides, and are experiencing societal change to a degree and of a depth unprecedented in our time:

> Youth are not just any youth, since they are experiencing the epochal transformation in their bodies [...]. Those of us who are elder feel doubts and uncertainties that have nothing to do with those of our sons and daughters; they are of a different caliber and type. [...] We had every dogma we wanted and they have nothing even beginning to resemble such dogmas – either in the religious, philosophical or political sense.

Martín-Barbero's remarks draw our attention to the fact that contemporary youth, immersed in a *glocal* reality (Hemer & Tufte, 2005), are living in a time of radical change, with intensified global transformations, fragmented ideologies and less fixed life cycles and trajectories.

In this context, the role of communication and media in young people's lives is an extremely dynamic object of study. Deliberation, social critique, advocacy, activism and protest are taking on multiple forms, and our challenge as social scientists is to conceptualize, understand and analyse the deeper meaning of these social and cultural practices, thereby revealing the polyphony of voices, the multiplicity of strategies and the multitude of arts, genres and languages through which youth, despite the many constraints outlined above, claim their rights and communicate for social change.

Notes

1. The Mexican-Argentinean anthropologist néstor García Canclini refers to the *different*, the *unequal* and the *disconnected* from a cross-disciplinary, intercultural perspective, and poses the problem of "how to acknowledge the *differences*, right the *inequalities* and *connect* the majorities to the globalized networks" (2006: 14). By *differences* he refers to ethnic, national or gender differences.
2. In 1996, Appadurai referred to media as "a complicated and interconnected repertoire of print, celluloid, electronic screens and billboards", emphasizing "television film and cassette forms". At present, attention is of course given also to the Internet and mobile telephones.
3. For an online version see http://www.un.org/en/mdg/summit2010/pdf/10-43282_MDG_2010%20% 28E%29%20WEBv2.pdf
4. Lise Grauenkær Jensen and Mette Grøndahl Hansen, both Danish, work in ADRA Denmark, the Danish sister organization to ADRA Malawi.

References

Alfaro, R.M. (2001/2006) Popular Cultures and Participatory Communication: On the Route to Redefinitions, in Gumucio-Dagron, A. & Tufte, T. (Eds) *The Communication for Social Change Anthology. Historical and Contemporary Readings*. New Jersey: Communication for Social Change Consortium, pp. 738-749

Algan, E. (2011) in this Yearbook

Appadurai, A. (1996) *Modernity at Large. Cultural Dimensions of Globalisation*. London and Minnesota: University of Minnesota Press

Bauman, Z. (2010) *Living on borrowed time*. Cambridge: Polity

Castells, M. (2009) *Communication Power*. Oxford: Oxford University Press

García Canclini, N. (2006) *Diferentes, desiguales y desconectados/Mapas de la interculturalidad*. Barcelona: Gedisa Editorial

Hansen, K. T. (2008) (Ed) *Youth and the City in the Global South*. Bloomington: Harcourt Trade Publishers

Hansen & Jensen (2011) in this Yearbook

Hemer, O. & Tufte, T. (Eds.) *Media & Glocal Change: Rethinking Communication for Development*. Buenos Aires/Gothenburg: CLACSO/NORDICOM

Herschmann, M. (2009) Brasil: Ciudadanía y Estética de los Jóvenes de las Periferias y Favelas (El Hip Hop en Brasil), in Martín-Barbero, J. (Ed) *Entre Saberes Desechables y Saberes Indispensables. Agendas de país desde la comunicación*. Bogotá: Centro de Competencia en Comunicación para América Latina, Friedrich Ebert Stiftung

Livingstone, S. (2002) *Young People and New Media*. London: Sage

Olsson, T. & Dahlgren, P. (Eds.) (2010) *Young People, ICTs and Democracy. Theories, Policies, Identities and Websites*. University of Gothenburg: Nordicom

Reguillo, R. (2009) The Warrior's Code? Youth, Communication and Social Change, in Tufte, T. & Enghel, F. (Eds.) *Youth Engaging with the World. Media, Communication and Social Change*. Yearbook 2009. The International Clearinghouse on Children, Youth and Media. University of Gothenburg; NORDICOM, pp. 21-39

Sassen, S. (2005) The repositioning of citizenship and alienage: Emergent subjects and spaces for politics, *Globalizations*, May, 2(1), pp. 79-94

Sassen, S. (2008, updated edition) *Territory, Authority, Rights: From medieval to global assemblages*. New Jersey: Princeton University Press

Silverstone, R. (2007) *Media and Morality. On the Rise of the Mediapolis*. Cambridge: Polity

Tufte, T. & Enghel, F. (Eds.) (2009) *Youth Engaging with the World. Media, Communication and Social Change*. Yearbook 2009. The International Clearinghouse on Children, Youth and Media. University of Gothenburg, NORDICOM

Tufte, T. (2010) Interview with Jesus Martín-Barbero. Unpublished, 10 May 2010, Roskilde, Denmark

UN (2010) Millennium Development Goal 8: The Global Partnership for Development at a Critical Juncture (MDG Gap Task Force Report 2010). New York: United Nations

Vidanava, I. (2011) in this Yearbook

Wildermuth, N. (2008) The Work of the Imagination: Young People's Media Appropriation in Three Cities, in Hansen, K.T. (Ed.) *Youth and the City in the Global South*. Bloomington: Harcourt Trade Publishers, pp. 174-206

The Authors

Ece Algan	Dr., Assistant Professor Department of Communication Studies California State University at San Bernardino San Bernardino, CA USA
Catharina Bucht	B.A., Information Co-ordinator The International Clearinghouse on Children, Youth and Media Nordicom University of Gothenburg Gothenburg Sweden
Ulla Carlsson	Dr., Professor, Director Nordicom University of Gothenburg Gothenburg Sweden
Kara Chan	Dr., Professor, Head Department of Communication Studies Hong Kong Baptist University Kowloon Tong Hong Kong China
Jeff Chester	MSW, Executive Director Center for Digital Democracy Washington, D.C. USA
Chi-Kim Cheung	Dr., Assistant Professor Faculty of Education The University of Hong Kong Hong Kong China

Henry Cohn-Geltner
Media Educator
Dorrance Hamilton Public Media Commons
WHYY-Channel 12
Philadelphia PA
USA

Lori Dorfman
DrPH, Director
Berkeley Media Studies Group
Berkeley, California
USA

Florencia Enghel
M.A., Ph.D. Candidate
Media and Communication Studies
Karlstad University
Karlstad
Sweden

Cecilia von Feilitzen
Dr., Professor, Scientific Co-ordinator
The International Clearinghouse on Children, Youth and Media
Nordicom
University of Gothenburg
Gothenburg
Sweden

Divina Frau-Meigs
Dr., Professor
University of Sorbonne Nouvelle
Paris
France

Lise Grauenkær
Program Coordinator
ADRA Denmark
Copenhagen
Denmark

Sonya Grier
Dr., Associate Professor
Kogod School of Business
American University
Washington, D.C.
USA

Alton Grizzle
Programme Specialist
Communication and Information Sector
UNESCO
Paris
France

Mette Grøndahl Hansen	M.A. in International Development Studies and Communication Studies Formerly at ADRA Denmark Communication Manager Copenhagen Denmark
Esther Hamburger	Dr., Professor, Chair Department of Cinema, Radio and Television School of Arts and Communications University of São Paulo São Paulo Brazil
Irma Hirsjärvi	Dr., Researcher Research Centre for Contemporary Culture University of Jyväskylä Jyväskylä Finland
Renee Hobbs	Dr., Professor Media Education Lab Temple University School of Communications and Theater Philadelphia, PA USA
Sara Kolomainen	Research Assistant Research Centre for Contemporary Culture University of Jyväskylä Jyväskylä Finland
Sirkku Kotilainen	Dr., Professor School of Communication, Media & Theatre University of Tampere Tampere and Adjunct Professor University of Jyväskylä & University of Turku Finland
John Landis	Technology Educator Russell Byers Charter School Philadelphia, PA USA

Dafna Lemish	Dr., Professor, Chair Department of Radio-TV College of Mass Communication & Media Arts Southern Illinois University Carbondale, Ill. USA and Department of Communication Tel Aviv University Tel Aviv Israel
Sonia Livingstone	Dr., Professor, Head Department of Media and Communications London School of Economics and Political Science London UK
Tatiana Merlo Flores	Dr., President Instituto de Investigación en Medios (IDIEM, Media Research Institute) Buenos Aires Argentina
Kathryn C. Montgomery	Dr., Professor School of Communication American University Washington, D.C. USA
Manisha Pathak-Shelat	Dr. School of Journalism and Mass Communication University of Wisconsin-Madison Madison USA
José Manuel Pérez Tornero	Dr., Professor, Director Communication and Education Center Facultad de Ciencias de la Comunicación Universitat Autònoma de Barcelona Barcelona Spain
Mireia Pi	Researcher Communication and Education Center Facultad de Ciencias de la Comunicación Universitat Autònoma de Barcelona Barcelona Spain

Ibrahim Saleh	Dr., Convenor of Political Communication Centre For Film and Media Studies University of Cape Town Cape Town South Africa
Arvind Singhal	Dr., Samuel Shirley and Edna Holt Marston Endowed Professor Department of Communication University of Texas @ El Paso El Paso, TX USA
Annikka Suoninen	Dr., Researcher Research Centre for Contemporary Culture University of Jyväskylä Jyväskylä Finland
Samy Tayie	Dr., Professor President of Mentor International Media Education Association Faculty of Mass Communication Cairo University Cairo Egypt
Jordi Torrent	Project Manager Media Literacy Education United Nations Alliance of Civilizations New York, NY USA
Thomas Tufte	Dr., Professor Department of Communication Business and Information Technologies Roskilde University Roskilde Denmark
Iryna Vidanava	Lecturer European Humanities University Minsk Belarus